CW00725815

THE ROMAN QUARRY

by David Jones
   (1895-1974)

IN PARENTHESIS (1937)

THE ANATHEMATA (1952)

EPOCH AND ARTIST (1959)
Selected Writings, edited by Harman Grisewood

THE SLEEPING LORD and other fragments (1974)

THE KENSINGTON MASS (1975)

THE DYING GAUL and other writings (1978)
edited by Harman Grisewood

CELTS

Celtic myth from 500 B.C.

Celtic & Pre-Celtic
Pre-Celtic

PREHISTORIC BRITAIN
A.D.60 ROMAN OCCUPATION to 5th C.
← Druidic Gnosis

Emigrations to BRITTANY c. 450 & also c. 550

537 trad. date of ARTHUR's death at Camlann.
Gildas 500-570

Histories of Eusebius Jerome Isidore Prosper

Irish & Saxon Annals

← Bede

MYTH + HISTORY + PSEUDO-HISTORY IN NORTH BRITAIN, WALES & S.W. BRITAIN

NENNIVS 800 A.D.
(Arthur already a marvel-maker)

IRELAND

Welsh-Irish Non-Arthurian Mythology

Union
Drystan
Peredur
Owain

Gawain
Grail?

King
Mark
of Meurion

?

GERMANIC
Weltanschauung

CORNWALL
(isolated from 685)
the Welsh Saints

WALES

1150
FRENCH
ROM

Pedeir Keine
Mabinogi
many Welsh & correspondences

WELSH MSS.

Ecclesiastical legend
Gallo-Roman
(from Lerins & Lyon)
Irish & Welsh
in 5th Century, proved

N.B.
refugees influence →
Pseudo
'Life of Gildas'
c.1100

in the earliest strata Arthur appears as a quasi-mythological figure in association with historical and mythological characters.
in two poems & two prose-tales he is a central figure.
& tends to be associated with the Dumnonian peninsular, but North Britain is associated with some of the most important figures.

Archdeacon Walter's 'book from Brittany'
Geoffreys avowed source.
?

'Blehri' 'Bledri' 'Breri'
'Cedhenicus' ille fabulator
'famosus'

Other Direct Welsh Influence on G.o.M. ?

GEOFFREY of M

via manuscripts

Metamorphosis of the characters.
Prose-tales in the new European Romance style.
(e.g. 'Geraint son of Erbin' 'The Lady of the Fountain' 'Peredur son of Evrawc')

the great influence of G.o.M.
The Hist. Reg. Brit. was translated by 12th C.
(also similar popular conviction in Brittany in 12th Cat.)

WAC
(a poet)

Layamon

the Early English
s...

Notes
① Riot in Bodmin, Cornwall in 1113 because a French monk said Arthur would never return.
② Existence not proved

Subsequent Welsh MSS. & tradition, Tudor & later pseudo-bardic invention, antiquarian & literary influences.

? ?
? ??

Red thus:
======
....
= Celtic Channels A.D.

NB. Arthur present in, but not central to main primitive...

* Though Trystan e.m. m. Romano, associated w. Cornwall
his name suggests a northern (Pictish) origin

ARYAN MYTH   Non-Aryan Myth

India (Waste-land motif)
RigVeda

...ORIC MEDITERRANEAN   NB
...CULTURES   PERSIA   3rd Cent A.D. Jewish
...EECE & ROME   & Arabian Knights
...ZANTIUM   Magian Gnosis   & troubadours at
                                       the Courts of the
...ts & Literature   Manichees   Ghassanids. (Petra-Palmyra)

...Late Empire   Arabian-Spanish complex
  mounted Knights →   Cathars ←
Madonna   PROVENÇAL COURTS of LOVE
WORSHIP

    Eleanor of Poitou (1122-1204) The Crusades
    Marie de Champagne   1095 onwards.
    (patroness of Chrétien)

...ERMAN   Western Catholic-Xtian Influences.
...ICE   ascetical and mystical.
        Metrical   The Cistercians.
        followed by
...Chrétien de Tr... Development of Eucharistic cultus (Corpus Xti 1264)
...Béroul, Thomas de Bretagne & its effect on the Western imagination & symbol.
...130 Eilhart von Oberge   (a pseudomorphosis in e.g. Grail material
...1190 Hartmann von Aue   i.e. the immemorial themes given forms
...1200 Gottfried von Strassburg   of Xtian significance.)
...1200 Wolfram von Eschenbach
        and other French & German versions (Metrical) of the separate
                                                            stories.
                              → Norwegian 1226
...t of Torigni   (Tristan)
...d copy in ... form)
...t Bec in Normandy)   → Italian 1300 (Tristan)
...n 1139
                            → Czech 1350 circa
...TH Hist. Reg. Britanniae   (Tristan)
        (present form before 1150)
...& Vita Merlini: German Prose circa 1450
...es Bretons: Rhyming chronicle was   Tristrant und
...de Brut 1155 (Just mention of Round   Isalde
...ayeux)   (in French)   Table.)

...t 1160 (Round Table theme developed
...n English & Arthur as English King   1469.
...Norman dialect) English folk-lore elements) MALORY   is a
...ion   synthesis of French material
...e & the Grene Knyghte   (Suite du Merlin etc. & insular material)
...orthern
...est...   14th Cent.
                                        XIX cent.
...t of Syr Gawayne   Richard Wagner
                                        (Tristan 1859)
...14th cent poem Mort Arthure   1809-1872   Tennyson
        a private source for Malory
...Chroniclers etc.
...   Late English Tradition ←
...   Drayton, Camden, Spencer,
...ition)   Milton, Dryden, Blake, etc.

DAVID JONES

THE ROMAN QUARRY

and other sequences

Edited by
Harman Grisewood
and
René Hague

THE SHEEP MEADOW PRESS
NEW YORK CITY

First published in MCMLXXXI by Agenda Editions,
5 Cranbourne Court, Albert Bridge Road,
London SW11 4PE, England

Text © Copyright the Estate of David Jones 1981
Editorial material © Copyright Agenda Editions 1981

ISBN   0–935296–24–7, paper
0–935296–25–5, cloth

Library of Congress Catalog Card Number: 81–52307
Published by The Sheep Meadow Press, New York
Distributed by Persea Books, 225 Lafayette St., New York, 10012

Printed in Great Britain by Poets' and Painters' Press,
146 Bridge Arch, Sutton Walk, London, S.E.1. 8XU.

DAVIDI NOSTRO
VIRO REI ROMANAE
SEMPER DILIGENTISSIMO
NUNC URBIS ILLIUS CIVI
UNDE CHRISTUS ROMANUS EST

"Qui sarai tu poco tempo silvano,
e sarai meco sanza fine cive
di quella Roma onde Cristo è Romano."
Purgatorio xxxii, 100-2*

* ("Here shalt thou be short time a forester, and with me
everlastingly shalt be a citizen of that Rome whereof Christ
is a Roman.")

CONTENTS

LIST OF ILLUSTRATIONS

frontispiece

A Genealogy of Myth
from a coloured diagram by David Jones

facing page 3

MS sheet ('Partee — party halt') from 'The Roman Quarry'
(1938-40)
(see page 49)

following page 83

MS sheet ('You still ask, where's the connection') from a
draft of 'Under Arcturus' (*c.* 1971)
(compare page 67)

facing page 87

MS sheet ('This one fetches more light') from a draft of
'The Grail Mass' (*c.* 1945-65)
(compare pages 109 and 113)

facing page 113

MS sheet ('a nice fork') from 'The Old Quarry' (*c.* 1939-40).
(see pages 131 and 155)

facing page 187

MS sheet ('I have watched the wheels go round') from
'The Book of Balaam's Ass' (*c.* 1938)
(see page 211)

page 283

Stray sheet of MS ('Commence Book on...')
(see Commentary, page 281)

FOREWORD

Some knowledge of how and why this book came to take the form it has is necessary to the reader's appreciation. The editors were not attempting to produce a volume which the poet himself would have compiled if he had lived. Our point of departure rather has been the belief that all of David's creative writing should be available, even though, in his lifetime, he was uncertain or reluctant about publishing much of what is here included. The recovery of manuscripts, the identification of the items, their arrangement and the preparation of the text — these aims were not achieved without much consultation among colleagues and hard work during five years.

David died on 28 October 1974. In the following year I was asked by his heirs to examine his papers and sort them into categories. I felt honoured by this assignment and delighted at the prospect. Visits to David's rooms for more than fifty years at his many addresses had prepared me for a large accumulation and much disorder. But when, on a fine spring day in 1975, the many boxes began to be unloaded I felt some apprehension at what lay ahead. I started work that evening. Not only the bulk but the miscellaneity was daunting. It was as if a reckless tornado had had its way with the many thousands of sheets, and had taken some impish pleasure in the companionship of a laundry list with page 68 of some early draft of *In Parenthesis*, while leaving page 69 to be found months later stuck by some unused postage stamps to an old catalogue of a Seven and Five Exhibition, inside the leaves of which were the unnumbered pages of a nameless typescript which turned out to be the missing sheets of 'Balaam's Ass'.

As this work of literary archaeology slowly progressed I concentrated my attention upon four piles of paper: the published prose, the published poetry, the unpublished prose and the unpublished poetry. After more than two years the work of classification was sufficiently advanced to begin the preparation of a volume of prose pieces. With the invaluable help of Catharine Carver this book (*The Dying Gaul*, Faber & Faber) appeared in 1978.

But the heap of unpublished poetry made a far more intractable task. I came to see that most of it had been first conceived as a large-scale epic poem with prose interludes. Later David detached passages of this work, still incomplete, and made them into the items which appear in *The Sleeping Lord*. Whether or not he was wise to isolate these particular pieces and present them separately is a question for the critics to discuss. I was confronted with the problem of what to do with the remainder, or 'the original' as it might properly be called. It is understandable that David should have quailed at the prospect of organizing this mass into a unity. It is understandable that I too trembled at the difficulty of making a presentable volume.

It was not only cowardice that made me turn to René Hague. It was the fact that he was a scholar of rare insight and he had studied the poetic writing of David more thoroughly than I. In telling him about the manuscripts which I had put together so far, I spoke of them as 'quarries' which David had subsequently used differently from their original intention. René in accepting the editorship explained that he had been asked first to produce a biographical volume which was to include a selection of David's letters. This book, *Dai Greatcoat* (Faber & Faber, 1980), duly appeared; no sooner was it finished than René fell upon the ziggurat of foolscap I had brought him, with astonishing zest. We corresponded about particular points on which he wanted my views but the main work of editorship is René's.

He brought to his editorship of *The Roman Quarry* a degree of energy and insight which younger men of comparable ability might envy; and he also brought a measure of self-sacrifice that should make us all humble. René was making plans for a book about the *Iliad*. I encouraged him.

I knew the result would be a lasting memorial to his varied gifts. All his friends wanted René to publish some creative work of his own. But he chose the self-effacing task of presenting the creative writing of his friend. He used all his strength in the completion of this work. In the last days of his life, while he was enduring much deprivation and discomfort, he concerned himself with the finishing touches to the book which he knew he would never see in print.

I was able to talk to him about these few remaining difficulties and to help in their solution. He told me how glad he was to have had the benefit of Catharine Carver's sensitive and practical mind in the preparation of the text, and how pleased he was that (Fabers having declined to publish) William Cookson of *Agenda* was to be the publisher.

In the last talk I had with him, two days before he died on 19 January 1981, René took his leave of the book, and of his friends, saying that he wanted me to explain that Catharine and I were to have a free hand in revising what he had done. 'You are the two editors now,' he said. But in fact he had done it all. Walter Shewring had composed the dedication in a form which he and René had agreed; we are most grateful to him for it and for agreeing to read the proofs. We are grateful too for the generous help and encouragement of René's other friends, and especially to Christopher Skelton, Peter Campbell and Leslie Hope. For all of us the completion of the book was felt as an expression of our admiration for René and of our concern at the loss to literature of a scholar with unique gifts of perception and sympathy.

H.J.G.

15 April 1981

INTRODUCTION

When David Jones died on 28 October 1974, his papers, correspondence and MSS were in a state of some confusion. After we had collected and examined them, we found that, apart from the MSS of printed works and of drafts associated with them, we had in all some 1,300 sheets of the poetry: nearly all foolscap, 13 × 8, written on one side, occasionally with notes on the back of the sheet. The disparity between the number of sheets and the extent of this book is accounted for by the presence among the former of numerous drafts of many passages, and of other versions of the pieces that appeared in *The Sleeping Lord* (1974).

The first thing we understand as we look at this collection is that we would be making a false distinction were we to speak of MSS of printed work and of the accompanying drafts, and MSS of unprinted work. We can, it is true, say of another collection, 'This is the MS of *In Parenthesis*, with its drafts, and that is *The Anathemata*'; but when we come to what we might be inclined to call MSS of unprinted work, we find that they are entangled with what has been printed in *The Sleeping Lord* and *The Kensington Mass*. There are even a few occasions when an 'unprinted' sheet will coincide with or come close to a passage in *The Anathemata*. The connection with the two later volumes is very much closer; and, what is more, even though the sheets with which we are now concerned fall into distinct groups, they are closely and intimately entangled with one another. We may, we believe, exclude *In Parenthesis* from this complexity and say that when David started to write again after that first book was more or less finished — that is, some time about 1935 — all that he produced, whether printed or unprinted, may be regarded as a draft for a wide-ranging poem which he was never able to complete. We then see what the poet meant when he described *The Anathemata* as 'fragments of an attempted writing' and later used the title *The Sleeping Lord and other fragments*. We might at first be inclined to say that 'The Kensington Mass' is fragmentary in another sense, because it was offered as an 'unfinished draft' and attempts were made to continue it. This is true; but that poem is also (as we shall be seeing) a fragment embedded in, and extracted from, the main body of work.

On the other hand, it cannot be denied that *The Anathemata* gives us a complete poem and that *The Sleeping Lord* gives us a sequence of complete poems — or even a complete sequence of poems. 'The Kensington Mass' too, if read without the attempts at continuation, is complete in itself. When we look at the 1,300 sheets we find that David had been following the same plan: they fall into connected groups, each of which may be seen as a section or part, showing varying degrees of progress towards what we may call either fragmentation or coalescence.

For three of these, 'The Narrows', 'The Kensington Mass' and 'The Book of Balaam's Ass', we already have titles, because they have appeared in print (the last as a section from an 'abandoned' work). For another, 'The Agent', we have adopted a title that appears in the MS as the heading to one of the sections or sub-sections. 'Under Arcturus' and 'Caillech' suggested themselves, the one from the scene and the other from the principal character, as obvious and convenient titles; and the reader can see for himself the appropriateness of the metaphor in 'The Roman Quarry' and 'The Old Quarry'.

The collection lends itself to division into four parts: First, three 'Roman' pieces. Secondly, three 'Mass' sequences. Thirdly, three 'Roman' pieces, with a strong link connecting them with what immediately precedes them. And finally, partly but by no means completely in isolation, 'The Book of Balaam's Ass'.

'The Roman Quarry' is taken from an almost complete MS,

the second part of which was rifled by David in order to extract and polish most of the pieces that appear in *The Sleeping Lord*. That second part contains versions — some of them very different from those printed by David — of 'The Hunt', 'The Sleeping Lord', 'The Tutelar of the Place', 'The Fatigue', and 'The Tribune's Visitation';* and of 'The Narrows', which has appeared only in periodicals.

Many readers will know, from an often-quoted letter of David's (in, for example, *Dai Greatcoat*, 1980, pp. 56-7), that the starting-point for all this type of writing was what David saw of Jerusalem under the British Mandate in 1934, and the analogy he drew with Judaea under a Roman Procurator at the time of the Passion. 'The Roman Quarry' starts, accordingly, with the bugle or trumpet-call that marks a change of guard. The bugler, Blondie Taranus, is a Celt. What does he think of as he blows? The Celts live in a world of illusion. Blondie is dreaming of the mists and legends of his own country. But even these Celts will be Romanized, they and their religion and imagery, by 'assimilation' and by trade that follows or accompanies the eagles. Rome will invade Britain again, and that will 'end their song'. The time is before the Claudian invasion of A.D. 43: the period, at about the end of the third decade of our era, in which are set all these Roman pieces.

So far, it is a Roman legionary who has been speaking, though somewhat as the poet's mouthpiece. The poet now begins to appear more openly, though he still speaks from the same point of view. On the other hand, much of the detail could not be known to the legionary. The poet's knowledge of the Celtic world is introduced gradually and skilfully, so that the reader accepts it and yet, when David wishes to return us to the guard-room, we can follow him without difficulty.

With invasion threatened, all that is most ancient in the Celtic world cries 'Beware!'. (This allows a pre-indication of the 'evolutionary' passages in the first part of *The Ana-themata. —* And the mention of that connection suggests

---

* These versions are printed here in their entirety, even when they differ only slightly from the form in which they appear in *The Sleeping Lord*, on the assumption that their sequence and position in David's MS will be of interest to the reader even when their content is familiar.

an explanation of a curious gap that some readers have doubtless found in *The Anathemata*: something akin to this 'Roman Quarry' might have laid stronger emphasis on the coming of Rome to Britain.) Here we meet our old friend the Dragon, standard and emblem.

Rome tames and masters the British (i.e. Welsh) streams; here the geographical writing is very careful. The mention of the Gwyddel (Irish) sea — David is always itching to get across that channel — suggests the birds of Rhiannon and their song that stopped the fighting; but even in this land of magic the 'wolf-cry' is heard. The legionary fades still more and the poet comes in more strongly. We enter the land of enchantment, and wonder as we look at the monuments of history. Who lies in the various types of tomb? ... And so we move into 'The Hunt', and the MS versions of some other interconnected pieces included in *The Sleeping Lord*.

In 'The Narrows' we continue with an allied piece which appears in a longer and more diffuse form in our MS, but which has already been printed (in the *Anglo-Welsh Review*, Autumn 1973, and in *Agenda*, Autumn-Winter 1973-4). Here we reproduce the printed text. There is no need to comment on this simple piece, but we may note that Spartacus, the Party Line, the 'withering away' of the State, the dialectic, take us back to the political climate of the years that led up to the Second World War; we glimpse, with no great pleasure, the other side of the totalitarian medal. We shall meet this again in 'The Agent', when Judas meditates on the despair of the final synthesis.

'Under Arcturus' (i.e. in the far north) completes the Romano-British part of this book. Some legionaries are talking to one another. They argue about the nature of Britain and its inhabitants. One of the speakers looks forward to the troubles from which the outskirts of the Empire will before long be suffering. He speculates about the possible emergence of an Arthurian figure, a leader of a mobile striking force who will become consecrated in legend. Another then insists on describing one of his own experiences in Britain, an attack on Hadrian's Wall. Unfortunately our MS breaks off and leaves the piece unfinished. The period is later than that of the other Roman pieces: probably at about the time of the abandonment of the Antonine Wall, from Forth to Clyde, towards the end of the second century A.D. It is clear that 'Under Arcturus' was written as a possible alternative to the attack on the Mill which forms the central part of 'The Book of Balaam's Ass'.

One of the sheets of the 'Under Arcturus' MS is dated 1971, when *The Sleeping Lord* was being prepared for press, and the handwriting shows that this MS is much later than that of 'The Roman Quarry' or 'Balaam's Ass'. This is not conclusive evidence for the date of composition: there may have been earlier versions in an earlier hand, but the presence of numerous alternative drafts suggests that this was a first trial. (About David's handwriting, we should add that with the years it became smaller and, particularly when a change was made from fountain-pen to ball-point, more crabbed. At the same time the neat and clear disposition on the page disappeared, the left-hand margin becoming wider and wider as it approached the foot of the page until only a very few tiny words can be read in the last lines.)

After these three linked pieces, we move, in Part II, to the three 'Mass' sequences. For the first, we have the printed *Kensington Mass* (Agenda Editions, 1975) in which are reproduced the fourteen sheets which appear to have been selected from the very many draft attempts as the basis for a continuation. For the second, 'Caillech', we have a comparatively straightforward (i.e. with few alternatives from which to choose) MS. It starts abruptly and ends in the middle of a sentence. For the third, 'The Grail Mass', we have the BBC duplicated script for a recording and David's fair copy.

The distinction we appear to draw between the 'Kensington Mass' and the other two Mass sequences may be misleading. It is clear that to the poet there was but one Mass poem. It dated from at least as early as January 1939, when he writes that he is absorbed in his 'Absalom, Mass, part' — an indication, moreover, that the Mass sequences are woven into the fabric of a larger work — so much so, indeed, that we may regard all that is printed here and has already been printed, after *In Parenthesis,* as parts of a single Mass poem. We may, however, treat the 'Kensington Mass' as a section that stands on its own, because it was the fruit of a deliberate fresh start, as will be explained below. It is further distinguished from other Mass writings in that it deals with a Low, as opposed to a High, Mass. The poem, as printed here, has been in circulation for some years, and we need say no more about what will be familiar to many readers.

The next two pieces are closely linked at their start and at their end, but follow different roads to the same end. In both we are present at a High Mass, in different places and with a different celebrant and a different congregation. Both converge upon the symbol of Lancelot outside the Grail chapel, for which the source was the *Morte Darthur,* Book xviii, ch. 15. 'Caillech', the first of these two, has a further link, with the *Anathemata,* for its opening lines are an elaboration of a passage in the 'Keel, Ram, Stauros' section (p. 180) in which girls of easy virtue — the courtesan had a fascination for our innocent poet — light candles before the crucifix in a church. Here again a definite statement may mislead: we may speak of 'Caillech' as an elaboration, but we cannot be sure that the passage in the *Anathemata* is not a distillation from 'Caillech'.

All the sheets of the 'Caillech' MS are headed 'Mass. Ken. m. J.O'C.' — which suggests that we should date it after the death of Fr. John O'Connor in February 1952. Neither 'Kensington' nor 'Fr. O'C.' appear on what are manifestly the earliest of the Mass drafts. The Caillech (old woman, as in the Old Woman of Beare in West Cork) is a great figure in Irish and Scottish legend: the source of mountains and lakes, the mother of countless children, time and again renewing her youth.

The third of these sequences is called for convenience 'The Grail Mass', from the reference to Lancelot and the Grail which it shares with 'Caillech'. In date of composition it precedes 'The Kensington Mass' and 'Caillech', but here it is placed after them because it overlaps with 'The Old Quarry', which follows.

'The Kensington Mass', and attempts to continue it, occupied David's last years. The first part, as printed in *Agenda* in 1974,* was completed to his satisfaction. Unhappily, it would be impossible, except in a very large book, to give a clear picture of the lines on which he sought to continue the poem. We have over 300 'Mass' sheets. Many of these are drafts of attempts at a continuation; of many it is difficult to say for which of the three sequences they were intended. The continuation sheets are particularly tantalizing. They are endlessly repetitive, and come to a halt precisely when we think a new step is about to be taken. If we look at 'The Kensington Mass' we can see how progress was effected when the poet hit upon the true line to follow. On p. 89 the priest's kissing of the altar-cloth suggests the kissing of the hem of Helen's garment, and this leads smoothly into the theme of the Emperor and his dream. That again introduces the meet at dawn, and so the dawn when the cock crowed for the third time, and so the blowing of the Olifant — associated with another betrayal, that of Ganelon — and the doom of the last line. Fourteen MS sheets, reproduced in the 1975 Agenda Edition, appear to have been put on one side as a final basis for a new line of departure. From these we gain the introduction of the notion of Absalom, hanging on the tree, as in some way — aptly or astonishingly? — signifying the other Son of David hanging on the Cross: signifying, too, the Golden Bough as the protective charm, the mark of Redemption.

This is one of the links that holds together all that is contained in this book, for the image appears both in the earliest and the latest writings. Another, which we shall meet when 'The Grail Mass' runs into 'The Old Quarry', is the parallel between the celebration of a Mass in our own day and the scene in the Cenacle, the Garden, and on Calvary. We may safely say that this notion occupied David's mind for the last forty years of his life, from 1934 to 1974, at

---

* *Agenda*, vol. 11, no. 4, vol. 12, no. 1 (Autumn–Winter 1973-4).

least. It lies behind *The Anathemata*, it is manifest in 'The Kensington Mass' and 'The Grail Mass', and in 'The Old Quarry'; it can be detected in 'Balaam's Ass'.

The 'Grail Mass' was recorded by the BBC in 1958. The quality of the recording was unsatisfactory, and it was never used. The BBC no longer have either the recording or the script, and it is only by chance that we have the latter. On the back of the last page of the fair copy we read — a further indication of the general coherence — 'Jerusalem in the first cent. A.D.'. On the paper wrapper sewn round the script is the title 'The Mass. A fragment' — a word whose correct interpretation we are beginning to understand — 'written (in part) in memory of the late Monsignor J.O'C., S.T.P. Note: An original version was made round about 1945 altered in 1958 and that printed here is a revised, corrected and somewhat altered version made in January 1965'. Then follows the BBC script, with the date, Saturday 8 March 1958. (The producer was Anna Kallin, whose memory is dear to many who were familiar with the Third Programme.) The note on the wrapper was written seven years after the recording; corrections, incorporated in the text printed in this book, have been made to the script, and they have been made with a view to the poem's being printed. We can find no trace of such printing. What is more, we strongly suspect that David mislaid both fair copy and script. In the Preface to the Agenda Editions *Kensington Mass*, William Cookson says that it is 'an entirely new version of a fragment he [David] first drafted *c.* 1940 but subsequently lost'. We may, therefore, conclude that in 'The Grail Mass' we have the lost draft.

When David later, at a date we cannot determine, returned to the Mass theme, he worked on the somewhat different lines of 'The Kensington Mass'. A further distinction between the two Masses is that the title 'Kensington Mass' does not appear in 'The Grail Mass', even though David must have been working on it when he was living in Sheffield Terrace during the war, and was attending the Carmelite church in Church Street, Kensington. The title first appears in a number of drafts which almost give the impression of there having been yet one more

Mass, intermediate between 'Kensington' and 'Grail'. The latter was written 'in part' for Fr. O'Connor, because it was started long before Fr. O'Connor's death in 1952.

If we associate 'The Grail Mass' with the Carmelite church in Kensington, we may also associate 'The Kensington Mass' with the church of Our Lady and St Thomas of Canterbury in Harrow, which David used to attend after his move to Northwick Lodge in 1947. At one time, the picture *A latere dextro* was called by David 'The Kensington Mass'. It represents, as can be seen by visiting the church, what David saw of the building from his position on the epistle side, in front of the Lady altar. 'Caillech' cannot be so localized. We have a church in Dublin (known to David only by passing through it for demobilization) and references to Bootle in Lancashire, to Bradford (suggesting the church of St Cuthbert where he was received into the Church by Fr. O'Connor), and, vaguely, to London.

We may, then, appropriately group these three Mass sequences together in our Part II.

Part III opens with the link between 'The Grail Mass' and 'The Old Quarry'. Our MS of the latter, which falls into two parts, contains 129 consecutive sheets, numbered by David 3-102 with a certain number of additions (17A, 17B etc.) which account for the difference in the two totals. The first two sheets are missing. However, the reader will see that towards the end of 'The Grail Mass' attention is turned to the congregation, and that 'The Old Quarry' starts in the same way — one of those present is trying to watch the actions of the celebrant at the altar. Fortunately, we have among the drafts for 'The Grail Mass' a sheet which fills the gap. This sheet is headed by three large asterisks and 'space of three lines'. The text then runs into the same words ('corbels, hangings, mouldings') as those which open 'The Old Quarry'. We are justified, then, in taking that overlap as the beginning of 'The Old Quarry'.

We have no difficulty in deciding where to end this first part. A line in David's sheet 25 reads 'a nice fork. That's the crux of it', and between 'fork' and 'That's' there is a large star, with a note in the margin 'Begin here Section XIV'. ('Section' is used in the MSS to indicate what we might call a separate 'piece'; thus the 'Roman Quarry' MS concludes with 'End of Section XII', indicating the end of 'The Tribune's Visitation'. We may reasonably regard the first part of 'The Old Quarry' as Section XIII.)

It is clear that David, almost unconsciously, as he wrote of the death on the Cross, ran on into an entirely different subject. He had led up to the final scene, with the division of Christ's garments, and, looking back later, found that he had moved into a conversation in which the whole affair was discussed.

The general movement of 'The Old Quarry', Part One, is clear enough. The modern Mass leads into the Last Supper, the betrayal, the Mount of Olives, the agony, the arrest, the appearance before the High Priest, Herod, Pilate and his wife's message, the humiliation in the Praetorium, Calvary. Interpretation of detail is more difficult. We may, it is true, keep in reserve the excuse that in this piece, even more than in other unpublished pieces, David's writing is unchecked. We might almost say — using the words in no disparaging sense — that he puts down the first thing that comes into his mind, almost without reflection. It is certainly true that in the early stages of composition his ideas and images proliferated, and that his chief concern when revising was to prune and introduce a strict logical succession. (A picture will be condemned, a piece of writing will be praised, for being 'tight'.) We may not be able at first to construct a completely satisfactory explanation of themes and details, but we must beware of falling back on the plea that what is an initial recording of thoughts is necessarily unintelligible. Those thoughts, and their expression, are always derived from his observation and, still more, his reading: and to these there are endless clues.

Still confining ourselves to generalities, we may then add that, as always, a number of separate strands are woven together. Here we have the celebration of a High Mass (where, as in the Mass sequences, considerable attention is paid to what is rapidly disappearing from common knowledge, the rubrics of the Tridentine Mass), the parallel with the Gospel narratives, comparisons with others who were victims or suffered 'misadventure' — in particular the puzzling Absalom — the various forms of the Waste Land (seen against the topography of Jerusalem: maps of Jerusalem in Biblical and New Testament times are useful — as is Schürer's *History of the Jewish People in the Time of Christ*), language and imagery from several of the Prophets, the Psalms and the historical books, the Prodigal Son, the *Mabinogion*. To see all these with true coherence would call for the sort of running commentary that the intelligent reader can construct for himself. In his accompanying notes to this, and to the next piece, the poet himself has made a beginning: but, as in *The Anathemata*, he is not concerned to explain his general intention.

Between the two parts of 'The Old Quarry' we interpolate 'The Agent'. This follows naturally as an elaboration of the references to the betrayal in 'The Old Quarry', Part One. It contains four clearly marked sections. Judas soliloquizes on the theme of his predestined treachery. The scene at the Last Supper — Judas has slipped out — the betrayal. Judas speaks with Caiaphas — Caiaphas looks into the future and back into the past. Judas with the armed party in the Garden — the arrest — the beginning of the Passion. David's notes are an indication of progress towards completion with a view to publication: and two readers, at least, find 'The Agent' the most finished, valuable and interesting piece in this collection.

We complete Part III with the second half of 'The Old Quarry'. This is first mentioned in letters in March 1940 (to H.J.G., 'I've been continuing my conversation at the time of the Passion'). Twenty-two years later he writes, again to H.J.G., 'I'm trying to re-write that thing you liked — the dinner party with the old Roman blimp and the girl and the subaltern in Jerusalem at the time of Our Lord's Passion. I used to feel it was crude and impious, but on re-reading it, I think I can make something of it — at least I hope so. I'm also trying to re-write a thing I did in 1940 (or thereabouts) about a conversation between Judas and Caiaphas' — i.e. 'The Agent'. 'The Old Quarry', Part Two, is one of the smoothest, most fluent and most easily followed of David's writings. The speakers are not identified in the MS. There are only one or two places where the reader may be in doubt, and we have thought it best to allow him to decide for himself who is speaking. Most of the talking comes from the old man. The girl Julia's fashionable interests will soon be apparent. The young man is altogether too inarticulate and conventional for her and, should they marry, we cannot but be apprehensive about their future.

We should note a parallel with *The Anathemata*, p. 89, in the reference to the Romans as letter-cutters; and in the last sentence the coincidence with Matthew 27: 45, 'from the sixth hour there was darkness over the whole earth, until the ninth hour'. The conversation was taking place as Christ was on the Cross.

That appropriately ends the third part of our book. 'The Book of Balaam's Ass' stands more on its own. David regarded it as experimental. It differs from other writings — apart, that is, from the central section — in that it is not a realization of what the poet has seen (supplementing his vision by his reading) but is purely imaginative. It is a 'rambling affair' about 'ideas', he says in a letter of May 1938, his problem being to express them in concrete imagery.

The first section leads into what will be more familiar in style to the reader, the attack on the Mill in the battle of Passchendaele. The version printed here differs slightly from that included in *The Sleeping Lord*. We may note in particular that the Melchisedec passage (pp. 108-9) was added in the later, printed version, and so provides another entry into the scheme of *The Anathemata* (p. 230). After the attack we return to the Balaam theme and the strange and unexpected 'Zone', in which camp life is, by analogy, the life and world of mechanized man. It is to this zone that the 'A, a, a, Domine Deus' which opens *The Sleeping Lord* was first, and appropriately, attached.

Anyone who has not read, or who has forgotten the details of, the story of Balaam's ass would do well to read Numbers 22-4 before reading this piece. David must have been impressed, too, by what is said of Balaam in 2 Peter

2 : 15-16: 'Leaving the right way they' — the children of malediction — have gone astray, having followed the way of Balaam of Bosor who loved the wages of iniquity, but had a check of his madness, the dumb beast used to the yoke, which, speaking with man's voice, 'forbade the folly of the prophet'.

From the story of Balaam was taken the idea that the animals are as much part of the cosmos which is loved by God as is man, and, further, that you may well imagine a situation in which the animal sees beyond the physical appearances that present themselves to man, and can so distinguish the divine. This idea is used in the third part of the poem as a way of expressing what on other occasions was presented as the difference between the utile and the gratuitous, the technical and the poetic, between use and sign. Those who are alive only to the first member of those three pairs are as Balaam; those who see beyond are as the donkey, who could see the angel when Balaam could not. They are alive to the 'sweet influence' that governs the world.

A further notion commended itself to the poet: that however much you feel called upon to curse your world as you look at it, your curse is expressed in an art-work; that work is of its nature a form of praise because it is directed towards a transcendent which we may call truth or being or beauty and which informs the work. The poet is therefore as Balaam, who was summoned to curse and was forced to bless.

There is a direction on the MS that the opening words shall be in capitals. Publication of the whole piece must, therefore, have been seriously considered. We know that David was working on 'Balaam's Ass' even before *In Parenthesis* was ready for the press. Of the central section he writes in December 1973, 'I've included some stuff that I made immediately after *In Parenthesis* was more or less finished, made partly at Sidmouth and Hartland Point and in that "cottage" on the Falmer estate' — i.e. the Mill House, Falmer, on the Stanmer estate — 'where Prudence and Lady Chichester lived, and was going to be called The Book of Balaam's Ass but I abandoned the project, as it would not come together.' Nevertheless, we feel that we are justified in closing our eyes to the 'cats-teeth' with which the seams have been sewn.

As so often, we start with a pronoun — no names, no pack drill; but in view of the time and place of composition, we think that there can be no doubt but that this opening sentence refers to Prudence Pelham. The Fort Hotel, Sidmouth, was very much a place of 'small conveniences' — tinned grapefruit? — though 'proud and rotten accidents' is a little hard on Sidmouth. While, however, the meaning is that the grace of one particular person will influence and give dignity to what is in itself (in spite of its pride) merely accidental (as opposed to substantial, and therefore rotten rather than real) yet this same person stands for more, for the principle of love and care, incarnate in Our Lady, which makes this vale of tears habitable.

Here, again, editors have to resist the temptation to offer, so far as they can, detailed exposition which most readers will prefer to provide for themselves.

Reference, necessarily vague, has been made above to dates. It may be well to record or repeat what precise knowledge we have:

1934. The visit to Jerusalem lies behind everything that was written after *In Parenthesis.* (See *Dai Greatcoat*, p. 56.)

22 November 1934. To R.H., 'I can almost hear his' — Canon Gray's — '*Nobis quoque peccatoribus* and the throat-clearing.' A trifle, but the mannerism, observed, too, in Fr. O'Connor, and the breaking of the silence of the Canon were to remain as detonators for forty years.

31 May 1938. A letter (to H.J.G.) of some length about 'taking up again' his first attempt in a new form of writing ('Balaam's Ass'). This is referred to again in letters of 17 January and 11 April 1939 (see *Dai Greatcoat*, pp. 86, 89-90). These letters show us what to expect in 'Balaam' and how to interpret it. A sentence in the last letter shows that we must take 'Balaam' as closely connected with the

'Mass' sequences, and therefore with 'The Roman Quarry' and 'The Old Quarry'.

1938-40. The back of the cover of the 'Roman Quarry' MS has the address 3 Glebe Place, Chelsea, S.W.3, which places it in those years.

January 1939. To H.J.G., 'I'm absorbed in my Absalom, Mass, part now.'

March 1940. To H.J.G., 'I've been continuing my "conversation at the time of the Passion".'

1941, or later. On the back of a sheet of 'The Agent' is a note, 'Back in a few minutes', addressed to Louis Bussell, who used to visit David at Sheffield Terrace, to which he moved in the autumn of 1941, and which he left in 1947.

Whitsun eve (27 May) 1944. A similar note on the back of a Mass sheet.

21-3 June 1944. This date is on the back of one of the sheets of 'The Agent'.

February 1952. Death of Mgr. John O'Connor. 'In memory of' is added to drafts of Mass sequences.

8 March 1958. BBC recording of 'The Grail Mass'.

28 May 1962. Letter to H.J.G., 're-writing the "conversation",' i.e. 'The Old Quarry', Part Two.

1971. On the back of an 'Under Arcturus' sheet David tries, unsuccessfully, to convert A.D. 1971 into A.U.C. *The Sleeping Lord* was published in 1974, and that David was working on 'Under Arcturus' in 1971 suggests that he may have considered using it in the extract from 'Balaam's Ass' instead of the Passchendaele episode.

Even this short list of certain dates shows how no single piece of writing can be separated chronologically from the others.

Finally, it will, we hope, be understood that we are reading the pages that follow in confidence, so to speak — a confidence that the poet is unable to withhold. So fastidious a writer would not have published these pieces unrevised. Nevertheless we are justified in printing them, both because of their many felicities and profundities, and because they illuminate and, even in this unfinished form, complement work that many readers have admired and loved and that David Jones himself was willing to make public.

H.J.G.
R.H.

July 1980

I

THE ROMAN QUARRY
THE NARROWS
UNDER ARCTURUS

Partee — party; halt.

Party — stand fast men detailed

re-mainder — steady.

Middle watch — to quaters — Dismiss.

* * *

(end of section, space of 5 lines)

Section XI

Sergeant, Sergeant! — where's the
sergeant of the guard.

He's about cock if you can find
him under his medals.

(Space of 2 lines)

What's your excitement, you jumping
Mercury — d'you want me or
holy Jupiter — or is it a double
issue you're after — or've y'r seen
the ghost of Jesus Maccabee.

(space of one line)

THE ROMAN QUARRY

There she blows, there she goes
the old tin tube rings clear
    Back to kip for section six
    The monkey's knackers for section seven

At the chill of the wind at the turn o' the wall
    Double up slow-boys
    Double up Seven
double to see Aurora's leg
kick back the starry blankets
You can break the hearts of gods and men
You won't break Caesar's
division of time
nor the august routine

There she goes again — sets term at long last to the middle-
vigil, calls these to the freshing wind at the third relief,
beckons these to stand down, harbingers for these the
guardhouse fug where the companions nod, where the black
billikin brews the dawn-broth, where the clear charcoal
glows for y'r stiffened palms and the stressed accents tell
bucolic song and the companion throats leave quantity
to cissy Greeks.[1]

---

[1] 'It is usually believed — but not universally — that the earliest
Latin poetry was scanned by stress, not by quantity; and that
the principle of scansion by quantity was adopted from Greek
poetry. There is evidence that the use of stress was never en-
tirely abandoned.' (W. F. Jackson Knight, *Vergil's Troy*, 17.)

3

There she goes — there she goes again — from Conduit
Keep — that's Blondie Taranus[2] I'll swear — he always
makes a bollocks of the first bar — sounds more like the
cock o' Gaul trumpeting the Britannic hen across the misty
Fretum.

Cushy job, those trumpeters, sweet fanny to do but swell
their cheeks a fine imperial hue at each vigilia's term.

An' the strut on 'em in their special clobber — and the
lip of 'em with their extra pay — they fancy they're the
Darlings of Athena — to bring all the world-walls down.

These west-wave Celts are all the same — tow-heads or red,
short arse or lankies, bond or freed — they all reckon on
celestial connections. The Julian line, the Claudian house,
the gens Cornelia — that's all jumped-up stuff to their way
of thinking — same with the muses and the invented in-
struments — there's nothing good in the world but what
there's better in the White Island.

To hear 'em talk you'ld suppose the Divine Julius was
blown from Thule back to Bononia by nothing but a barrage
of British horns.

Blondie can blow his Roman horn and pocket Roman
pay — but what does he see from his fronted eyes when
he sounds the vigilia call?

Most like his mind's on the canteen with the rest of us —
but in his mind within his mind are other eyes that see not
quadrilateral shapes as ours do, but broken contours and
drifting things and confluences between small hills where the
Degeangli[3] grope between the sea-damps and the mountain-
damps, with swords like leaves and horses wear coats of

Tanarus [accent on first syllable]. See Collingwood and Myres,
Roman Britain, 262. [See *The Sleeping Lord*, 55, n. 1, for D.'s
explanation of how 'Tanarus' became 'Taranus'.]

[3] The Degeangli were a tribe which in Roman times occupied
Flintshire. Cantref Tegeingl was still the district name in the
Middle Ages. At Mold (in Tegeingl) early in the last century,
there was found the great and exceedingly beautiful horse-
peytrel (pectoral) now in the British Museum. The beaver was
hunted in Wales until the Middle Ages.

river-gold and men wear coats of river-beast — so they do say.

How I figure it out is they open their mothers' wombs on a misty bed — some say the cold's not over horrible and some there's no true night year in year out, and others that it's dusk at high noon — but all say of the far isles that walls of fog drift all day and every day and the salt sea they say reaches their inmost valleys and all is a maze of meeting damps and ebb and flow of mist and tide so that the waters are, in a manner of speaking, lord of all.

From infancy they feed on illusion — the very elements refract their thoughts — their brain-pans are as full of mist as their hill-circles. When they step in our ordered light and know the clear sky where Caesar reigns they yet walk like men in a dream and in their puzzled heads there yet rings the tumbling of the waters and estuary fret.

And they do say that in the country of the Demetae, in another west-hill track of that March hare's island there is a black mountain and on the black mountain a black water and under the black water a race of naiads, as it were, who sometimes come to surface and, so they do say, will leave their water-kin and celebrate the rites with mortals and share the griefs of mortals and conform all ways to the pattern of mortals, both as to the comfortable things, as flesh with kindly flesh and as to what they call their *cyfraith*, what a civilized party 'ld call *lex*.

And all seems festal in the green valley and economically on the up-tack too, for these naiads of Dyfed bring dower of milch-cows and plough-bullocks what's more, so they do say. Till one fine day the inadvertent iron contacts the fairy skin and back goes water-bride to water-lord and back goes water-kine to water-byre — and that surprises all; and no thing left, but the twin fruit of vanished water-wife, mewling for breasts that are not and a bewildered mortal man moaning for those same breasts and for his lost cattle-dower, groping his native mists alone to bark his dreamer's head on the hard edge of fact.

These things, comrade, are said for an allegory: as soft-smelted Belgic iron is to water-bride, so is Roman steel to the Britanni, so is continental fact to island dreams, so is the world-sun to Thule mist, so are our shock formations to their loose deployments.

But by assimilation most of all we conquer them and by equation too, comrade. Their Sulis[4] we can juxtapose with great Minerva, and she how dim she'll shine down the history-paths — how bright the other. Nodens by the water and the wood must learn that even gods can be decoyed within, and have a roof and tessellated floor — he'll hardly recognize himself in bronze.

Briginda,[5] her cause approved, — the Army for her devotees, — why, she'll cut a more substantial figure as Dea Brigantia — darling of the unlucky ninth.[6]

We'll mix their Bride-lights with the lights of Syriac God-bearers, and gusty flames they coax within the wattle

---

[4] Sulis, the female Celtic deity associated with Bath, was under Roman patronage linked with Minerva, and a Sulis-Minera cult developed in connection with the warm springs — fire-rites were part of the ritual.

[5] Briginda is one form of the Dea Brigantia of the Roman altar inscription found in Yorkshire. She seems to have some affinity with the cult-deity Brigit.
The fore-associations of Brigit are well known, and the possible relationship of those Celtic fire-rites with the Mediterranean has been noted by scholars. In Scotland the 'Bleeye of Brigit' was kept on 1 February, the eve of Candlemas. At Kildare, the burial-place of the Christian Brigit, a fire-ceremonial persisted into the Middle Ages. The titles 'Mary of the Gael', 'Mother of the King', are Irish titles applied to Brigit as saint. The river Braint in Anglesey is thought to get its name from the Celtic cult-deity. The elements brig and braint imply what is high and what is privileged. So perhaps we can go so far as to suppose that we are dealing with variations of a great cult-figure, sometimes associated with fire, sometimes not; and like Minerva and Demeter and other Mediterranean figures, of many aspects. At Birrens in Dumfriesshire a Romano-British statue has been found of Dea Brigantia in the guise of Minerva. It is precisely these interchanges and approximations that concern us.

[6] [See Graham Webster's The Roman Imperial Army, 82-3, where he speaks of the 'romantic aura of mystery and imagination which has surrounded the disappearance of IX — a great Roman defeat has been visualized, leading to its replacement by VI Victrix', and discusses other possibilities. R.H.]

6

hedge shall call to carried flame lit from Demeter's torch —
till, in the woof of time there'll be but one queen of the
candles, and by whatever name they call her she'll be in
Roman rig.

I wouldn't be hard on 'em — after the steel comes the
softer wares, indeed before, to soft 'em up a bit to make
the steel's work more certain — corrupt their economies
before we break their wills — that's already under way —
the peaceful penetration's doing well, there are some who
say.

Once your Briton sees his drooped moustaches in a Corin-
thian mirror, sold him by a Greek Massiliot, off they'll
come. Once his women finger the baled linen from Scytho-
polis,[7] a length of tawny silk from Cos,[8] what's a mere man
to do? What's freedom, what's autarchy, compared with
smooth Sidonian glass. Next his sons 'll pawn their golden
collars to buy a white length of toga-cloth — and shear
their milk-white necks of golden locks, and into the salvage
bin goes the striped war-coat and the madder sagulum.
Who'ld be an island hobbadehoy in home-cut trews when
the world-mode can rig you out as flash as a Syro-Phoeni-
cian jockey.[9]

Once cats freighted at Nisibis or striped Hyrcanian ones[10]
that the wind begets on a cat-mother, and Mauretanian
lions shipped from Alex, throw up the British mud under

---

[7] Scythopolis (Bethshan) in Batanaea, 20 miles S.E. of Nazareth,
one of the towns of the Decapolis, an important centre of the
linen industry.

[8] Cos, famed for silk manufacture (yellow as opposed to white
from China).

[9] Many Syro-Phoenicians were to be found supplying the pro-
fessional sport and entertainment markets of the Empire.

[11] Nisibis, on the Mesopotamian trade-route. This district pro-
vided many of the leopards used in the games.
Tigers from Hyrcania (Armenia) were sometimes obtained.
There was a belief that all tigers were tigresses and that the
wind was the male parent, because of the agility of these
animals. The traffic from India came to Charax on the Persian
Gulf, thence through Palmyra to the West.

7

the stretched velarium that's meant for sun but sagged and
limp in the prevailing soaker, rows of damp Britons make
Roman holiday to pile the takings of a syndicate co-
terminous with ocean[11] — once these things are, the mission
of empire is accomplished.

What, then, susceptible Britannia, when any tout from
Miletus can unpack his pretty wares[12] by soft Thames run.

That will end their song, when sandy-floored Sabrina
breaks on Illyrian keels,[13] and narrow Nedd between the
mud-flats — and even the far sinuses of Rhôs feel a flow
across the ebb, know a new tide that floods all tides — and
the submerging suck from far-out wash of galleys laden:
    when the flotillas white the tide that washes tidal Isca
and Severn-flood floods to *hendre*-height with tides of
empire.

And the aged ousel of Cilgwri pipes beware to fauna more
aged still, and from the rotted flora of heaped ages the
ancient antlers lift the grey hunched sleeper that never moves
his stance for flint-head flight or flying bronze hoots at
the oldest carnivores of all
    who saw the world-woods three times change from
acorn-shoot to lignite bed, from whose weary pinions, the
last grey moultings fall to the secret pool
    and the primordial fish that was before them all — long
long before and before again, before the whirling sticks
caught the worm of fire — much, far before, far again

[11] To 'make the empire co-terminous with ocean' was said to
be the aim of Julius Caesar.

[12] Miletus had a name for disreputable traffic: sexual goods
(*olisbos, baubôn*).

[13] Roman biremes were called *liburnae* after the name of the
light fast vessels of Illyrian pirates. Subsequently the word was
applied to any Roman naval ship. The Illyrian name, I imagine,
conjured up for the Romans good sailors and sea-faring, just as
the word 'Devon' does for us — a British man-of-war might easily
have become known as 'a Devonian', and the engine-room of
any ship might well be called 'Scotland'.

who kept slow amoeboid vigils on world-bed, who heard
the dumb anaphoras from creatures crawling world-slime,
who bears the barbed name of Ichthus,
  the king-salmon of Glevum,[14]
with his fish-eye that saw the ages die
tells the water-darks,
Beware!
and as quick light he glides the water-paths, down, down
deeps, deep down by deep ulterior water-track below, yes
— far it is below again, where, past where, the secret prison
is, where the lamenting trembles the waters deep under world-
floor, deep beneath world-flow, to where the captive ages
wait
and all cry, Beware!
Ichthus comes, all cry Ichthus comes who knows all
things — so old he is who is by water and by slime, who
knows the mutations and the silent metamorphoses, who is
by water and by blood — who shines like the nine darting
choirs.
Transfixed and burdened with the fifty spears he is, yet
so quick he is and agile as light when he turns in the dark
tracks.
Ichthus of the three liaisons, who mirrors in his saucer-eye
the feathered things and the things of fur when he breaks
the rippled filament of the water-sphere to drink the
atmosphere.

---

[14] The salmon of Llyn Llwy, the eagle of Gwern Abwy, the owl
of Cwm Cawlyd, the stag of Redynfre, the ousel of Cilgwri:
these, in tradition, are the five oldest existing creatures — I give
them in order of age, the ousel being the youngest.
  In *Kulhch and Olwen* they are each questioned (from
youngest to oldest) as to the whereabouts of Mabon ap Modron,
who is imprisoned beneath the waters of the Severn at Glevum
(Gloucester). The order of their age is somewhat suggestive of
the 'evolutionary stages' of modern science. And in the idea
of water being the element of the earliest form of life and the
womb of all terrestrial forms we have a more accurate guess.
  The ancient salmon fish had in his sides 'fifty fish-spears'.
He carried the heroes of 'Arthur' on his back to the relief of
Mabon from his underworld prison.

9

His solitary eye that slipped the first fisher's double-barb, has seen what the falling feathers tell that tell what the owl of the cwm was told by the stag of the thousand winters, what the water-ousel saw above the estuary-bar on world-floor,

where anthropos walks so proud — so young he is — O yes, so young and late in time he is he thinks he can measure all things that are before he was

the fledgling of earth-time so young he is he knows nothing, yes yes, so young he is he has not yet learned to sit still.

And all cry: beware, the most young of these youngest, these come, more active than any yet that have come, they borrow from all, and because of their ingenuity they surpass all, and they understand less than any.

The new Arya treads world-shoal with gilt-pinioned creatures of the air and the winged beast of Parthia,[15] his silver jaws drinking the world-wind to enlarge himself, held at rigid leash on numbered and medallioned poles, by men in lion-pelts[16] and these several, whose directional movements pivot the massed direction of these many whose ribs the iron laminations brace, — and all move as though one iron thorax caged the even pulse of one organism, whose iron cheek-guards cause the many eyes fixed single-eyed on one immediate mark.

And these many walk not as many but as one out of the sea. Their iron-shod feet toil the draining shingle not as many feet but as one man's feet moving on one articulation,

---

[15] The *Draco* standard was borrowed from the Parthians, under Trajan. The jaws were made of a rigid material and the body was a coloured silk bag which inflated in the wind in the form of a dragon.

[16] 'In place of a helmet they' — the *signiferi* — 'wore a head-dress made of a lion's skin ... the words of command were directed to them, being given by the general to the trumpeters ...' (H. Stuart Jones, *Companion to Roman History*, 213.) The title, number and battle-honours of the unit were signified by those saucer-shaped discs characteristic of Roman standards.

heavy they are and their many weights are as one weight bearing on one objective.

And these some red-combed like the cock[17] bark like the grey dog, and these many, for that dog-cry, pattern strict formations as if the ordered pleiad deployed earth-floor — so shine their surly order does.[18]

And their related unities grid a hard beauty from torrid Pharphar et fluvii Damasci to fierce Ebro flood, from Cyrene shore to the cool washed weirs of Rhôs.[19]

Because comrade:

at the disembarkation point, the green-gilled details fall in, as best they may on the shivering markers, with a bawling *optio* barking 'em into some sort of shape, and at the usual command the sea-doused signifier, spitting out the briny, doubles to his column station and ports the section's *draco* and she droops like a wet Monday wash on an old mare's prop — but now for a cupful o' wind she flaps a bit, but now the bright jaws drink

and now she bellies fine to the breeze of Guenedota,[20] and they see for the first time their destined totem.

---

[17] It is true that ordinary legionary soldiers wore, in some periods, a helmet crest; but I mean here the distinctive plume of the officers and N.C.O.s — all with parade-ground lungs.

[18] [The odd construction at the end of the paragraph should be read as 'so does their surly order shine'. R.H.]

[19] The wattled weir at Llandillo yn Rhôs functioned until quite recent times; but, revisiting it in 1937 [cf. *Epoch and Artist*, 27], I found it in complete decay. The hill behind is called Bryn Euryn or the Golden Hill, perhaps because of the gorse on its slopes and below. From this hill across the bay one sees the Little Orme, a name of Viking origin. On this shore, when a child, I saw the bodies of two persons washed up from the sea.

[20] Guenedota = Gwynedd = N.W. Wales. The destined totem is the Red Dragon. It is most probable that this emblem derived from the late-Roman military ensign called the *Draco* [see n. 15 above]. It is now known from Bede (*Eccl. Hist.*, ch. xvi) that Roman insignia were adapted or retained by barbarians, so that it is only to be expected that semi-barbarians, semi-Roman leaders such as Cadwaladar, should be found to be associated with a Roman signum. It has been

So mate, their very signa we fetch for them — let history
weave but long enough: their special boasts down the dim
history-paths where the race-memories fork and criss-cross
are boasts of our begetting.

When the tumbled caer above Seiont[21] sees the squared
castellum pile, and from the river-massif the river-matres[22]
whisper:
    the race which is the pontifex
    need find no ford
    for all our westing-flows, for any of
    our easting daughters
    that scour the primal beds

---

suggested that the name of the flag came to be applied to the
officer or chief who employed it: hence 'Pendragon' as a rank-
name.

It might be further suggested that long afterwards under
quite other conditions the symbol was re-employed or assumed
new prominence as a 'national' flag. Some supposition of this
nature suggests itself, because there appears to be no evidence
for the actual use of the dragon, whether as a flag or official
title, among the Welsh under the native princes in Norman
or Plantagenet times (ruling out possible poetic references and
legendary associations). On the other hand, one English king,
it seems, employed it in campaigning against them. Glyn Dwr
is said to have raised it as the sign of his national rising; and
Henry Richmond, for his own propagandist purposes, used it;
and from Tudor times onwards it has been regarded as
specifically the emblem of Wales.

[21] There was a native hill-fort at Llanbeblig above the river
Saint or Seiont, where the Romans built Segontium (Carnar-
von). Whatever is the relationship between Segontium, the
name of the Roman military station, and the river Seiont or
Saint, the native Y Gaer Saint yr Arfon, or Caer yn Arfon,
Carnarvon, the fort in Arvon, remains the name of the site,
or sites, for the succession of fortresses. It is of some interest
that the native word Caer should have been retained to de-
scribe both the hill-forts and the new military stations, so that
today 'Caer', not only for the Welsh but for all of us, evokes
the feeling of defence no less than 'dun' or 'burg' or 'burh'.

[22] From the main N.-S. mass of the Cambrian mountains rise
many streams; the Pumlumon ('Plynlymon') group is called,
on this account, 'The Mother of Rivers'.

12

and score the tilted floors
that sweep the talus down and
mock the failing grey wackes
(that once had mocked all waters, so hard they came from the ancient fires).

All the bounding naiad-ways break their frolics on the centred piles, cease their laughing liberties at the curbing piers, dance to a stricter tune for the dark conduits where the vaulted sluices sewer and regulate

Because the men with the groma[23] align the Via Helena from Kai's fort to Maridunum, because the Men of the Strider must walk the via they'll call Julia south and beyond Merlin's burg,[24] with culverts for Towy, a filed-pontoon for Cowyn, with a sapper's quick span for little Cynin and the same for twisting Tâf[25]

with lashed fascines or a duck-board each for all the winding courses that ambulate the virid ways, where the subsidiary viae fork to the forward stations.

For all the gay eroders that lush the draining valley-troughs to Narberth, where the *palas* is[26]

[23] *Groma*: an instrument for taking measurements and angles.

[24] Via Helena: The Welsh call sections of the Roman road from N. to S. Wales the *Sarn Elen,* Helen's way or road. The name commemorates Helen, wife of Maximus; she is important in Welsh tradition.

Kai's fort: Caergai, the Roman fort near Bala lake. Maridunum, Carmarthen, seems to have been a tribal centre before the Romans built their *castellum.* Caer Fyrddin, the native form, means 'Merlin's fort'. The Via Julia is a name applied to some sections of road reputed to be Roman, but this naming seems to be an invention of antiquarians.

[25] Each of the small streams mentioned must have been crossed by Roman field-companies and other detachments (if not by lesser military ways no longer traceable) to the routine relief of such forward posts as that of Castle Flemish; but the Ordnance Survey *Map of Roman Britain* (1931) marks no Roman road south-west of Carmarthen, as the positive archaeological evidence is lacking. [Nor does the current, 1956, 3rd edition.]

[26] Narberth has mythological and historical associations as an important site, and we have such expressions as 'at Narberth his chief palace' from where 'originated all honour'.

and by the dark boundary-stream:
where the prince who hunted, met
the Jack of Hunters
in the woof of grey[27]
and the pale dogs deep under earth-floor lit the dim chase.

Even at the confines
    where this is that, that, perhaps was this,
even there, where is the moving wall of mist where
was the pillared hall

because of the inversions and the transmogrifications
where the illusions bind and loose, where the inadver-
tent word binds the word-looser
    where every barrier shifts:

does the confine-stream define the upper from the
lower commote or is Afon Cych Cocytus?
Cothi[28] of the quickset hedge Acheron?
Does meandering Gwaun[29] flow to the Gwyddel Sea, or
does she empty in that under-flood where the eternal
bargain holds Proserpine from fall to crocus-time?

Where, they do say, the singing birds yet sing the song the
ported weapons heard gripped still, for the eight sweet
decades in the stilled grip of listening warriors
    the song the tough spear-stocks heard that faltered, at the
ready.

[27] Readers of the *Mabinogion* will recall how Pwyll, Prince of
Dyfed, met Arawn, Lord of the underworld, hunting at the
boundary-stream called the Cuch (the river Cych at the modern
Carmarthenshire–Cardiganshire border) and how the mortal
prince and the king of Hades exchanged dominions and iden-
tities for one year, and how such transpositions and meta-
morphoses are typical of those tales. The immortal hunter was,
like John Peel, in 'a coat of grey'.

[28] Cothi: this is with reference to an ancient farm holding in
the Cothi valley, called Maes-y-Bidieu, 'the field of the quick-
set hedges'.

[29] The river Gwaun, apart from a sharp bend near its source in
the Presely hills, describes a gentle curve to reach the Irish
Sea near Fishguard (Abergwaun).

The song that checked the hafted iron at long point, that stayed the close-handed upward jab, that withheld at middle drive the maiming butt-stroke.[30]

The winged-spell of the creatures of Rhiannon the Mother,[31] that deflects the arissed shaft-heads, that holds back the socketted axes from the blue-enamelled shields,[32] from the dear bodies anxious behind the shields, from the pierced limbs of the sweet sons.

The song the lifted weapons heard: the long dark-tempered blades and the holed hammers of polished felsite[33] lifted at the stroke that never fell
    because of the song-spell.

The song the tendoned limbs heard and the articulations of bone and corded sinew that implement the weapons
    the song the fisted knuckles heard that are taut and pale

[30] I use the terms of bayonet-drill because they are the only terms of which we have experiential acquaintance, and so the only ones with emotional validity; and also because of the genealogy: spear — pike — bayonet, and because of the common elements: haft, butt, blade. The sequence of movements in that drill may possibly disclose a very remote technique. In this connection it has been remarked how similar, for example, was the Roman arms-drill to our own.

[31] The 'song of the birds of Rhiannon' is a recurring theme. Rhiannon is queen and wife and mother; her son is 'Anxiety' (Pryderi). All beauty 'was as nothing compared to her beauty'. Her mysterious quality whereby no pursuer could gain upon her, though her gait appeared to be tranquil and not in haste, her acceptance of the abominable penance of the horse-block, the vengeance-spell cast upon her at the marble fountain, her bondage in the asses' cellar, her trials, her wisdom and her patience are famous, but her singing birds and the sweetness and efficacy of their song are more famous. Battles ceased because the warriors became immobilized by the sound-spell, but as a late Triad bitterly observes, that song is seldom heard. As seldom, says the Triad, as wisdom from a Saxon, or largesse from a miser, is the sound of those birds.

[32] Shields decorated with blue enamel are listed and priced in the codes.

[33] Stone hammers: see Wheeler, *Pre-Historic Wales*.

15

for pressure of the white-hilted iron;[34] that the jointed fingers heard, pressed to the round hand-grips.

The song the obliquely positioned bodies heard, bent heavily to the anxious technics of defence.

The song the fast-beating hearts heard that drum within the crouched bodies, of those who wait the zero-hour.

The song the faster-drumming hearts heard that beat within the alert bodies hunched at the weapon-vent.

The song that changed the hard eyes of the sons that looked into the eyes of the other sons

across the enormous floor that is the narrow space of yards that separates the crouched and waiting sons from the hunched and ready other sons.

The spell-song that was heard when the enormous floor contracted.

When the traversing flint-heads and the aligned shafts measure to a nicety the place of separation

when the narrow yards narrow to that shrunk space where the hard breathing is of the embraced sons begetting anguish upon each other

and the sound is of the reaping blades toiling for the dragon-crop (for the swords of the sons must garner at furrows the fathers tilled)

and the sound of the rough-ground iron of the brothers, reaping down the white harvest of the brothers

ceased for the song-spell.

And for the eight decades, because of the song of the birds of the Mother of Penances

the war stood still.

Because of the melody and the melodic spell, because of the shrill harmonies of the melodious birds.

Because of the spell that binds by reason of the unities when the diverse throat-strings bind and loose the creature of air.

because of the sound-spell, because of the clear-voiced song.

[34] The codes speak, in the pricing of articles, of swords with 'white hilts' and swords with 'round hilts'.

Because of the spells and the enchantments, because
   this is the zone
   here are the marches
   where such things may be.

Yet, even here,
   where the mixed-men most mix their magic, where the
exchanges[35] are:
   if it can be palace-queen into field-rodent, is the wolf-cry
from the grey stone the spell-changed voice of the palace
prince under bondage of the beast-spell.
   Are these fragrant limbs meadow-blossom and is she
very flesh or would her bright boughs break bent at the
sink-drift, or rocking the Dioscuri.

Is he lord of the sparse commote or lord of illusion? Do
the leaning gorsedd-stones rest heavy on the hill or does
the potent and exact circle draw the elusive contours to
itself of the lights upon the mountain, which is uncreate?
   Is she unborn, is he begotten, or is this of the eternal
precessions?
   Ah! *Gwlad y Hûd*, and where the *lledrith* binds and
looses,[36] even there, where west-land slowly drains to west-
sea and hills like insubstantial vapours float — is this by
some dissolving word or by straight erosion?

---

[35] Cf. among the many transformations effected by magic: the
changing of the women of the court into field-mice to destroy
Manawyddan's harvest, the turning of the sons Don into
wolves and the fashioning of a girl from meadowsweet, broom
and oak-blossom to provide a suitable housewife for the youth,
Llew of the Skilled Hand.

[36] *Gwlad y Hud:* Land of Enchantment; *lledrith,* illusion. The
expression *hud a lledrith,* 'enchantment and illusion', is an
often recurring one in the traditional literature wherever the
magic processes are referred to.
   The south-west part of Wales was denominated *Gwlad y hud*
by tradition, and by the poets, and was particularly associated
with the earlier mythology, much of which is common to
Ireland and Wales — the myth of a purely Celtic pantheon.
We say 'Celtic', but just as grammarians tell us there is a

Are they Goidel marks for Pretani monolith or do the *mamau* with the adze of night incise the standing stones?[37]

Does the riding queen recede from the pursuer or does the unbridled pursuit recede from the still queen?

In this place of questioning where you must ask the question and the answer questions you

where race sleeps on dreaming race and under-myth and over-myth, like the leaf-layered forest-floor, are the uncertain crust, which there has firm hold, but here the mildewed tod-roots trip you at the fungus-tread.

Here in Kemais, igneous and adamant and high — there in Penvro, the high trees are low under Manannan's tide, where the Diesi foray who converse with incubi.[38]

---

marked pre-Celtic and non-Aryan influence in Welsh syntax, so, no doubt, there are non-Aryan, pre-Celtic elements in Welsh myth.

It is the land of Pryderi and Rhiannon and Pwyll, of magicians and demigods, a world removed from the later struggle-legends of the Dark Ages; neither Saxon nor Roman are as yet in evidence. It was into this world of the archaic tabus and the primitive magics that the later 'Arthur' stories infiltrated, but it seems likely that the Arthur-motif, in some form or other, may have been present from very remote times. There is, for instance, the suggestion that the Gaulish inscriptions commemorating an agricultural deity, Artaius (later on a war-god) and the female deity Artio (associated with a bear-symbol) may connect with a bear-totem of a still earlier society; that many centuries later the name of an historical leader, Artorius (and centuries later again the romances which gathered round that name) became associated with the immemorial, primeval cult-figure or figures — at least with regard to the protector and saviour motifs, to the dying-and-living-deity concept.

[37] The grouped strokes which form the characters of the Ogham alphabet are found incised on many stones in Wales. They are indicative of the Irish infiltrations and occupations, and are assigned to the post-Roman period.

[38] Cemais was an ancient division of Pembrokeshire; it included the high ground of the Presely hills. Penfro was the lower land south of Milford Haven as far as Amroth, where the remains of a primeval forest have been identified under the shallows of Carmarthen Bay. From the middle Bronze Age onwards to

Does this tifted coverlet drape the shifting scree or do we
tread the palaeozoic certainties?
   Where, hard strata lean on leaning strata harder yet, and
with each greater hardness the slow gradient falls, slowly
falls to where the basalts dark gull's isle, beyond the fretted
knuckles of Pebidiog[39]
   where the brittle rim of the lithosphere hangs and jutties
between water-cloud and water
   where the last grey tokens are.[40]

And does the tilted capstone, do the triliths, move in a
space of mist, or does the veiling mist recede and come
again, now closely wreathe and now disclose the fixed,
positioned dolerites
   that stone-drags dragged from augite-brighted dyke for
love of his sacred body?

Where the magnate of the sea-roads is in his red-daubed
cist[41] where silence is, in his sea-slope chamber, where the

---

sub-Roman times Irish raiders made settlements on the coastal
parts of Wales, the Deisi of Meath being particularly associated
with these activities in Pembrokeshire, both during and after
the Roman period.

[39] The rock formations become successively older and harder
as the contours fall from the Presely hills to the sea, and basalt
itself occurs beyond the last mainland on Ramsey Island. The
ancient cantref of Pebidiog included this last mainland.

[40] This district of Pebidiog is remarkable for the large number
of funerary monuments. The stones of some of the cromlechs
were quarried from the dolerite sills in their immediate vicinity.
Dolerite rock can contain crystals.
   In his chapter on the megalithic world in *The Age of the Gods*
Christopher Dawson has written, 'It is only in dying civiliza-
tions that men forget their dead.' It was because of the sacred-
ness of bodies that this labour was expended.

[41] The chamber tombs were sometimes painted red on the
interior surfaces. Examples occur in Spain, and red colouring
material has been found in one such tomb in Wales.

narrow-skulled prospector[42] lies, under the ritual cup-marks,[43] in the valley's narrow cup, where the resounding is of the baffled wave-sound and the screaming wave-birds tack for the backing gale
— and does the stone mastaba cairn the negotiator? Does the false entry guard the mercator? Does the holed slab within the darkened passage[44] keep the dark Promoter?
Or does it kennel the bitch hounds? Are these the name-bearing stones of the Arya of Britain, are they the night-yards of the dogs of the Island — the rest-kennels of the hog-quest? Do they mark his froth-track and the wounds of his brood from the foam at Porth Cleis to the confluence at the boundary where Wye stream wars with tidal Severn
when the dog-cry and the shout of the Arya shouting the hunt-cry fractured the hollow sky-vault because of the impetuous unison when the dog-throats and the horn-throats of the Arya were lifted as one.
When he doubled his tracks and doubled again and stood and withstood in the high hollow, where the first slaughter was.
Was he over Preselau top and down where the nymph

[42] The expression 'narrow-skulled prospector' may seem a contradiction in terms to those who are familiar with the theory that the broad-skulled race, christened the 'prospectors', was responsible for the diffusion of the megaliths. But as far as Wales is concerned, evidence seems to show that a narrow-skulled type was responsible. The word 'prospectors', however, has a poetic appropriateness with regard to the dissemination of that culture, for some form of commercialism seems to have been bound up with it, and, like the 'prospectors' of more ramshackle [cf. Ana., 59] and more recent 'cultures', this solemn burial-culture was semi-global in extent, and tended to be maritime. In Wales the monuments are more often on the lower slopes near the sea, rather than actually on the highest headlands.

[43] The name 'cup-marks' has been given to the small circular artificial pittings found on some megaliths— they are presumably of ritual intention.

[44] A large hole (or holes) piercing the entrance-slab is a characteristic of some chamber tombs.

pours out the Nevern, where the Arya waited with boar-spears and the second slaughter was
  and was it in Teify dun where he sorrowed the foreign queen,[45] and where was he thence that no one could tell?

Is the Sumer director within the hewn circle or is this the dark pent for the mottled hill-pack with the wall-eyed leader? What is it that glints from the holed-stone? Is it the collar of honour with the jewelled thong that leashes the glistening hound of the hunter-lord
  or is it the dark signet of the lord of barter — was world-gain the quarry or the world-hog?

What of the grouped stones by alluvial Towy?
  Did they shelter the nurtured dogs of the trained venators when the innate men of the equal kindreds and the men of equal privilege, and the men who wed the kin and feud with the stranger
  and the torque-wearing high-men on the named steeds and the small elusive men from the bond trevs,[46] who,

---

[45] At Aberteify (Cardigan) the boar killed 'the King of France'.

[46] Here we meet some ideas and terms derived from the Welsh Laws of the early Middle Ages; and although they necessarily are in the main of that period they do in some respects reflect a far earlier society, the society of Celtic antiquity, pre-Christian and pre-Roman. What was envisaged at the late date of the codification was still 'an aggregation of kins'. All rights derived from the blood tie and a common ancestry. These were the 'co-proprietors' of full privilege.
  Professor Lloyd has illuminated one use of the vexed word 'Cymry' in suggesting that it may well have meant 'the co-proprietors' before it was used to describe a race or was employed in its now generally accepted sense of 'comrades'. These free men were termed the 'innate gentlemen'. The codes know of no 'nobility' in any way separate from these free tribesmen, but the 'high-men' and the 'lords' and 'kings', together with some officials, had dignities and 'worths' attaching to them in virtue of their various functions. The remainder of the nation were 'unfree' men who had a limited but real participation in the society of 'co-proprietors'. The conception of freedom was 'freedom to move at will', and this freedom

before the Arya was, knew the beast-way and the elusive tracks of the island, without whom the Arya could not follow the questing beast, because they knew the secret ways of the Island and the ingrained habits of the fauna and the paths of the water-courses and the fissures and the rock-strike, and the properties of the flora before the Arya came, and the ministering sons who uncover the father's fires,[47] whose charge is the bright seed under the piled ash which is the life of the people.[48]

And the hundred and twenties of oath-taking riders, who closely hedge with a wattle of weapons the first of the equals from the wattled palaces, the lords of calamitous jealousy,
   and the fetter-locked riders, and the faithless riders, the riders who receive the shaft-shock instead of their lords and the riders who slip the column whose lords alone receive the shafts,[49] when the men of proud spirit and the

---

was withheld from this numerically smaller class. They were, it is supposed, largely of that aboriginal stock which the Celtic Arya had conquered. 'Bond-trevs' refers to the grouped dwellings of these men (tref = dwelling). Beneath these again were a certain number of persons who, either as captives or for some other reason, had lost all rights, and might be the property of either 'free' or 'unfree' tribesmen; they were termed caethion (slaves).

[47] To the eldest son belonged the privilege of 'uncovering' the household fire when the head of the household was dead. He did so ritually and as minister to the hearth-spirits of his ancestors, in accordance with common Indo-Germanic practice with regard to kin and place and continuity.

[48] [Here the text of the MS runs into a version of 'The Hunt' (cf. The Sleeping Lord, 65–9).]

[49] The teulu (house-host), the warband of the leaders and petty kings, traditionally consisted of 120 horsemen vowed to protect their lord and supported and maintained by him.
   The Triad of 'The Three Fettered Warbands' describes how one warband tied the fetterlocks of their horses to their own ankles, making flight from the battle impossible.
   The Triad of 'The Three Faithless Warbands' describes how

men of mean spirit, the named and unnamed of the island
and the dogs of the island and the silent lords and the lords
who shout and the laughing leaders with the familiar faces
from the known dear-sites and the adjuvant stranger lords,
with aid for the hog-hunt from over the Sleeve,

and the wand-bearing lords that are kin to Fferyllt[50] who
learnt from the Sibyl the Change-Date and the Turn of
Time, the lords who ride after deep consideration and the
lords whose inveterate habit is to ride,

the riders who ride from interior compulsion and the
riders who fear the narrow glances of the kindred,

those who would stay for the dung-bailiff's daughter and
those who would ride though the shining matres, three by
three, sought to stay them,

the riders who would mount though the green wound
unstitched and those who would leave their mounts in stall
if the bite of a gad-fly could excuse them, when the Arya
by father and mother,[51] without bond, without foreign,
without mean descent,

and the lords from the co-equals and the bondmen of
limited privilege whose insult-price is unequal but whose
limb-price is equal, for all the disproportion as to comeliness
and power, because the dignity belonging to the white

---

among the men of one warband no one at all could be found
who would stand substitute for their lord and receive in his
place the accurate darts of his special enemy; and how the
entire personnel of two other warbands deserted their leaders
on the road to battle.

[50] Fferylt = Vergil. The mediaeval conception of that poet as
a magician was so dominant that in Middle Welsh *fferylt* is
the word for any alchemist, and in modern Welsh the word
for 'chemist' is still *fferyllydd*; so Hughes, Cash Chemist, is 'a
vergil' even if his female assistant is far from being a *Sibli* [?].
It will be recalled how Ceridwen in the Taliesin story con-
cocted her cauldron 'according to the arts of the books of
Vergil (*Fferyllt*)'.

[51] 'by father by mother' is a translation given by T. P. Ellis in
Welsh Tribal Law and Custom, from the Dimentian Code,
describing the legal ideal of a free tribesman.

limbs and innate in the shining members, annuls inequality
of status and disallows distinctions of appearance,[52]

when the free and the bond and the mountain mares and
the fettled horses and the fourpenny curs and the hounds
of status in the wide jewelled collars,[53]

when all the shining Arya rode
with the diademed leader
who directs the toil
whose face is furrowed with the
weight of the enterprise
the lord of the conspicious scars whose visage is fouled
with the hog-spittle, whose cheeks are fretted with the
grime of the hunt-toil.

If his forehead is radiant like the smooth hill in the lateral
light, it is corrugated like the defence of the hill, because of
his care for the land and for the men of the land.

If his eyes are narrowed for the stress of the hunt and
because of the hog, they are moist for the ruin and for the
love of the recumbent bodies that strew the ruin.

If his embroidered habit is clearly from a palace ward-

---

[52] The codes say: 'The limbs of all persons are of equal worth,
whether of king or villein.' As in the *Jus Gentium* of all
Western Europe, status determined 'insult-price' and 'blood-
debt', but, in apparent divergence from the general rule, the
Welsh codes allowed no variation of status to influence the
'limb-price'.
This conception of the common dignity due to the organs,
limbs and ornaments of the human body is a unique character
of these codes, whether or no it reflects a primitive conception,
or is a modification peculiar to Wales in the post-Christian
times.
The body was for this assessment divided into fourteen
parts, and the payment was made in head of cattle plus so
many pennies. The tongue was half the value of the sum total
of all the other parts, because, the codes say, 'It defends the
whole body.'

[53] Any nondescript cur was assessed at four pennies, no
matter who owned it, but kinds of hounds were assessed ac-
cording to the owner's status, a king's covert-hound at twenty
shillings, four times the value of a sheep dog.

robe, it is mired and rent and his bruised limbs gleam
between the rents by reason of the excessive fury of his
riding when he rode the close thicket as though it were an
open launde;
    (indeed, was it he riding the forest-ride or was the
tangled forest riding?)
For the thorns and flowers of the forest and the bright
elm-shoots and the twisted tanglewood and stamen and
stem clung and meshed him and starred him with variety
and green tendrils gartered him, with splinter-slikes and
broken blossom twining his royal needlework
    and ruby petal-points counter the
countless points of his wounds
    and from his lifted cranium, where the priced tresses
dragged with sweat stray his straight furrows under the
twisted diadem
    to the numbered bones of his scarred feet,[54] and from
the saturated forelock of his maned mare to her streaming
flanks and in broken festoons for her quivering fetlocks,
    he was decked in the flora of the woodlands of Britain;

    and like a stricken numen of the woods he rode, with the
trophies of the woods upon him, who rode for the healing
of the woods and because of the hog.

    Like the breast of the cock-thrush that is torn in the hedge-
war when bright on the native mottling deeper the mottle
is and the briar points cling and brighting the diversity of
textures and crystal-bright on the delicate fret the clear
dewdrops gleam: so was his dappling and his dreadful
variety — the speckled lord of the Priten[55] in the twice
embroidered coat — the bleeding man-in-the-green.

[54] In the codes the locks over the brow were priced higher
than any others. The several bones in the hands and feet
were severally priced.

[55] Priten: I chose this word on the following account: from the
fourth century B.C. until the time of Caesar geographers called
these islands the Pretanic Isles, implying Pretani for the in-
habitants. This word can be identified with an early native
form, i.e. Priten, and it is supposed that the later writers, in
using the word Picti of the northern inhabitants, were only

If through the trellis of green and between the rents of the needlework, the whiteness of his body shone, so did the dark wounds glisten.

And if his eyes, from looking toward the hog-track and from considering the hog turned to consider the men of the host and the eyes of the men of the host met his eyes, it would be difficult to speak of so extreme a metamorphosis
>   when they paused at the check
>   when they drew breath
and the sweat of the men of the host and of the horses salted the dew on the forest-floor and the hard breathing of the many men and the many creatures woke the many-voiced fauna of the Great Forest[56] and shook the silent flora and the extremity of anger alternating with sorrow on the furrowed faces of the Arya transmogrified the calm face of the morning as when the change-wind stirs and the colours change in the boding thunder-calm

---

translating into late Latin this native word for painted or speckled by which originally the men of the whole island were known. The authorities say that Pretani cannot be equated with the familiar Britanni.

The latter was the name of a people on the continental shore of the Straits, and this, or rather a kindred people, had invaded the insular shore and conquered part of the island during the century before Caesar's expeditions. It is perhaps because of the westward drive of these Britanni — the last westward expansion of the Celtic-speaking Arya — that today [i.e. *c.* 1940] Mr Churchill is a Briton and not a Pict and Britannia rules Pretania's waves. The Welsh, who owe their language (and so much besides) to the successive waves of conquering Galatae, have nevertheless retained in that language the older form: they still call this island, Ynys Prydain — the Pictish Isle, i.e. the Pretanic Isle of Ptolemy and Diodorus of Sicily, and all the world before Rome set the fashion of 'Britannia'. Some scholars have observed that a similar Roman inaccuracy makes us still call the Hellenes, 'Greeks'.

[56] Great Forest: Fforest Fawr is the district name for a tract which includes the country between the upper Tawe and the upper Usk and which separates the two groups of Black Mountains.

because this was the day of the passion of the men of Britain, when they hunted the hog life for life.[57]

* * *

When they paused at the check
when they drew breath
when they lost the scent.
Was the thing already as far as Taff or was it wasting the trevs of Teify had it broke north and away oblique to the chase was it through the virgin scrub back beyond Cothi, was the stench-track blighting the Iscoed oaks
  does the red spot pale on the high boned cheeks in Ceredigion because the cleft feet stamp out the seed of fire, is the fire-back stone split with the riving tusk in the white dwellings
  while they pause at the check
  while they draw breath
to take the ford of Amman flow, to ride the high track of the Amman hill-scent to find the grit-beds of the Vans[58]
  (where the leader rested from toil).

* * *

And is his bed wide
          is his bed deep on the folded strata
is his bed long
          where is his bed and where have they laid him from Buelt to Gower?[59]

[57] [After a version of 'The Hunt' not very different from that printed in The Sleeping Lord, a short connecting passage leads into a version of 'The Sleeping Lord' that differs significantly from the one in The Sleeping Lord, 70–96.]

[58] The 'Carmarthenshire Vans' — Fan Fawr, Fan Llia, etc., the heights of the Carms–Brecon boundary district. This whole district is called Fforest Fawr — Great Forest.

[59] Gwely Arthur, 'Arthur's Bed', is associated with this same Brycheiniog district, but I have associated it with a whole cross-section of South Wales, with the Twrch Hunt and with the general theme of the long sleep of the Arthur-types and with Plutarch's story of how Cronus sleeps in Britain and with later adaptations of the same or similar themes in historic times (cf. Owen of the Red Hand, Glyn Dŵr, Richard II, Frederick

27

Is the tump by Honddu his tilted pillow does the grit-stone outcrop incommode him does the deep syncline sag beneath him

or does his strata'd mattress and his rug of shaly grey ease for his royal dorsals the caving under-floor?

If his strong spine rests on the bald heights, where would you say his foot-chafer[60] leans?

Are his wounded ankles lapped by the ferric waters that all through the night hear the song from the long night-sheds of Ystalyfera where the narrow-skulled Kaethion of the lowest price and the Kaethion of mixed breed,[61] labour the changing shifts for the cosmocrats of the dark aeon.

Is the Usk a drain for his gleaming tears when he weeps for the land — who dreams his bitter dream for the folk of the land. Does Tawe clog for his sorrows, do the parallel dark-seam drainers mingle his anguish-stream with the scored valleys' tilted refuse

does his freight of woe flood easterly on Sirhgwi and Ebwy, is it southly borne on double Rhonddha's fall to Taff.

Is his royal anger ferriaged when black-rimed Rhymni[62]

Barbarossa, Achilles etc.), all the 'heroes who shall come again' from their secret places to restore the land and the people of the land. There is the further conception of the hidden saviour becoming as it were the *genius loci* of a district, and a further identification of the actual land with the presiding genius. In the Cantref of Buellt there rests another Arthur-type: somewhere near Builth Wells lies the body of the last representative of the Brythonic Arya to rule as a *princeps* in Britain; the exact site is, very characteristically, mountain; though local traditions and later writers have pretended to some exactitude and have embroidered the sparse certainties.

[60] The office of foot-holder was to hold in his lap and to keep warm the king's feet when he sat at meat in the hall, and to keep the king from mishap during the mead-drinking.

[61] *Caeth* = slave ($c = k$). A native slave was priced lower than a foreign one because theoretically all men 'of the Island of the Mighty' were free from bondage, except through their own fault. So by the logic of the fiction a Briton who was a slave was largely non-existent.

[62] The river Rhymni divided Cantref Breiniol from Cantref Gwynllwg; it now, in part, divides Glamorgan from Monmouthshire.

soils her marcher-banks. Do the bells of St Nellons toll his
detour; are his sighs canalled where the Mountain Ash
drops her bright head for the black pall of Merthyr? Do
Afon and Nedd west it away does grimed Ogwr toss on
a fouled ripple his broken-hearted flow out to widening
Hafren[63]
and does she, the confluence queen, queenly bear on her
spumy frock a maimed king's sleep-bane?
Do the long white hands, would you think, of Ierne
queans unloose galloons to let the black stray web the wet
death-wind — does the wake-dole mingle the cormorant-
scream, does man-sidhe to fay-queen bemoan the passage of
a king's griefs?
(who drank the torrent-way?)
westing far
            out to unchoosing Oceanus.
Does the blind and shapeless creature of sea know the
marking and indelible balm from flotsamed sewage and
the seeped valley-waste?
Does the tide-beast's maw drain down the princely tears
with the mullock'd slag-wash of Special Areas? Can the
tumbling and gregarious porpoises, does the aloof and in-
frequent seal that suns his puckered back and barks from
Pirus' rock,[64] tell a drowned taeog's dole-tally from a
gwledig's golden collar refracted in Giltar[65] shoal?
Or is the dying gull on her sea-hearse that drifts the oily
brown to tomb at turning tide, her own stricken cantor? —
or is it for the royal tokens that with her drift jagg'd Morben
echoes and the hollows of Yr Ogof echo: *Dírige dírige.*[66]
Does in-shore Dylan hear —
Whose son is he,
            and does no wave break under him

[63] The Bristol Channel.

[64] *Pirus Insula* or Ynys Pyr, Caldy Island.

[65] *taeog* = villein, a man bound to a district, a semi-free
labourer. Giltar Point, Pembrokeshire.

[66] First Nocturn, Matins of the Dead, Antiphon, *Dirige, Domine
Deus meus, in conspectu tuo viam meam.*

or is he each breaking crest and what can he hear but his own sullen death-wash — himself on himself broken

and in chorus with him and as for a wave-mate of theirs the keening waves of Iwerddon and the Manaur wave, the world-wave of the White Island and the glaucous wave of glass from Orc-night[67] and ice-feld, that four'll heed no laut-king's griefs who grieve for the dying water-boy.

But where's that tribious[68] conjuror who is both steady steer-board hand and heaving keel-track, gunnel-wash and handy at the thole-pin, wave-lord and lord of the wheat-waves, mercator and sky-plotter, — where's Manannan, deep of counsel

Is he to west — do his three shanks wheel the Leinster brume,[69] or is he on circuit nording the whale-track, leagued with the Gynt,[70] or is he homing scudding the quartz on the Eastern pontiff's western cure or is he sounding the narrows at fifty fathoms where Dalriada whites to Kintyre, with a sidling incline, dipping his tufas does he gravely asperge the southing seals, off Larne, or, is he sud of the Mull and thudding the Bradda, or, lolled asleep — not winking a limpid ripple from Bride to Maughold to bluff the porphyry sills on his nomen-isle;[71] or, with a long snook for Halcyone, quit by his south-port

[67] Orc = Orkney.

[68] [For 'tribious' read 'tribulous' or 'tribulus'? D. is speaking of Manannan and the three-legged emblem of the Isle of Man, which was his operational centre. He must have had in mind the Latin *tribulus* (Gk. *tribolos*), a caltrop. One of the four spikes was pushed into the ground, leaving three projecting. Another draft reads 'trubious', suggesting the 'u' sound. R.H.]

[69] In Ireland the three-legged man of Man was said to cartwheel in the mists of Leinster.

[70] The Gynt (*gentes*) was the Welsh term for the Northern peoples. This is an association arising from the later Norwegian ecclesiastical jurisdiction over 'Sodor and Man', which was in a way a fading symbol of the various pervasions and influences of the Nordic sea peoples over all the western sea fringes.

[71] Dalriada was the name for the parts of Ulster opposite the coast of Kintyre. The North Channel registers there a depth

his paddy up
his grey coat on
him phantom-daffled
brume-white
under the hurrying scud
on Solstice-night
straight for the Wirral
    Wave is rough and
    cold is wind
    but
    bright is candela
God! he'll not douce with Deva-water their Plugin[72]
lights! nor brackish her Well for 'Frida Hygeia nor blight
his Mary-berries[73] for Caisar o Pen-y-Bal, neat and measured
are his leeks to the *passus*, whose squared, kept plot looks
on the twin estuaries — He'll not havoc those *strigae*!
That's no jest for a Lar of the grain-stalks, for a consort
of dawn-riding queens — or is he the moon's mate? he's a
fine one for craftsmen to pray to!
Is that what he learns from his black Schleswig gentes
when he takes his three legs aboard, easting to Gokstad —
he'd better by half stay at home in the West
    (no wonder the Matres keep sons from the sea-spell

---

of 50 fathoms. The arctic seals pass through this channel to
their breeding grounds further south; for instance, to Lambay
off Dublin. Bradda Head on the west coast, Maughold Head
on the east, of the Isle of Man.

[72] I have anglicized *Plygain* into 'Plugin' as that is more or less
how it sounds to an English ear as pronounced in one border
district. The significance of *Plygain*, 'cock-crow', is to be found
in its application to the matins service of many candle-lights
and singing which lasted from the small hours until daylight
on 25 December. Here I am concerned with my father's district
(Holywell), where the lights and the singing of 'the Plugins'
(so spelt in one parish accounts-book) remained a memory into
the '60s or '70s of the last century. At Hope Church the practice
was discontinued as early as 1770 on account of drunkenness
and fire; similar disorders appear to have been not uncommon,
according to Pennant.

[73] Mary-berries = gooseberries (*eirinen Fair*).

small wonder the sisters weep when the youngest-born
brother sits long on the aged mariner's knee and drops his
bright toy and bawls for wet sea-shell — that tender skin
'll harden on the splintered thwarts — he'll waste land yet
for all their beads)

Or, is he teaming his sea-tithes for Trillo — a giving and
beneficient lord! or over the drowned lands smiling placid
for the death of Helig; or does he cry Dylan's woe where
down-coming Conwy,[74] channeled to left-bank, wars with
the moon-drag, or three leagues west by north is he rocking
the puffins, off Glannog — will he try the fjord... [MS
torn: probably one word] clincher-built or circumam-
bulate the world of Mother Mona[75] to wheat her furrows
for Camber's mess.

[74] Conway Bay has, like other coastal districts, a tradition of
submerged lands — associated in this case with the name of
Helig. It used to be said in the Conwy district that the noise
of the river and tide at the estuary was the cry of the dying
sea-god Dylan.

[75] The 'angle' in Anglesey derives from the Norse *öngull*, a
fjord [marginal note corrects, or adds, 'Ongul, a Viking proper-
name']. It is the Island of the Strait, or fjord, not, as William
of Malmesbury supposed, the 'Island of the English'. This makes
historical sense and shows that Ynys Fôn, as with Ynys Pyr
(Caldy) and Ynys Weir (Lundy), received the latter name from
the Vikings, as one would suppose. It has always been a
mystery to me why Anglesey of all places should be associated
with the English, who, except for a very brief interlude, never
controlled it until the end of the thirteenth century.
Anglesey was known as Môm fam Cymru, 'Mona the Mother
of Wales', on account, it is supposed, of the corn grown on
the island. We have already noted the association of the sea-
god Manawyddan with the soil. The great fabulist Geoffrey of
Monmouth, in order to provide suitable founders for England,
Scotland and Wales respectively, names as the sons of Brute:
Locrine, Albanact and Camber. Camber no more than the
other two has any place in earlier tradition or mythology. He
is, I suppose, a literary invention of the Angevin age. Geoffrey
was trying to provide an *Aerued* for Henry of Anjou's empire.
We can, however, at this date afford to utilize his inventions,
for he himself has become part of our deposit. (Incidentally,
what a tragedy it was for Britain as a whole that Angevin

Is he whiting the Maldraeth for the Aberfraw queens —
for Tegau to lave with her breasts of gold, to get his brine
in the Gwynedd milk that Madoc the Voyager may drink
his wanderer-potion.
Or has [he] southed the reaching sleeve of narrow Llyn,
does he fret a cancellus of spray at Ogof Dilyn[76] for the
kneeling thegns of Mair — is he deeping the Camlas, or,
is he come to Big Traeth[77]
to gusset green the jagged seam of Eifion's côte, racing
the troughs of Donatus for progenitor Cunedda to rinse the
Goidel stains from the Tyrian pexa of Padarn the Wall, for
Triphum the son of Ane the Mother to wet his decurian
boot on his Combroges leg, for Urbigena, to gird his toga
close when he drags his sea-weir in his wild Gwynodog
diocese.[78]

hegemony ever disintegrated — for had it continued the unity
between this island and French civilization would have been
assured.)

[76] Ogof Dilyn (Deep Cave), on Ynys Enlli (Bardsey). This island
was a place of intense religious life. From a remote period its
caves (ogof = cave) were the habitations of dedicated men in
Christian and, it is presumed, in pre-Christian times. Called
by the poets 'the beauteous Isle of Mary (Mair)'.

[77] Traeth Fawr. The triangular lowland that stretches to the
sea between the Merioneth and Carnarvonshire mountains.

[78] When Cunedda son of Eternus, during Stilicho's military
reorganization of the Province (c. 398), moved with his foede-
rati from a district near the Antonine Wall in Lothian and
expelled the 'Irish' from North Wales and founded a dynasty
(which continued as the ruling Welsh line for nine centuries),
his several sons took over the newly settled land, and Donatus
was allotted this district called Dunoding, later in parts Eif-
ionydd after Eifion his son. Marianus gave his name to Mariana
(Merionethshire), and Romanus to Romaniaca (Rhufoniog).
Thus do the Celtic forms mix with Latin ones. Cunedda's
grandfather Paternus (Padarn) is known to tradition as Padarn
Beisnidd, 'Paternus of the Red Pexa' — on account, it is reason-
ably supposed, of his official Roman position. Sometimes the
title is transferred to Cunedda.
'Triphun' and 'Urbigena' are proper names derived from
'tribune' and 'city-born'. We find Urbigena hidden in the Celtic

33

Or, is he white-fretting a foam-fringe with his cirrus wavelets extra frilled and gloriously broad for the trailing hem of lovely Mariania.

Is he high-seas over Sarn Badrig, his back streamers lavering Gwaelod — five fathoms high-over the drowned caerau (where Lyr has multiplied his holdings) and speaking of Lear, where's Nuada, where's the Roarer, or was he the Strider, or what, by his shape-shifting name, is he properly called?

They're all shape-shifters — all a changeling bunch of amphibious hierarchs refracted in a misted prism — there's none stays put in their changing phantomsphere. Is he their lord-Director of the Cisterns with aboriginal command of the west approaches? But whoever he is, where is he?

He's busied under, far and deep under.

Who'll fetch him from his under-heights? Where's their wandering Ogma — he's the next thing they can swim for, a fleet Mercury — let him be liaison.

He'll neither come nor heed, he's busied under, piling his Spolia Opima, draping with slippery sea-flora his second trophies gained in his bice-dark terrain — there too his fluxing war is total.

Call him as may be: Lodens of Lydney, Nodens the horned the hunter of Dean, with his Hafren salmon, his classical Tritons, his Phoebus-tensa, rayed and afire; Nudd the Generous, Ludd of Fleet Streams — Good King Lud of Londinium wharf, loving, with a loving brother.[79]

---

form Urbgen and Urien — the 'King Uriens' of Romance.

The Welsh genealogies, though tracing the Imperial descent, also give another clue — where they include on the female side Anna the cousin of Our Lady, in reality, perhaps, Ane the Celtic Mother Goddess.

[79] The god Nodens whose Romano-British shrine at Lydney on the Severn is well known, is equatable with the Irish Nuada (of the Silver Hand). Lludd (of the story Lludd and Llevelys) and Nudd are variations of the same god. Rhys mentions also the form Lodens; we all are familiar with him as Lud of Ludgate. He is of many aspects, sometimes appearing to be a Mars and sometimes a Neptune; he is sometimes compared to the Norse Tyr and with Wotan and Zeus himself.

(for romancer boy back by-the-fire, over his birthday
fairy-Brut)
    but
Nuada he is
of west-waters
a Wotan of deeps
a wolf-meeter, a hand-loser
his heaving war-field swept by the
Westerlies
    the barque of his godhead jackass-rigged — he's a sinister
build from whatever his slip-way,
    denominate him once for all, hand him a fish-spear, treble-
barbed and call him Poseidon, but
    remember,
he's half a Mars, if not Father Thunderer gone for a sailor.
Not he will heed a land-king's grief-flow.

But what's this Bright?

Who's quit the wine-darks and the pseudo-deeps? Who's
broke middle-sea? Who's braved the pillars to drench her
navel in West-brine, to witch with a cast eye the axile star?

She's left her dolphins for the spotted seal — lets her
doves and peacocks pine for great-pinioned grey gulls and
the sea-lammergeyer. She's put on the northern diaphane
— to that brumous shift how well she's suited.

The West casts her his pluvial — that damp drape makes
ceaseless metamorphosis the only constant.

West-gowned she looks her best. From west-wardrobe
her changes are for each vagrant light and each becomes
her — not by dawdling Kalendar — no moping dowdy till
the season's turn, nor yet a forenoon drab and frilled for
afterwards — each day the same; but, with any hour's
chance of wind or flow her frock is new.

Who'd not choose her lit by the sea-candles. West-
light's best for escaping contours; in the West we find and
love as can none under the star-gaze meridian sun

We saline his eye for Phoebus in the West so that he
smiles only through his tears. These rough rises of our
western air, hurt him — but learn him and learn him beauty
too and teach him less abrupt approach and

what does he know of beauty who
does not know Thule[80]
and the laddered lights that change
on Thule sea?
Here's a sea for beauty's best.
Here then's the sea for white Gwener.[81]
She's a mirror for her streamers! Who gave her the
mirror if not the King of Pictland to comb her streamers.
Did she stretch for his comb from the white rock or did
he give her that too, along with the Pictish lunula she wears
for tiara purled with the spray of the Isles.[82]
She'll know a Trojan's tear. Gwener will find the King's
grief-flow. She'll bear it on her sea-Veronica out to the
glass tower where they sing their West *In Paradisum* and
the Corposants toss for the dying flax-flames and West-
world glory in transit is.

*   *   *

But yet he sleeps. Do the stripped boughs grapple above
the troubled streams when he dream-fights alone with the
hog in the wilderness, when the eighteen twilights and the
nine midnights and the equal light of the nine mornings
were equally lit with the light of the saviour's fury and
the dark fires of the hog's eye.[83]
When he moved in his fretful sleep did the covering
stone dislodge and roll to Reynoldstone.
Are the clamming ferns his rustling valance, does the
berried rowan ward him from evil or does he ward the

[80] I use the word Thule here and elsewhere to denote the
lands and isles of the western sea, not in the accurate and
precise sense of the Shetland Islands.

[81] Gwener: Venus.

[82] It will be remembered that among the earliest (Pictish) incised
stones in Scotland, about which there is some debate, the
symbols found include the mirror, the comb and the crescent.
(See introductory text to the Ordnance Survey's *Map of
Britain in the Dark Ages*, North Sheet.)

[83] Arthur fought the beast in single combat for nine days and
nine nights in the 'Irish wilderness' — neither combatant gained
the advantage.

36

tanglewood and the divisions of the wood. Are the stunted oaks his gnarled guard or are their knarred limbs strong with his sap.

Do the small black horses grass on the hunch of his shoulders — are the hills his couch or is he the couchant hills? Are the slumbering valleys him in slumber, are the still undulations the still limbs of him sleeping — is the configuration of the land the furrowed body of the lord, are the scarred ridges his dented greaves, do the trickling gulleys drain his hog-wounds?

Does the land wait the sleeping lord or is the wasted land that very lord who sleeps?

*   *   *

What was he called — was his womb-name Cronus or had he another — was he always the stern Maristuran. How did they ask for the wheat-yield? Was the nomen's ending he or she? What did he answer to, lord or ma'am — was he breaker or creatrix?

At the other reaping, before they sowed the dragon's teeth what love-word wakened him?

Is he of the Arya after all or was he the gentle lord? Is that why he smiles behind his eyes and from the mobile lines between chin and nostril — and does he make hares of them all in his iron and bronze and his enamelled gilt — in his Arya-rig?

Is his descent agnatic at all[84] — or is that tale too a woof he's wrought to hide his peculiarity — the divine old hoaxer?

---

[84] The emphasis on the agnatic principle of descent is usually associated more with the Aryan Celts than with the non-Aryan 'aborigines'. Though the well-known instances of queens among the Celts of Britain (Boudicca and Cartimandua) seem to suggest that they were not averse to feminine rule. Nothing of the sort occurs at all in later Welsh history. In no instance did a queen reign, and as we all know the tables of descent were always exclusively of the male line. But for that matter so were the tables of some non-Aryan peoples; cf. the genealogical table of Our Lord, in Luke 3, regardless of the theological fact that a legal, not a blood, connection made him Joseph's son.

Will they bless him a font-cup at the Turn of Time, will they call him the lord of the chalice-hunt, who sleeps?

Is this the land where the sleeper sleeps, the sleeper who shall wake, is he in his island cave — does Briareus guard him yet, are the single standing stones divinities about him?

In this charged land of under-myth and over-myth where lord rests on greater lord and by lesser names the greater named are called; where the inversions are and the high anticlines are hid by newer valley ways.[85] And the under-strike of the ultimate folds — how does it run? What ageless Mabon recollects, which long-winded Nestor knows the axile line of the first of the sleepers? and from what exertion was he fain to lie down? and what commotion faulted him through and through?

But in this place of myth on wonder-myth, in this place of questions — where the deepest thing outcrops on the highest hill, where the gods are beneath and the men are above

even here, where the known and the unknown traffic together at the ultimate tilt of Thule where the gods of Thule rest by the ninth wave,

in the last cantrevs, at the brink of the lithosphere

even here

the factual gromatici,[86] peevish in the hill-gods' driving piss, wipe their tablets and plain-table the hill-gods' knob

and back to valley-quarters, past the valley-trevs — and see the valley Fuzzwuzzies togged antique like Hallstatt duces[87]

---

[85] E.g. the valleys of the Towy and the Teify both in part contradict the under-structure, which is anticlinal.

[86] Roman surveyors, the men who used the *groma*.

[87] A Roman soldier serving in Wales at the time of the Conquest would find vestigial evidence of that technique and aesthetic for which the Iron Age Celts are now praised.

Exactly three centuries earlier, other Roman soldiers had seen the splendours of those techniques at the battle of Clastidium; and that 'third trophy', the *Spolia opima*, which the 'great Marcellus' won, was the accoutrement, though not of a 'Hallstatt dux', at least of a La Tène one. The successive forms of the prehistoric cultures were late and incomplete in infiltrat-

— arse over tip for the heads an' tails when they toss 'em
Caesar's dimes, to see what magic Caesar's image works
(whose clear superscription cuts square and across the
faltering Oghams)
Even here
    the casual sappers stand and watch the borrowed
infantry labour the pontoons and the Corps Survey strike
the levels true — from the 200 line up and along the last
long gradient down to Promontory Post[88] where the for-
ward details contact Coast Command.
Who watch the nearing speck become the scouting
actuaria that brings the blank report, but brings from
Manapia shoal[89] the tallest tale of all.

So we grid the green shadow-floor whether of failing
land or gaining sea, and change our picquets at the Ivory
Gate[90] and trim the fast liburnae for service on West Styx
and test with flesh the word to beyond world-ends over
the world-edge.

*　　*　　*

When Calibans of Logia Sinus[91] swear by Bron that tree-
tops walk the spume because the green troughs hide all but
the top-trees of our cruising biremes pooping the after swell

---

ing the valleys of Wales, only to be superseded by or fused
with the products of classical derivation which everywhere
followed the flag.

[88] I was thinking of the road called *Fford Fleming*, which runs
from the river Cych and follows the line of the Presely hills
and drops down towards St Davids. It used to have the reputa-
tion of being of Roman origin (but see n. 24). St Davids
Head was called by the Romans the *Octapitarum Promon-
torium*.

[89] According to the early geographers the Manapii occupied
the Irish coast nearest to the extremity of South Wales, the
parts around Wexford.

[90] Cf. Vergil's ivory gate, whence the Manes send delusive
dreams (*Aeneid*, Bk. VI).

[91] Logia Sinus: Belfast Loch.

and sea-watchers on Mona tell that boding corpse-lights
hover Cantref Manawyddan[92]

When the truth is that on the factual and charted sea,
from the stern-post of our leading quadrireme sways the
light of admiralty[93] and a Middle-Sea trierarchus checks his
log under his dipping sea-lantern as cosy as if his bearing
was on the Ostia light or he was snug at anchor behind the
fifteen piers of Puteoli mole[94] — the Sibyl's desolate shoal,
so near now, easily forgot for growling pilots and the gay
stolas on the bund.

So, near, or very far — by Aenaria straits, plumbed and
piloted, or by the vatic shallows back side Britannia, the
mantic spells give over, once the factual and material light
that lights the work-a-day and waking world, our world,
is ascendant. So let the agnosis work by us the appointed
channel.

Some see Ghosts, comrade, but seldom when the cooked
udders[95] are milky on the dressed dish and the lamps are
filled and the friends congenial, some they do say — there
are some in Taprobane, they say, who see turbaned boys
clamber to the sun's eye on ropes as bolt straight as this
stick rises from butt — there's no end to it, comrade — no
end to it — why they say that the Troy Games[95] what our

---

[92] The 'corpse-candle' is a phenomenon which foretells death.
It is common to all parts of Wales. Belief in such lights sur-
vived into this century. Manannan [Manawyddan] being a sea-
god, the sea can be called his *cantref*, his 'hundred'.

[93] The admiral's light on the flag-ship of a Roman squadron
hung from the decorated *aplustre*, which curved inwards far
over the after deck.

[94] The port and base of Puteoli, a few miles from Naples, had
a harbour mole of fifteen piers to check the Tyrrhenian storms.
Just north of the bay, round the headland, lay the Sibyl's cave,
past the island of Aenaria, the Ischia of our present com-
muniqués (1 September 1943).

[95] Cooked udders. Cf. Martial, Bk. XII, 44.

[95] The Ludus Troiae, one of the public games of the earliest
Roman period, having fallen into disuse, was revived by Augus-
tus. In Wales a game called Caerdroea was played on the

Augustus did but late years cause to be [kept], is figured out, and always has been, on west hills by the remembered *disciplinae* of migrated savages — such as Blondie might yet be, had he not got bagged by the Greek mercator, and so by one mischance fell in with many fortunes and made into a more or less civilized party, and so finds himself at last in a nice billet — all because he's got a pair of lungs on him and can blow his trumpet like a Brigantian bull — he's well out of that Honey Isle[97] of his — they're going to get a nasty packet soonish, soonish that is, as soonish goes, when it's the great long labour of making the world-people, that all may be one in us.

*   *   *

Ah, mate, so Iuppiter me succour — you can watch the bugger flourish — more and more — out to the world-ends — till the world end.

So long mate, so long china, dear friend — it'ld be a whoreson indeed but for war-friends on the traverse of the wall who redeem each other on the traverse of the wall.

So long, comrade. Roll on the guard-house fug, roll on relief and the guard-house snooze and the songs of known-site that we sing together in all the guard-houses of the world-wall.

Cripes comrade, kind comrade smile — smile comrade smile! there'll be no end to it comrade, no end to it — no end at all — no end to the song! — in all the guard-houses on the world-walls, in all the traverses world-without-end they'll sing the songs of known-site, they'll sing the womb-songs and the songs the fathers told — the songs of origin — the real songs.

May be comrade, may be — but may be no as like as bloody not. We're 'listed be numbers to drill be numbers as part of a sum of numbers and we who are ourselves

mountains — figures being cut in the turf; perhaps it is yet played in some remote places. Mr Jackson Knight, in *Cumaean Gates,* refers to the Welsh version, and Sir Laurence Gomme lists a Game of Troy in his *Dictionary of English Folk Games.*

[97] One of the names for Britain, in Welsh tradition, is 'the Honey Isle'.

numbered and who do all things to numbers, balls-up be
numbers the orbis bloody terrarum —

I'll layne we'll sing to numbers the numbered songs the
C.3's file in hypocausted offices graded be Cuthberts-in-
curia as suitable to the throats of auxilia.

O man, this is but a beginning — we, who reckon we suffer
so late in urbs-time, who come late in time, when times
have gone to the bad, are but at the initiation days of megalo-
politan time — Caesar is but a pallid prototype of what
shall be, and what is shall pale for what is to come. Take a
common instance, mate: A laureate — supposing him well
lined, primed, dined, and well boosted, can yet, with a
cheek full of tongue, sing In Praise of the World; but
laureates shall need two tongues and double-bandaged eyes,
and hemlock for the prescient faculties and counter-magic
against the vengeance of disgusted Muses, who shall presume
to sing in praise of the world yet to be.

Our time is Strider's time — and what's world-time but
Caesar's time. When Caesar's clock is wound it runs not
down, but rather accelerates — fast and faster the wheels
go round — till the Crixuses and Oenomauses, the you's
and me's at the world-end, in the last millenniums, shall
think of us as living in an Age of Gold, as almost human,
as relatively free, as children playing at empire.

What if the senate is Caesar as once was, or Caesar the
senate as now is, or by some other name than Caesar,
Caesar is, as in times yet to be? If the dictatorship is
Caesar's, the dictated are the people, no less are the dictated
the people if the people make themselves Caesar and the
Dictatorship is of themselves — for still they can but dictate
their own deaths as does our life-giving Caesar — no man
— there's no end to it nor no way out, neither.

I'll be off, china — I've gone — can you hear them at the
turn of the wall — that's his lovely voice and all.

Sure mate, that's his delectable word of command on the
wind that tells the middle vigilia's term — or I'm as plug-
eared as suffraged Jupiter.

As, sweet mate — this lord — this Thunderer, this God
the Father of Heaven, did he lend ears when Turnus by the

Fury doped and gaffer Aeneas egged on their common folk to bleed for the warring bosses and the spites of heaven's radiant whores — the Olympian syndicate is as all syndicates — remote from all our cries and like the gentry of the Boarium, deaf on ferial days to all but the venereal whim and deaf on transaction days to all but gold.

Should ever the men of rule with the masters of the covenant come to a profitable pact, should universal Caesar kiss the indivisible baal, then farewell hearth, and farewell home for all the gods of place and the sweet name-numina. Unless some Lars named of all the names and master of them in very flesh on known-hill drags their convenient abstractions down and with hooks pinions the sky-plan to place and time.

Then in such a one on one hill the hill-war gathers to itself all struggle ever, denominates the site by which all sites are named. Now is restored to each help-height to each dear site the ancient efficacies.

Not on far fair-height, unbodied, where men of mind clamber the steep concepts, grope the damps of unknowing, but now on named tump, known to the kith where this kin made this mound without this tun, beyond this vallum — now is he lord of each locality, who lets blood of this body moist here this cranny of this rock on this parched alien hill far side Our Sea. Not on any hill nor not on unseen unknown other-height the masters of concept postulate, but here in this demarcated place to touch and cross with iron, to see with this flesh-eye. Back to the womb of Tellus drips the fertile flood.

*   *   *

Wherefore Sergeant on this sacred night keep y'r eyes skinned for the Man in the Mock
   like Grass of Troy that queens meander gilt, taut on the loom-timbers for the swift-shuttled blows
    you'll see
    taut on world-loom
    brighting the mortised tree
       the radiant abb for the dark warp

the crimson *fila* in and out
woof the five medallions for his pallium
  on the leaning lignum see the spolia-bloom

Arbor axed from arbour-side
that now stript is more arrayed
more than in the silvan ride
  when, to pierce the green
and tangled tenebrae
comes Apollo's ray.
  See what sheen the lopped boughs
now lift high,
fronde, flore, germine.[98]

*   *   *

Relief details — halt — fall out first file for this post — remainder, order arms. Nothing to report?

Nothing, Sergeant — all correct sergeant — bar-a-movement-out-beyond-round-be-the-water-gate a bit back.

Water Gate — wot's that to you — that's for Virgin Post area you save your eyes for where the're detailed, d'you reckon you're tutelar deity of the whole of Salem City — Upper and Lower and extra-mural picquet as well — not Water Gate nor Fish Gate, but from left of Old Gate to right of the Arx — Birket Post West inclusive — with y'r centre on Skull Hill — that's your bit — left an' right of Skull Hill — Skull Hill's your lode — the tump without-the-wall. Project an imaginary line from that tump cutting Cheese Gully back to this same block of silex where you now stand and you've got y'r median point of vision — now hold it man, hold it.[99] That's how we keep the walls

---

[98] [The lines beginning 'Arbour axed' (cf. *The Sleeping Lord*, 27) introduce a version of 'The Fatigue' (cf. *The Sleeping Lord*, 24–41); however, in the MS this section is headed 'The Tribune's Visitation' — indicating that the two were once a single piece.]

[99] A sentry looking across the shallow depression which divides Jerusalem, called the Vallis Tyropoeon, the Valley of the Cheesemakers, from his post on the S.W. angle of the Antonia Fortress and having for his front an area stretching from the Arx (Herod's Palace) to the Porta Vetus, would have for his

of the world, by sector and sub-sector, by exact allocation, unit by unit, man by man. Each man as mans the wall is like each square stone fronting the wall — but one way, according to the run of the wall.

— It's whoresons like you who can't keep those swivel eyes to front one short vigilia through as cancel and properly bitch all the world-plan — and keep that weapon at the proper slope when you're receiving orders from a *principalis* on his way to promotion — and report for optio's reserve on relief of guard — he wants two extra details at the Water Gate and seeing you're so attracted to the Water Gate, why then, y'r duties, for once in y'r twenty years service, shall fit your desires — and where's that other beauty — where's Castor for our Pollux

where's Crixus?

On his beat, Sergeant, along be the hoist — optio's strict orders, Sergeant — man at hoist stands fast at hoist.

Crixus!

Coming Sergeant.

Nothing to report?

Nothing Sergeant bar a movement left of Water Gate Post.

Ho! So! — that's how it is. O admirable collaboration! The celestial pair see with one eye tonight — the synchronization perfect — the eagle-eyes of Caesar's horse-marines see through stone and all at movements that are no

---

centre the slight rise outside the then west wall of the city — the traditional site of Golgotha. He could not, without leaving his post, observe any movements in the area of the Porta Aquarum and the Mount of Olives — these would be round to his left beyond the roofs of the Temple buildings. By Birket Post West I suggest some military post near Birket Hammam al Batrak, water supply, within such a sentry's view, toward the west wall. The references are to the small map 'Jerusalem, tempore Jesu Christi' in the Desclée edition of the Vulgate Bible, it being the only map I have by me, purporting to show the lines of the city at that date; for the rest I have my own confused memories of the place, as viewed from a top window of the Austrian Hospice, which, it so happens, is not so very far north [west, rather, and a trifle north] of where the Antonia stood.

concern of theirs — you can make number two for optio's reserve.

New guard — take over.

Party! — fall in behind you two — remainder, in file — to quarters — march!

Mind that step the leading file — This is the Procurator of Judea's night relief stepping the smooth-laid silex of the wall — not the radiant Cymbeline's Catuvellani having a cut at the passo Romano — pick 'em up in front — keep the regulation step . . .

On the narrow beat of the wall
this relief of all
and two of you chosen
and the least of you[100]
for escort without the gate
    where the *optio* waits
his full complement
 And others of you to be detailed
    (not on other fatigues)
for the spectacle
    at the sixth hour
in Supplementary Orders
    not yet drafted
to furnish, for the *speculatores*
    those who handle the instruments
who *are* the instruments
to hang the gleaming Trophy
on the Dreaming Tree
and to see
for the pluvial blossoms and
the taut knotted thongs
his strong wrists more arrayed
than field lilies
and his fair ankles the feet shod
with the tidings
purpled for the dark staple-heads
brighting the mortised tree.

[100] [The rest of the sheet is torn away here, and we must fill in the following 12 lines from *The Sleeping Lord*, 31.]

46

From where, behind the Composite façade off the second quadrangle, past the third invisible cordon covered by the screened vent in the new oblique wall far side the temporary barrier close the convenient niche where the sentinel has dumped his shiny dark, tight-rolled *paenula* and the emergency buckets dress by the night, without entablature flush with the drab cement
 the inconspicious door
 within the spiked gate
 gives inward on a stair that's narrow,
 but of polished Lunic and ornate,
 from where beyond the antechambers across the greater atrium through the double hangings within the interior room on the wide bevelled table the advices pile and the outgoing documents must wait his initials,
 from where in the adapted wing the ply partitions cubicle the marble spaces and the utile fittings plug the gilt volutes and the night rota is tacked to the fluted pilaster,
 from where in the corridor's annexe the newly assembled parts and the convenient furnitures already need replacement they sit the regulated hours and enclose with each directing chit a root of Saturn's Loathing[101] special spined, for every Jack man,
 from where a high administration deals in world-routine down through the departmental meander winding the necessities and accidents the ball rolls slowly — but it rolls
 and on it your name and number.
 By how an inner cabinet plot the mappa mundi when key-officials and security agents forward their overlapping but discrepant graphs,

[101] Saturn's Loathing is an English folk-name for one of the Ranunculaceae. The *ranunculus arvensis*, corn buttercup, is listed as a cornfield weed and is described in the botanical textbooks as characterized by its 'spiny outgrowth'. It is therefore hated of Saturn, who hates all things which hurt the grain. Burne-Jones, in his series of allegorical designs based on flower-names, chose, with poetic exactitude, to depict under this title, an armed encounter in a harvest-field. As we know, wars tend to commence in the late summer.

by whether the session is called for after or before noon
by whether a hypocaust has fouled its flues
by how long the amphora is off the ice
by whether the prevailing wind
blows moderate from trans-Tiber or with a nasty edge, straight up the Tiburtina,[102] to nip his special buns on Esquiline — and really find his kidneys,
by whether there's an 'r' in the month
by how the shuffled pack divides
by how her intuition works
by the celestial conjunctions and the journeying stars
by which side he gets out of bed,
by routine decrees gone out from a central curia, re Imperial Provinces, East Command
by how a legate's executive complies in detail, by the disposition of groups and units of groups
by regimental strength, by personnel available to an orderly officer
by the personnel available to the Orderly Officer for the week ending Friday tomorrow.
by your place on a sergeant's roster
by where you stand in your section
by when you fall in
by if they check you from left or right
by a chance numbering-off
by a corporal's whim:
YOU WILL FURNISH
THAT FATIGUE.

Perhaps as digger's mate, perhaps to carry the heavier pick, perhaps the heavy maul, the steadying wedges, the securing tackle of lift and lean and fall
or, perhaps, if you hang back behind Lanky, or make yourself scarce at the hand-out you'll get away with the

[102] The Via Tiburtina, the road from Tivoli, runs roughly from E. to W. toward the Esquiline, in which district were many gardens and palaces. The wind from that quarter is, like our own east wind, bad 'for man and beast' — and blossom.

lighter essentials: the four hooks of Danubian iron[103] to-
gether with the spares in the wattle basket brought from
Thames[104]

so light a child might carry up a hill with briary-gifts for
the hill-god — who from the iron briars plucks flowers for
all, — so clinking light they are to staple such a burdened
bough on world-orchard wall.

Or, if you can play old soldier really well there are things
they tend to be forgetting: the dried reed from up-stream
reaches, with that creature of sea-sponge from tidal Syrtis,
and the small crock of permitted dope, that compassioning
Rachels fetch from their Judaean Jove's Mercy Seat.

Partee — party halt
Party — stand fast men detailed
re-mainder — steady.
Middle Watch — to quarters — Dismiss.

Sergeant, Sergeant! — where's the sergeant of the guard.
He's about cock if you can find him under his medals.

What's your excitement you jumping Mercury — d'you
want me or holy Jupiter — or is it a double issue you're
after — or've y'r seen the ghost of Jesus Maccabee.

Officer of the Watch, sergeant, doing his rounds sergeant
— out o' season and on his lonesome — dekkoed his lordly
crest by the Medium Donkey[105] — no sergeant, no — the

[103] Much Roman iron came from the Danubian and Illyrian
Provinces. See Stuart Jones, *Companion to Roman History,*
ch. V, production and distribution, sec. 5.

[104] Martial (Ep., Bk. XIV, 99) refers to basket-ware brought
from the painted Britons.

[105] The *Onager,* 'donkey', for casting missiles; so called from
the kick of its recoil. 'Medium' on the analogy of our 'heavy',
'medium', 'light' mortars etc.

Mark IV below — and he's stepping it — and — sergeant —
he wears that lean and thoughtful look.[106]

*   *   *

Sir!
No sir, yes sir — Middle Watch relief, sir — just come off,
sir.
Well sir no sir — half an hour back sir.
No sir — some from last levy — some re-drafted.
No sir — from all parts sir.
In particular?
I see — and you, sergeant?
The Urbs — District IV, sir.
Fifteen years sir, come next October Games.[107]
October Games! — and whose games, pray, are these?
Some Judy-show
to make the flowers grow
the April mocked-man crowned and cloaked — I suppose
going rustic are they
under y'r very nose
   and you good Cockney bred born well in sound of the
wolf-cry — and with the Corona up, I see, and of the 1st
Grade.
Where won? — or was it an issue, sergeant?
On the German *limes*, sir, — North Sector.
And the two torques?
On the same *limes*, sir, — South Sub-Sector, sir, in front
of Fosse 60, sir, — the other . . .
Enough! I'm not asking for back-filed awards or Press
Communiqués, — no doubt the *Acta* gave you half a column
— on how plebeian blood's no bar to bravery — I know it
all — and backwards.
   But come — all this is good — yet, not quite good enough.
Distinctions can tarnish, and, so can you and I. Remember
that, sergeant — always remember it.

---

[106] [From this point onward, 'The Roman Quarry' consists of a
version of 'The Tribune's Visitation' not greatly different from
that printed in *The Sleeping Lord*, 45–58.]

[107] The *Ludi Augustales* were held from 3rd October to the
12th; they were instituted in memory of Augustus Caesar.

For now — where's this mixed bunch of yours — I have
a word to say.
Very good sir — Guard! Guard — for Inspection . . .
Cease man, cease! — a liturgy too late is best not sung
    Stand them at ease — stand them easy
    let each of you stand, each as you are
    let these sleep on and take their rest if any man can sleep
to equinoctial runes and full-moon incantations.
    You corporal — stand yourself easy. You — whose face
I know — a good Samnite face — Private what? Pontius
what? a rare name too for trouble. And you with the
Etruscan look — 'o6 Tullius is it?[108] — with a taste for the
boards, eh? We must remember that at the reg'mental binge[109]
— that lorica back to front and y'r bare backside becomes
you well — extremely funny — and very like your noble
ancestors.
    But all of you stand — I have a word to say: First a
routine word — a gloss on the book and no more — a
sergeant's word.
    Men, when you are dismissed to quarters, it is to quarter-
duties, not to Saturnalia — the regulation rest's allowed —
now get onto those kits, onto those brasses. D'you think
that steel's brought from Toletum at some expense for you
to let to rust — and those back-rivets and under those frogs
— but
    must I do a corporal's nagging — shall I scold like a
second cook to pallid sluts beneath her, must I read out a
rookie's list of does and don'ts and speak of overlaps and
where to buy metal polish — are there no lance-jacks to
demonstrate standing orders
    Does the legate need to do what he delegates — must
those with Curial charge be ever prying on a swarm of
vicars or nothing goes forward must tribunes bring gun-fire
to centurions or else there's no parade?

---

[108] The Pontii were a Samnite gens. The name of Tullius would
indicate that a person was of Tuscan extraction.

[109] As with ourselves, Roman units had an annual regimental
supper, called the saturnalicium. Contributions from each
soldier's pay were deposited in the regimental savings bank
to defray the cost of this celebration.

But enough — analogies are wearisome — I could ana-
logize to the end of time — my Transpadane grandma's
friend taught me the tricks, I'ld beat the rhetoric of Carnutic
conjurors and out-poet ovates from druid bangors far side
the Gaulish Strait — but I'll be forthright Roman as the
saying goes — but seldom goes beyond the saying — let's
fit our usage to the tag for once.

The loricas of Caesar's men should shine like Caesar,
back and front, whose thorax shines all ways and to all
quarters to the world-ends — whether he face unstable
Britain, or the weighty Persians — so that all of 'em say:
Rome's back is never turned.

But a word more: This chitty's fire is built for section's
rations — not for warming backsides. Is Jerusalem on Cauca-
sus — are your Roman loins so starved that Caledonian
trews were best indented for, should all the aunts on
Palatine knit you Canusian comforts,[110] or shall we skin the
bear of Lebanon and mount guard in muffs.

Come! leave that chatter and that witch-wife song — that
charcoal can well tend itself — now do you attend your
several duties.

Guard! guard — At ease! Guard! ...

No Sergeant, no! — not so anxious — I have yet a word
to say — I have a more necessary word — I would bring
you to attention not liturgically but in actuality.

The legate has spoken of a misplaced objectivity — I
trust a serving officer may know how to both be objective
and judge the time and place — for me, the time is now
and here is the place.

You Sergeant — you junior N.C.O.s, my order was stand
easy — men less at ease I've seldom seen. It belongs to the
virtue of rank to command — if I, by virtue of my rank
deem it prudent to command composure — then compose
yourselves — I have a word to say, to say to you as men
and as a man speaking to men, but, and a necessary but, as

---

[110] Canosa was famous for the good quality of its wool (Martial,
Ep., Bk. IV, 127).

a special sort of man speaking to a particular sort of men at a recurring moment in urbs-time.

Is this a hut on Apennine where valley gossips munch the chestnuts and croak Saturnian spells — is this how guard details stand-by for duties who guard the world-utilities?

Old rhyme no doubt makes beautiful the older fantasies, but leave the stuff to the men in skirts who beat the bounds of small localities — all that's done with for the likes of us, in urbs, throughout orbis. It's not the brotherhood of the fields or the lares of a remembered hearth, or the consecrated wands bending in the fertile light to transubstantiate for child-man the material vents and flows of nature into the breasts and milk of the goddess.

Suchlike bumpkin sacraments are for the young time, for the dream-watches — now we serve contemporary fact. It's the world-bounds we're detailed to beat, to discipline the world-floor to a common level — till everything presuming difference and all the sweet remembered demarcations wither to the touch of us — and know the fact of Empire.

The remembered things of origins and stream-head, the things of the beginnings, of our beginnings, of our own small beginnings — the loved parts of that whole, which when whole subdued to wholeness all the world — these several streams and local growths, all that belongs to the fields of Latium, to the Italic fatherland: surely, these things, these dear pieties, should be remembered? It stands to reason, you'll say, these things, deep things, integral to ourselves, make for efficiency, steady the reg'mental will, make the better men, the better soldiers, so the better friends of Caesar.

No, not so! — cut it out: only the neurotic look to their beginnings — we are men of now, and must strip, as the facts of now would have it, step from the caul of fantasy — even though it be the fantasy of sweet Italy. Spurn if need be our mothers' wombs, if memory of them, or our sisters' paps raise some signum or call up some embodiment of early loyalty, which, by a subconscious trick softens the edge of our world-intention.

Now listen: Soldiers, comrades and brothers — men of

the Cohors Italica,[111] men of my command, guard details —
I address you: I've never been one for the vine-stick, I've
never been a Sergeant-Major Hand-us-another to any man,
and we can do without the likes of Lucilius in this mob, — but
let there be no Private Vibulenuses neither.[112] I would address
as one soldier to others — I would speak as Caesar's friend
to Caesar's friends — I would say my heart, for I am in a
like condemnation. I too could weep for these Saturnian
spells and for the remembered things. If you are latins, so
am I, if the glowing charcoal draws your hearts to braziers
far from this parched Judaean wall — does it not so draw
my heart? If the sour issue tot,[113] hardly enough to wet the
whistle, yet calls up for each of you some remembered
fuller cup from Luna vats, do not I too remember cups so
filled among companions — womb-companions and sisters
dear — the brews of known-site and the vintage hymn,
within a white enclosure our side Our Sea? No dying Gaul

---

[111] *Cohors Italica.* As pointed out in the Preface [see *The
Sleeping Lord,* 45], contrary to the historic facts I have, for my
own reasons, made the guard seem to be regular legionary
soldiers of no particular period; in changing them here into a
specific body of auxiliary troops, i.e. the 'Italian Cohort' (com-
posed of free citizens raised in the Italian homeland), I again
belie history, and again have the interior requirements of this
writing as reason.

There is evidence from inscribed monuments that a *cohors
Italica* did serve in Syria at some later date, and there is the
'Italian band' of Acts 10 : 1; but the troops composing the
Jerusalem garrison under Pilate were Palestinian gentile levies
(probably of the Sebastian Cohort, i.e. auxiliaries drafted in
Samaria), Jews being exempt from military service. See Schürer,
History of the Jewish People in the Time of Jesus Christ,
Div. I, vol. 2, 49–56 (Eng. trans., 1890 edition).

[112] Cf. Tacitus, Annals I, 22–3, the centurion Lucilius, nick-
named 'Cedo alteram'. The mutinous Vibulenus comes in this
same section of the Annals.

[113] When writing this I was thinking of some cheap ration wine
such as I supposed might be issued, but I find that at one time
vinegar mixed with water was a regulation issue drink in the
Roman army — so 'sour issue tot' was more fortunate than I
had supposed.

figures in the rucked circus sand his far green valley more clear than I figure from this guard-house door a little porch below Albanus. No grave Teuton of the Agrippian *ala* rides to death on stifling marl-banks where malarial Jordan falls to the Dead Meer thinking of broad salubrious Rhine,[114] more tenderly than do I think of mudded Tiber and of lesser streams than Tiber, and more loved, more loved because more known, more known because our mothers' wombs were opened on their margins and our sisters' shifts were laved in the upper pools and pommelled snowy on the launder-banks. These tributary streams we love so well make confluence with Tiber and so lose all identity and Tiber flows to Ostia and is lost in the indifferent sea.

But, *Our* sea, you'll say — still our sea! you raise the impatient shout — still the Roman sea! — that bears up all the virtues of the middle world; is tideless and constant, bringing the norm, without variation, to the several shores. Bah! — are you Party members doped with your own propaganda, or poets who must need weave dreams and yet more dreams, saleable dreams, to keep the duns from door-step — or have you hearts as doting as those elder ministers who think the race of gods wear togas? But you are soldiers with no need for illusion, for willy-nilly you must play the appointed part. Listen! — be silent — you shall be silent — you shall understand the horror of the thing.

Dear brothers, sweet men, Italian loves, it may not be!

We speak of ends and not of origins when Tiber flows by Ostia: the place is ill-named — for mouths receive to nourish bodies; but here the maw of the world sucks down all the variant sweets of Mother Italy and drains to world-

[114] See George Adam Smith, *Historical Geography of the Holy Land,* 626, on the tombs of the Hauran district: 'Sometimes it is a native of Germany or Gaul drafted for service on the Arabian border whose epitaph tells how he died thinking of his fatherland: "born (?) and a lover of his country, having come from Germany and died in the Agrippian troop was taken back to his own".' He points out that the Jordan Valley, where the river enters the Dead Sea, is particularly unhealthy. In historic fact, of course, the 'Agrippian *ala*' belongs to a period subsequent to the times of Christ (see n. 111 above).

sea the blessed differences. No longer the Veneti, no more Campanian, not the Samnite summer pipes nor Apulian winter-song, not the Use of Lavinium, nor the *Etrusca disciplina,* not Vetulonia of the iron fasces, not the Arya of Praeneste in the gold fibulas, nor any of the things of known-site — our world-Maristuran marshals all to his world-sea.[115]

As bucinator Taranus, swilling his week's pay with his Combrogean 'listing-mates, tough Lugobelinus and the radiant Maponus[116] — an outlandish trio to wear the Roman lorica — maudlin in their barrack-cups, remember some high hill-cymanfa[117] and the valley tippling-bouts and cry:

> No more in dear Orddwy
> We drink the dear metheglin,

Now we, for whom their Ordovician hills are yet outside the world (but shortly to be levelled to the world-plain) must think no more of our dear sites or brews of this dear pagus,[118] this known enclosure loved of Pales, lest thinking of our own our bowels turn when we are commanded to storm the palisades of others and the world-plan be undone by plebeian pity.

As wine of the country, sweet if drawn from wood near to the living wood that bore the grape, sours if taken far, so

---

[115] Vetulonia was traditionally connected with the origin of the fasces, and, as Christopher Dawson points out in *The Age of the Gods,* a singular corroboration of tradition occurred when an iron fascis was discovered on the actual site of that place.

Praeneste was a very early foundation of the Latin nobles, and the sixth-century B.C. gold fibula discovered on the site is engraved with the oldest known inscription in the Latin language. Maristuran = 'Mars the Lord'.

[116] The names of these Celtic recruits are also the names of Celtic divinities. Taranus [Tanarus], a thunder god; Magons, a Mars; Maponus, an Apollo.

[117] A *cymanfa* is an assembly or festival.

[118] Stuart Jones in *Companion to Roman History,* 15, says, 'We can only define *pagus* by saying that it was a primitive division of land in Italy where inhabitants were united by social and religious ties and possessed a corporate organization.'

56

can all virtue curdle in transit, so vice may be but virtue uprooted, so is the honey-root of known-site bitter fruit for world-floor.

The cultural obsequies must be already sung before Empire can masquerade a kind of life. What! — does Caesar mime — are the world-boards his stage — do we his actors but mimic for a podium full of jeering gods what once was real? This is about the shape of it, O great Autokrator, whose commission I hold — but hold it I do, over and above the sacramentum that binds you all.

What then? are we the ministers of death, of life-in-death? do we but supervise the world-death, being dead ourselves long since? Do we but organize the extension of death, whose organisms withered with the old economies behind the living fences of the small localities?

Men of my command — guard-details of the Antonia, soldiers of Our Greater Europa, saviours of our world-hegemony, tiros or veterans, whichever you be, guardians of the perennial order, I have called you brothers, and so you are, I am your elder brother, and I would speak and command fraternally. Already I have said enough to strip me of my office, but comrades I did so from a full heart — from a bursting heart and knowing your hearts

but set the doors to — let's stand within and altogether — let's shut out the prying dawn: the dawn-wind carries far and I have things to say not for the world-wind to bear away but for your ears alone to hear.

I have spoken from a burning heart I speak now more cold (if even less advised) within these guard-house walls, which do, here and for us, enclose our home; and we one family of one *gens* — and I, the *paterfamilias*, these standards, the penates — however shorn to satisfy the desert taboos of jealous baals.[119] This chitty's fire our paternal

---

[119] It will be recalled that the standards of all the troop-detachments posted within Jerusalem were stripped of the silver effigies of Caesar as a concession to Levitical law. Although this was in keeping with the general Roman policy toward religious cults, yet, considering the special sacred character of the *signa,* it must have seemed a unique concession to the average Roman and an impious one to those who put a serious

hearth, these fatigue-men, our sisters, busy with the pots —
so then, within this sacred college we can speak sub rosa
and the rose which seals our confidence is that red scar
which shines on the limbs of each of us who have had
contact with the fire of Caesar's enemies; and if on some of
us that scar burns, then on all — on you tiros nc less than
these veterani for all are members of the Strider's body

and if not of one hope then of one necessity for we are
all attested to one calling — not any more several, but one.
And one to what purpose and by what necessity?

See! — I break this barrack bread I drink with you this
issue cup I salute with you these mutilated signa — I, with
you, have cried with all of us the ratifying formula, *Idem
in me.*[120]

So if the same oath serve, why, let the same illusions fall
away. Let the gnosis of necessity infuse our hearts — for
we have purged out the leaven of illusion

if then, we are dead to nature,
yet,
we live to Caesar
from Caesar's womb we issue
by a second birth.
Ah, Lucina! what irradiance
can you bring to this parturition
What light brights
this deliverance?

---

interpretation on the cult of flag and **Emperor**. Caesar was
Salvator mundi. and these were the symbols of the only con-
ceivable world-order.

[120] Seyffert says under *sacramentum:* '... swore to the same
oath with the words *idem in me,* i.e. "the same (holds good)
for me"... after the introduction of the twenty years' service...
the men... took the oath... all together and for the whole
time of service, in the name of the State, afterwards in that
of the Emperor.'

THE NARROWS

This year's call-up? why for sure
          and well before they're time-expired
There's no end to it, comrade Porrex
no end at all.
No end nor no known beginnings to these
Mystery-cults some of these learnéd do say
others among them argue differently — so that's
as may be.

No end to these wars, no end, no end
at all. No end to the world-enrolments
that extend the war-shape, to police the
extending *limes*, that's a certainty.

No end nor no cessation to the
          convoking bucina-call[1]
nor the harsh-bray'd dictat
of the tuba's táratántará.

From Pontus where Euxinus laps her shore
how many milliaria west
          to Corbilo-on-Liger.[2]

---

[1] The bucina was a large instrument, curving in serpentine form and used to convoke assemblies, both civic and military. The tuba was a straight tubular instrument used as a military bugle is with us today.

[2] Corbilo-on-Liger was a town at the mouth of the Loire. Near or on the site of the much bombed by us St Nazaire in World War II. It had been very important as a place to which tin was brought from Cornwall before Roman times.

How many paces of
the regulation step
                    graded exact for
the marching mules of Marius
determined by the armipotent Lars Ultor the
exact Avenger, the lorica'd Gradivus himself.[3]

How many, how countless many
                    of the Strider's measured paces
from the Galatic confines
                    to the Fretum Gallicum
          and beyond?

At the Narrows
                    it is but ten leagues or less
of briny *mare*.
So, leastways, a freedman of the Morini[4]
                    (and he not unversed in nautics)
did tell to me.
                    Further, that for some mileage of
the coastal *via* north of Gesoriácum
the Gaulish land inclines very gradual
to a point more westerly and
thereabouts, in a fairish weather
you best can mark where
                    the son of Lir's foam
breaks white on the KANTION shore.

---

[3] One of the titles of the war-god Mars was Ultor, another was Gradivus, the Strider. Lar or Lars was the ordinary Etruscan word for Lord. Ultor, the Avenger. — It is odd how sometimes a word or words from very disparate sources link in one's mind. Thus the agnomen Ultor of Roman Antiquity, the exact avenger, evokes for me a line in the sixth stanza of that most stupendous hymn the *Dies Irae,* used, until yesterday, as a sequence in all Masses for the Dead, *Nil inultum remanebit* assuring us that no evil thing will be left unrighted.

[4] The Morini were a people of Gaul on the coastal belt north of Gesoriacum; or Bononia, now Boulogne. Lir or Llyr was the father of Manannan or Manawyddan, the Celtic sea-god Manannán mac Lir.

And on the heights above the spume-fret
the albescent chalk
cliffs gleam-bright
her sea-ward parapets.
It was, he said, as though the White Island
lay at anchor
riding a mooring
just off Europa's main.
And had so lain
for countless millennia back
and would so lie
hodiern, modern, sempitern.

All, all, the total sum of all
even the very baritus[5]
of blond, great-limbed, berserk savages
of the dense Hercynian dark arbor-lands
is ours now for barrack liturgy
to keep our peckers up when on West Front
we mingle the blood built of
the destined commerce of
Ilia and the Strider
nourished of the Faunine she-wolf
with the blood that Teutoburgan paps
were bared to nourish.
Our hinged check-pieces of tough
resistant work of iron
hide the green-gilled aspect of
the Optio of Maniple IV
or of Legionary '59 Artox, but lately
posted back to his forward station, from
his job as farrier's mate at
Cohort H.Q. horse-lines.

[5] The war-cry of barbarian tribes, called the baritus, was adopted
by the legions — which may seem odd but, after all, there are
modern instances of soldiers of one country borrowing from
the enemy, if not a war-cry at least a favoured song. Cf. 'Lili
Marlene', and in the Peninsular War a French song borrowed
by the English forces.

But it would serve little to note
the pallid hue visaged on, may be
best part of half of us.
And we easily the victors
what then of the broken vanquished?
There's no end to it. No end at all.
Suppose we'd failed, as well we might, well
                    that'ld not serve, neither.

There's been more than one Caudine Forks,[6] more
by a long chalk and more to come
More when we're on the upgrade, as now
                    (so they reckon).
Still more, and internecine too
                    when the cosmocrats of the dark aeon
find themselves
                    wholly at a loss
in the meandered labyrinth of
their own monopolies.
And the Celestials themselves
                    begin to weary
of our bickering imperium and turn
plug-eared to all our suffrages.

All our swords
                    ring in the heads of mothers, and
the world-mother knows the iron thrust
that gives not life
                    but reaps down the fragile womb-fruit
like early barley.
Green and beardless is the barley-mow
that the world-mother weeps for.

So long, Porrex, we'd best not long
                    be found together twice in one vigilia, or

[6] Caudine Forks: in 321 B.C., in a defile known as Furculae
Caudinae in Samnia, a Roman field army was trapped and
forced to surrender to the Samnite leader.

they'll suppose we tell together
                    the beads of Comrade Spartacus.[7]

I wonder how the Dialectic
                    works far-side the Styx
or if blithe Helen toes the Party Line
and white Iope and the Dog
                    if the withering away
is more remarked
                    than hereabouts.

[7] The Thracian gladiator Spartacus, the leader of the great
slave revolt of 73 B.C., for two years defeated the powerful
legionary armies sent against him. Many of his very mixed
force are said to have been of Celtic affinity. Eventually Marcus
Licinius Crassus, a man of great wealth, as praetor in 71 B.C.,
broke the insurrection.

UNDER ARCTURUS

...like Emeritus Nodens of the 2nd Adjutrix, who regaled them with tales of the elusive Pict (with half his face vermilion) that burned through the creeping brume, sleuthing geistish-white the dim mirk of that Ultimate Province.

They came over, he said, in front of Vercovicium, he said. It's pretty much perpetual gloom up there. Votodini? Yes, largely, anyhow. He supposed they came cat-eyed from the womb, so should Phoebus in his bright quadriga chance to stray his trackway above their accustomed pall of leaden sky, they'ld scarcely be aware — they saline his eye for him so that should he smile 'twould be but through a dimming mist of tears. Bordered on the dexter side the breaking surf and the sea-fret of leaden Cronos, and more inland the damp mists of upland pools... that's the general situation of the run of the Wall and thereabouts.

At this Varro raised his eyebrows and muttered: 'That's a good one, for a start-off.' But Lucia whispered, 'Not to argue, for that would but make the tedium longer yet.'

He next averred that further forward in the signal stations it was black as the inside of a Capitol wolf, and north of the Bodotria Aestuarium more Stygian still.
But this was too much for Crixus:
Come off it mate, don't every pedagogue in the universal orbis, who scarce stirs from his books, know how the light of day lengthens in those parts under Arctophylax? How much more, then, do we, who in our own bodies have kept the Strider's *passus* in issue *caligae* for the Lord Mythras knows how many *centum* of *milia*, in column order, aside from forming line in *acies ordinata*?

But at every numbered *milliarium* set up by the Survey along the northing *viae* you feel a nearing of celestial Arcturus.

The further north from the now abandoned *limes* of Lollius Urbicus (may the blessed *manes* shine perpetual light on his strategic soul), so much, however gradually, is the influence of Arctophylax to be observed. The exact reverse of what Emeritus Nodens has declared. — Neither his service with the 2nd Adjutrix, nor his now ageing years, could keep me silent.

Fairish mirk, he says, in Votodinian territory, in the area of the Wall, and to the north of that a Stygian darkness. I myself have read a parade-state in the Middle Vigilia with scarce more trouble than at high noon, and that was at an isolated post a tidy few thousand of the hobnailed paces of the Gradivus — at a rough guess I'ld suppose CCLX *milia*[1] from the Wall at Vercovicium, and that's another XC *milia* from our base at Eboracum — so, all told, a terrain of some length: best part of more easterly Lower Britain, as fair a land as a man could ask for.

Well yes, on the chilly side; not by any means of sun-baked slopes, as in the Province, and dusky olives that pattern the tawny soil both sides our Middle Sea. But temperate in the main. Though truly it can and does get chill and more so to the north — but just as five *pedes* of one *passus* become a thousand *passus*, you begin to appreciate the permission, 'The men may fall out at the next *milliarium* and put on the *sagum*, pending counter-orders.'

No, of course, a wild land indeed, little agriculture, in small patches, and but lightly furrowed. No, few, if any, nucleated sites, but scattered dwellings held by men of equal privilege[2] in the folds of the wide rolling uplands.

---

[1] [The most northerly 'temporary camp' marked on the Ordnance Survey *Map of Roman Britain* is at Glenmailen in Aberdeenshire, about 170 miles as the crow flies north of the Wall. R.H.]

[2] [See D.'s n. 46 in 'The Roman Quarry', on the Welsh codes and 'men of equal privilege'.]

Quercus? Why yes, tangled grey virgin sylvae of immemorial age here and there. *Fraxinus?* Ah indeed, and many, their fair-leaved branches that stem from tall boles tossed in the freshing breeze, against the clarity of sky, these more than all else are for me signa of that bright land — the sea-light reflected upward to the caelian arc reflected downward illumines the contours of the wide-spaced hill-lands and these fair-headed ash.

Once, after a night of tempest, of wind of gale strength, my cohort was held up for many hours, for right across the *agger* that carried a half-laid *via*, a great *ulmus*, rotten within, had tangled in its fall a fair flexing fraxinus, and snapped it right at the middle bole, as though some still small voice unheard for the crowing of wind and weather had from outside time quietly commanded, *frangit per medium*. The sound of that rending is with me yet: the gods alone know why, for often enough I have heard the curious cleavage-cry of breaking living timber.

We were in a fine fix. No lifting-gear to get a free passage of the heavy baulks of tangled elm and ash — there was nothing for it but chain the heavier boles to the few horses of the command, and to tug by hand the tangle of lesser boughs; the work took hours, and only under sharp vine-stick threats of a couple of reluctant *optiones*. Eventually the thing was done, and six hours late we arrived at our destination.

[But for] our friend Nodens [so] to envelop even the Votodinian territory in the neighbourhood of the Wall, and, what is even more a matter for ridicule, to suggest that further north the dimness becomes Stygian — whereas the exact reverse is true, and, as I've said, far beyond the Bodotria, the light of day more and more takes over from the night, till Arctophylax brights the Bear of the Island. At certain phases of the year this is more evident than at other times. This, till the cycle of the cosmos is subjected to some new and unimagined metamorphosis, must needs be so. There's no mystery in the matter — as factual and of this material world as some chance observation in *De Rerum Natura*.

Yet I've a hunch that, maybe, in some centuries yet to come, when all our order and rationality have, by pressures from without and defected oracles of our own within [not declined but fallen], [there] may, by what circumstances as yet unguessed, [be] create[d] an association between the constellation of Arcturus and a mortal man of our tradition of arms but of outstanding genius, and using some mobile tactic yet barely conceived today (yet I have heard purely theoretic talk of how, in principle, heavily armed but highly mobile groups of *equites* under a central command, might some day be the answer to the cumbersome and already slow to move masses of legionaries). I speculate of a time as remote from ours as ours is from Homer's Troy? Yes, of course: but history returns in least expected of guises, and it is not outside the bounds of factual possibility that some *dux* or *comes*, by chance accident of the Artorian gens but a family long rooted in Britain, should save this island for maybe half a century, and most certainly be thought of as the celestial Arcturus, and by a complex twist of etymology, be known as *arctos*, 'the Bear', in the dialect of the Neltoi, and centuries after that, by men of a culture wholly other again, we may come full circle and have a cooked-up *quondam lux, luxque futura.*

You still ask, where's the connection between celestial Arctophylax and my hypothetic strategos. Well, Arctophylax is one with our Arcturus as guard or ward of Arktos, and should this Director of Toil chance to be nominated Artorius...

Hold on! how many 'ifs', 'perhapses' and 'possibilities' clutter that one?

Not so unlikely as may appear. Chancy, of course, very chancy, but a number of our nomina have already caught on, as: Constantinus, Ambrosius, Tacitus, Paternus — if, maybe, these loans have in some cases taken on a native form as Custennin, Emrys, Tegid, Edern and the like. And who would expect to find a man, as I myself did, a subregulus of sorts, called Aeternus, in the western area of Lower Britain, a princeps he was of Petra Clota[3] that, like

---

[3] [The Rock of Dumbarton.]

the mound of traversed Hissarlik, rises abrupt and sheer, but here is basalt hard; it guards the wide estuary that westwards beyond insulae and tongues of lands [where] lies the nearest shore of the Scotti of Iverna, but eastwards it is but few miles to [the] median area of Lower Britain — a well-sited *petra* of defence. This Aeternus or Edern, which native form he also used, told me he'd seen naiads on the east shore of his defences, while nereids contended in the tidal currents of the western side. His analogy required no stress. He used the native name Alltglud, though he lacked no Latin, elsewise we could have had no converse. Indeed his was of cultivation far above mine; but one thing I noticed was that his mode of speech had a curious somewhat pedantic turn — very other from the groping colloquialism you get in Gaul. That came to me as a great surprise, from this outland man, in this remote region.

It so chances that when my mob were in Gallia Lugdu-nensis, a Gaul of Latin speech, whose praenomen was, he said, Artorius, and that his mother's mother had insisted on this (you know how in Gaul the women rule in such matters and in a good deal besides), and that far back a cult-figure called Arctaius, I think, to whom oblations were made for the soil to yield good harvesting — but that like our Marmor he suffered the metamorphosis of ceasing to be tutelar of the bronze plough-share's furrowed and sus-taining line, and became the especial tutelary of the men who form in line of battle, not to sustain, but, according to how chancy fortune ran, to pile high the bodies pierced by the pitiless bronze — true, there's here sustenance of a sort, supposing the mounded dead were left for long enough to become one with the humus of the field where they fell — these would be those of the younger, the eager *principes* who fell like green barley to nourish a lesser order of being: but 'tis said that where the battle has been of most contention, there, given time, the grain gives fullest yield. So, may be, the metamorphosis from Lord of the furrowed line to Marmor or Arctaius makes little difference after all — but here [we] are in deeper waters than I care for.

68

The Gaul, Artorius, said moreover that a female counter-part Arctio, a stone set up to whom he'd seen in childhood, a stone of immemorial antiquity, had incised or moulded upon it the signum of a bear — *ursus* as we say, but for all Keltoi *artos*; so back we are to the celestial Arctophylax as ward and adjutrix — I can but think that her splendour makes her feminine — a kind of Virgo Potens, as we say of Heaven's Queen, the darling armed Parthenos — the Guard of Arktos, so the guard of Artorius, the Bear of the Island.

Sheer dreaming and invention, you say?

Look to your own past, before you dismiss the possi-bilities of an unknown future.

Do you suppose that at the Lupercalia the shouting mob believe themselves to have sprung from the rape of Rhea Silvia by Mars, and so have forebears suckled by the she-wolf on the slope of Palatine? Or [that] the Palladium fell from Jove's Heaven to Troy at the suffrages of the founder of Ilium, and when Troy fell our father Aeneas contrived to bring [it] to the Urbs, where it's still in the keeping of the Vestals as maintain the eternal flame?

And what of Cloelia, given by our civvy authorities — those bloody politicians of the Senate, as a hostage to the king of Clusium, but who took her chance and breasted the Tiber, only to be returned (I suppose they had the wind up), but was surrendered by Porsenna in admiration for her courage — I must say *he* has *my* admiration. I can't see any of these Celestials coming anywhere near that for sheer magnanimity, can you? Wonder what's behind it all. Even today it'ld take a courageous bloke to question the matter of the twins, or the Palladium and the Vestal fires, and much besides.

But, to the *general* situation throughout our world im-perium, I doubt if the necessary changes will or can ever now be implemented. Our rooted tradition of the Strider — the ordered files of marching men in column and exact alignment, maniple by maniple, legion on legion, or at the crucial moment formed in line, the invincible *triplex acies ordinata* by which we brought down the proud — that and much more — it's all too deep set to suffer the required adjustments.

We'll fade away all right, Clio alone knows *when* or for how long the *when* may drag on. But at least we can be sure that they'll die with their *caligae* on their feet and thong-tied according to regulation requirements, and be beyond the Styx well before the 'required adjustments' are made and the 'impending exigencies' (as old Brasso has it) are upon us.

But mercifully Lethe's stream will (let's hope) have washed away regrets for what might have been.

We all know the conscription of more and more legionaries and auxiliaries, heavier and heavier siege-trains stationed at larger and larger bases, is no answer to the growing need of weight swiftly required, maybe on the Illyrian front or the Limes Rhaetica or here in Britannia — in our set-up the mobility can't exceed the Strider's *passus* of a thousand paces to the mile, and that's covered no more by six legions than it is by a maniple of sixty men — that's the basic problem they can't face — weight plus mobility. It's a real poser, and can't and won't be solved without some radical re-fashioning — and the will to welcome rather than impede what, if not implemented within a decade or two, will bring down the whole bleeding fabric.

But can you see 'em at it?

No, nor me.

But what I *can* envisage is some such figure as I've tried to indicate operating in a limited terrain, here in this island, for half a century perhaps — he'll go down in the end, of course, and with him such order as he's managed to achieve.

A futile effort, you'll say: inutile, seeing that by then our own imperium will be, [as I've said], not declined but fallen.

That's rather the point; from the inevitable failure the splendour of the extra-utile will shine out.

I'd guess it might be some centuries from the time of his effort (supposing such a man to exist at all) before the weave of marvel gathered round his name. So that the extra-utile will lend him fame and mysterium other than what his actual achievement as *dux bellorum* may have been.

From his many wounds that gleamed from his tunica of
Grass of Troy or from where the rivets of his Roman lorica
were wrenched askew by spear-thrusts of tow-haired men
wading-in from the surf-break could be left an after-image
of a native *imperator* of strange qualities — did Arcturus
the celestial Bear lend his light to Artorius the Bear of the
Island, or did he lend greater light to constella'd Arcto-
phylax?

Of his hordes of foe, whether from Engle or from Pict-
land or the Scotti of green Eriu, his mere name would be
unrecorded and unknown.

Yet, maybe, five centuries yet again, [from] men of a
culture and interplay of mixed traditions, as differing from
an actual Artorius as is our present set-up from his, there
may arise a whole body of *materia poetica* centred round
a Rex Arturus, using, in forms incomprehensible to us, the
twisted nomina of his *equites* — whereby not the actual
deeds, not the highly utile and effective operations of our
dux bellorum, but rather the inutile attaching to his name
fused with historia and tales from half the orbis would give
undying and wholly unexpected continuity to that name
and those of his men —

*   *   *

Well, Crixus, you've weaved a long enough tale, largely *ex
nihilo*, in part what's known to all of us — but seemingly
sparked off [a] bit by old Nodens' account of his ex-
perience in some scuffle at Vercovicium — and we've yet
to hear his account, for once on to a track he'll never be
silenced — that would take the intervention of the gods.
So far all I've gathered is that he's insistent on the gloom
and mirk of those parts, while you depict a land of singular
fairness and clarity of a unique sort: never having been
stationed in those parts it serves no purpose to assess which
of you is nearer the actualities. As for the remainder of
your bloody meander touching the unknown future, well,
crystal-gazing's never been up my street. My wife once
consulted the Cumaean Sibyl with nothing but ill effect —
she took up with [a] merchant from Syria Palestina, from
the part we call the Ten Towns, and he convinced her that

71

one of his people's earliest kings, a kind of chrism'd Daphnis whose songs they greatly venerate to this day, testified to much the same thing as the Sibyl, only long anterior, maybe three hundred years before the year of the Foundation of the City.

But to return to your outburst immediately Old Nodens began his tale of the gloom and general half-light where the Votodini grope — beats me, it sounded as if you had some innate affinity with the place.

Well, what if I have? But what I could not and would not stomach was his absurd falsification of that fair land — and, incidentally, though not in our time, the Votodini in particular, the peoples to their westward, as those of that bloke I told you of whose *oppidum* was at Petra Clota — most of the peoples of what we call the inter-vallum area, yes, and south on the western side, will yet become numeri within the forces of our imperium...

No, may the Furies rend you! More of the stuff? No! not a syllable, not one word more, of y'r imagined future. We've had enough of that, and suffered it with too much patience — its tedium excels that of Nodens himself, and his tale's but scarce begun.

So be it. If you prefer Nodens' tales of increased gloom as against known facts to the contrary, I'll pack up. In any case, he'd never retract an iota of his tale — his mulish nature rules that out — he's a proper 'mule of Marius' in a sense not generally meant.

Was the ter-nox at great Hercules' begetting given a repeat performance here in Lower Britain for the special benefit of this particular emeritus of the 2nd Adjutrix, or for the gods to have a fine jape, the time being heavy on their celestial hands? Poor Alcmena! whose womb-burden, I've heard say, was by omnipotent Iuppiter himself —

* * *

Nodens took no heed of any of this, except to lift his ancient head and say: If you gentlemen have concluded your debate, if debate it was, I will continue my account of what I chanced to experience at the Wall.

As I've already said, they came over in front of Vercovicium — or to be more exact to the dexter side of the *castellum*, where the Wall changes its alignment a bit, to conjoin with the angulation of a buttress of the fort. Some details of the last day-watch were handing over to those of the first vigilia, so dusk was beginning to fall. In fact the notes of the evening bugle were already thinning-out among the heavy clouds and purpling uplands to westwards.

It happened that I was off duty, and no fatigues, along with a mate of mine from the same maniple; a Silurian he was, Morgant by name, and as the tuba-notes faded away he said with a wry grin: Not much of y'r *terribili sonitu* in that *taratantara*.

No, I said, but we're fairly plug-eared to these routine calls, and anyhow in this heavy muffle of air it'ld take a trifle more effort and pouting of cheeks than can be expected of these bucinators — they take it pretty casual, and especially when old Brasso's not around.

By now the fall of evening was more upon us, but with it thicks of white mists made a shifting diaphane. Here, maybe, the further barrack-wall was defined, if darkening; there a shrouding of thick brume made insubstantial a solid bank a few *passus* from where you walked, only to clear after you'd come slap against some familiar edging.

I was saying to Morgant, the Silurian, that we'd best remember that every bugle is but a routine and in no way indicates what may be the fortunes of the night.

But what about the chances of that *Pegasus* as against *Auster* we both fancied for the show at Eboracum next Thursday fortnight. 'I still reckon Auster will make it, because a Syro-Phoenician jockey is riding her, and if you want a slap-up jockey go to the Phoenician littoral — round about Tyre. I don't deny Pegasus is the more favoured, but I still fancy Auster will make it, owing to this Syro-Phoenician jockey.'

I know nothing of horse-flesh and less of jockeys, but

by the fleet-foot, wing-shod Mercury or, for that matter, lune-bright Artemis, who, like Arctophylax, has in her train, by the will of Zeus, the celestial bear-nymphs, and so is tutelary of y'r Bear of the Island, should he ever materialize — and it sounds to me we could do with him right now, for I don't like the sound of that sudden racket that started up while you were on the topic of Pegasus and Auster and the races at Eboracum we reckoned to be at in a fortnight's time with a bit of luck — well, *I* reckon we've other matters to occupy us, very immediate. All was quiet enough, a bit too quiet, a few moments back, but unless you're uncommon hard of hearing, what do you make of that confused but gathering flare-up away on our extreme right?

Some say that among my people, from Siluria (we call it Morgannwg in our lingo, which means no more than Pelasgian), there are those whose ears are alerted so that from Isca, even when deeply entrenched, they could hear an insect rise from an anthill in Glevum, which is over fifty thousand marching paces distant. However that may be, the uncertain clamour I heard a moment back is now deafening enough. Has half Pictland massed unseen to storm this one sector of the Wall, under plucked boughs of twelve times sixty Birnam woods, a millennium before an imagined date? Is Vercovicium fort mistook for Dunsínane yet to be? Does Clio lark about to that extent? Maybe those Muses, all of the feminine gender, transferred in locale by a hundred thousand paces, as well as by pre-dating of every circumstance evoked by great Dunsínane yet to be weaved of cooked and lying historias?

Have the level-eyed, exact and tranquil Treasury officials, prototypic of Roman virtue, who did not hesitate to raise objections to the falsification of the agreed amount paid into the scales of the *libra* as ransom price of the fallen Urbs, only to cause the victor, Brennus, to toss in his *cleddyf fawr* upon the piled coin, and so increase the amount due out of all proportion: the city was wholly in his power and nothing whatever could be done, but their inutile act rises from the sordid story of Roman power as the redemptive hour, splendid and implacable in their total defeat. Not again did the singular fortitude and indifference to consequences shine quite so brightly; the swaying *libra* became as the *statera* on which the Victim became Victor. Across the long long long centuries, and though more of Brennus and his Keltoi, we salute these tribunes of the helpless Urbs —

Must this be played-out again by Clio's whim?

History, they say, repeats herself, but never in the expected accidents. Is Julius not yet fallen, his mantle muffling his face in the Senate House? How or when? Ah, but when is when?

For Morgant the Silurian, inly and within the tortoise of his skull, who'd talked much with a *felid* from the Desi of Iwerddon, who had already partly established themselves in the neighbourhood of the Octapitarum Promontorium, and from his native Brythonic foster-parents, in the hills above Venta, this mode of thought was native enough. Outwardly he was in all respects a legionary, of the forces of the empire, for since Hadrian's time the enlistment of men into regiments stationed in their own native land was permitted. Once among men of intermingled tradition, the cults and beliefs of the Middle Sea mingled with his own basically Celtic conceptions, and in his case both Goidelic and Brythonic.

But now no man of us had thought for inward thoughts, but immediate matters only; the tuba-blare refracted by the shifting walls of mist, so far from fading out, became sustained, and with it a quite differing war-horn bray from seemingly beyond the Wall, and with this c[ame] what sounded like weapon on weapon and harsh command and counter-command and muffled fall of heavy bodies and grunts of anguish mingled with exultant shouts, all, too, fused with the bugle-bray; and the increasing thicks of fog-drift made it impossible to guess with any certainty how matters stood, but as a slight lull seemed to follow, I took it that the few of his first wave to reach our parapets had been dealt with.

So far, so good; but even if this was the case, it must necessarily be no more than a fortunate beginning — a probe, as we would say, at one point of our defences, and at the easiest point.

We were greatly under strength; the new drafts urgently required by the Commandant had, as yet, not materialized, beyond assurances from the authorities that the situation was understood, and the re-dispositioning of units was in process, so that he could expect replacements within a matter of days. This much we knew, for Morgant, when detailed for special guard duty at the door, within the *praetorium*, of that room in which the Commander confers with various officers, had heard every bloody word said. Moreover he got on matey terms with one of those blokes on orderly room staff, and what he got out of him checked up on what he heard, and a bit more.

The Silurian and I were hastening now to our manipular station, somewhat to the left of where the first assault had failed, and as we crossed a few paces of our barrack-square we noticed that here and there missiles with heavier war-heads than were usual had fallen within the compass of our *castellum* area. We took little heed of them, nor was there time to think of anything but our immediate business. But we did wonder from what sites these had been discharged — their trajectory line must have been exceptionally high for them to fall at such a steep angulation to our parade-ground. Perhaps they'd got the hang of some new technique — anyhow, no damage done so far.

Then came a sight that drove to the furthest ebb the rising tide of our fortitude.

The Commandant, having come from his quarters to enquire if the sudden commotion was of any consequence, chanced to cross from another angle the paved space where our maniple had fallen-in in line.

Out of the heavens it came, a few paces from where I stood. He was the first to get it. I stood but three paces from him, and Morgant the Silurian next me.

He dropt like a stone at our very feet, no word or groan, without even knowing whether the racket at the dexter parapet was of any significance or not. With the Divine Imperator's [signum] muffled about his face, he fell: Caesar's Legatus Militum in the scarlet *paludamentum* reserved for the High Command, and he in a special sense Caesar's vicar, for on him the responsibility of the entire Wall from sea to sea, the *limes* of the empire in this island.

This is how it was, best known to us much later. He was in his quarters at supper or about to sup with the Lady Elena Creiddylad his wife (Yes, of mixed Brittonic and Roman blood, the latter quite recent, but on the Brittonic side she's a genealogy of their high men, sub-reguli and princesses, stretching back for many centuries: Cunebelinos, yes and Catavalaunos too were, for her, but recent). Anyway, on hearing the sudden and continuing tuba-blare and the general run to our far right flank, he is said to have listened awhile, and then, returning to the Lady Elena: Sorry about this, Creiddylad, but I think I must step without to assess better what's afoot — shall be but little time, during which would you instruct that idiot [Conall[4]] to bring the amphora I ordered — Oh, yes, he understood all right. I know he's a recent acquisition from that raiding party we caught off-shore from Dalriada, poor devil, and has scarce a word of either Latin or Brittonic, but I marked it — he understood all right — it's of that vintage for which you have a special liking, and this is, I know, one of your special days. We'll drink together of the fruit of that vine in spite of these guttering candelae, gusty wick'd in this insufferable brume that creeps through every vent, no matter how heavily curtained. We'll see to that tomorrow, but for the moment I'd best make some enquiries, just in case certain dispositions I've in mind need implementing.

Of course I'll see [Conall] about that amphora — how like you to think of that. But if you are going to wear that cloak, which is, after all, Caesar's *signum* of your office, wear [it] in the proper manner; and such a night as this [it] is necessary anyway, so fasten that fibula. Moreover, it's proof against rain and damps, which is more than can be said of the issue *pallia* doled out to Caesar's chosen. I myself saw to it that it was made of British goat-hair and lamb's wool by the best staplers of this island, and dyed

---

[4] [Conall is inserted for the blank in the MS, as being an Ulster (Dalriada) name.]

of madder from British lichen, and interlined with flattened pelts of British wild-cat, stitched with my own hands. Not the Vicar of Britain nor the Praetorian Prefect of Gaul can boast of anything touching that. But won't you get Tryphon to arm you properly, or at least carry your gladius, won't you?

A gladius would be of little use, my dear, when all I propose to do is to enquire in my own barrack-square as to this evening's commotion.

So through the heavy curtained door he passed out from his private quarters along [a] covered colonnade of sorts to the paved way that led to the drill-yard.

* * *

As I have said, we were now in some haste, for our maniple was already forming in line along its allotted space of the *via quintana* before moving off to our positions in the fire-bays of the Wall, which chanced to be just to the left of where the racket had been — and there was still some stuff in progress — a mopping-up party, maybe. Anyway, we had just numbered-off — by no means, not b' a long chalk, anywhere near manipular strength as reckoned and wrote down by H.Q. staff-clerks at Eboracum or elsewhere. Morgant, who stood next me as we numbered-off, said from the corner of his apparently tight-closed lips (very asymmetric was his whole visage, his mouth permanently askew, his dark eyes only — and they were as dark as pitch — gave any indication of his changing mood), Tell me, he says, what in your judgement is the bleedin' distinction between a skeletal maniple and a maniple of skeletons. A question very real it is, not a tom-fool conundrum or riddling rhymes.

But before I could utter a word, our *Optio* snapt out the order that brought us from single file to sections in column, the more quickly to reach our allotted sector of the Wall; and even as our hobnailed *caligae* [were] striking the stone setts as one in the swing round — enough to satisfy old Brasso, had he been present — there loomed upon us out of the drifting thicks of mist and gathering fall of nearing night, the tall figure of the Commandant himself: [he]

was but a pace or two [from] us. There was no mistaking that gleaming *pexa*-surfaced madder-red paludament. He had come upon us at an acute angle and from the far left of our turning files. The *Optio* stood fast and saluted.

Out of upper thicks it came at an acute angle. He dropt without a cry, and without ever knowing the answer to the matter of his enquiry. With the Lady Elena's paludament muffled to his face, he fell within a pace of my Silurian's *caligae*, [by] the base-beam of a Mark IV Onager, pinned between the shoulder-blades to the stone setts by the long-hasped, heavy-headed Votodinian spear.

The Onager is jammed.
The Commandant is dead.
The Senior Centurion takes over.

Somehow or other he must master his grief and at the same time assume command of a situation the gravity of which he alone chanced to be aware. During the engagement that had held the enemy from forcing the parapets of one small sector of the Wall, and which was still in progress, he had seen massed forces, if massed ill, away on the further slope. This was precisely what his now dead General had himself come to enquire about.

For some time he looked down on the shrunken form who should have now been as the Winged Victory — this was the very hour for which they'd together made certain dispositions — taking into full account the 'skeletal' state of troops available, far worse than even Pte Morgant had supposed, with his Silurian intuition.

The General had the solid facts, the actual statistics, and these alone would have caused a lesser man a paralysis of will, except that we regarded the thing as of extreme improbability — but what he had seen with his own eyes in a break in the mist was a massing of the enemy in great numbers on the slope of the hill facing our porta principalis, and that means that this affair an hour back was merely a tryout on a small scale to test our defences, and we only with difficulty flung that few from our parapets.

But there's no getting round it:
'The Senior Centurion takes over.'

He continued to gaze carefully at every detail in the fallen
Commander's pierced figure. One long, steady, glance ob-
served in the thrown-back paludament the broken stitches of
the interlining that laid bare the markings of the Lady
Elena's skilfully sewn-in pelts of wild-cat. He even had a
guess at where, from its markings, one at least of these had
graced the thick wood-ways of a particular area of Britain
— from round about Uriconium, and this other maybe from
Varae of the Deceangli on the *via* that takes you west to
Segontium: a land he'd heard the Domina speak of, and he
himself had been at one time stationed with a small con-
tingent in those parts, from the legionary fortress at Deva
— indeed, the fauna and flora of Britain were pretty well
known to him — woodland cats were but *cattae* to be
trapped for their pelts, but he had noted that their markings
varied, not that the matter had been of any consequence to
him, but because his life as a centurion had conditioned him
to note with precision this from that to a nicety — no matter
whether it was an affair of parade-states, two inches over-
laps, precise height of parapet, or, as here, the variant
markings on cat-pelts.

But those broken stitches displaying the Domina's superbly
managed contriving whereby her husband, his Commander,
if he must wear Caesar's paludament as signum of his
authority, here *yn yr ynys hon*, then it shall be of the finest
weave Britain can provide, and radiant with the madder-
dye the receipt of which was known only to great ones
years since before Cunobelin, before [Catavalaun] — and if
we raid the deepest *coed*-ways and sylvae of Britain for the
finest cat-pelts to interline more warm the shoulder-pieces,
while retaining the required military cut, it shall be done,
much as I love the quick-limbed denizens (of flaming fury
are they, and unknown to fear when men would corner
them), the most perfected leaping beauties of our dense
woodlands, other than the gentle does that desire the water-
brooks.

The Centurion knew this much of her thoughts, though

he could not comprehend them — but she had suppressed her innate feelings for his dead Commander — and the thought of it all broke his hard-fibred will. But 'the Senior Centurion takes over': there was no escape.

But how 'take over'? — he a Primus Pilus Prior, and the dead General of senatorial rank and responsible for the entire middle defences of the Wall.

His face it would be hard to delineate in that hour.

No word to those about him.

Then to some legionary: Tell my *Optio* I require him at once.

Is he: well, he can leave fooling around with whatever's happened at the Wall. I require him here, and instantly.

Yes sir.

Yes, it had better be 'Yes sir'.

'79 Porrox of Maniple VI took one quick glance and heard the tone of voice refracted in choking mist, and as he turned, then the single word *Vade!* sped him off as though the Thunderer himself were on his track. Nor for his life after could he ever forget the inscrutable and terrible metamorphosis that was imaged in the visage of [him] that commanded him.

The Senior Centurion remained fast, his eyes reverting to their gaze on the Medium Mark IV, the post-holes and the heavy beam left askew by the work-gang for the night. He remained silent and then, forced as it were to consider a matter of dire misery linked with that inescapable formula, 'the Senior Centurion takes over', he beckoned four, no, it must be six men and indicated to them to stand by and carry the pierced body of the General to his quarters in the *praetorium*. He would not suffer any but himself to free the body from the spear-shaft of high trajectory, whereby through vertebrae and fractured sternum a Roman General Officer, and his own beloved Commander, was transfixed to the earth of his own parade-ground.

Mercifully, this task, requiring technical ability equal to its grimness, was familiar to him — you don't climb from taking y'r *sacramentum* as a tiro, twenty years back, to steady progress through the *primi ordines* to become a *primus pilus prior*, without some experience in the extraction of spear-heads.

That done, he fixed his whole attention on the onager.

His assistant centurion, the *optio*, had now come up, saluted from the required pace, and stood fast.

He lifted his eyes from the onager, and returned his subordinate's salute; managed a smile, for the two were long old friends.

Come closer, Caius, as close as may be, and speak softly.

Well, Caius, that was quick work, that man Porrox has more to him than I'd supposed — half-way between a stoat and feathered Mercury — where did he come to you?

Well, sir . . .

Come, Caius, between you and me we can cut out the sir — but what I bloody well won't stand for not even from you is any evasive answer to my questions. I repeat: where precisely did he give you my command — S.O.S. would best describe it?

Very good, we'll cut what you will, but no shade of disobedience will you get from me. As a matter of fact, we came upon one another in the most literal sense — collided, one might say, at the turn of the revetment of fosse B, you know, by where the Field Survey (withdrawn six Kalends back) had engineered a recess for reserve supplies. That is the precise spot y'r Mercury gasped out to me your orders — the last the poor sod will ever deliver this side Dis. For it chanced that thereabouts the thicks of white mist swathed extra solid — the confined way runs a bit low thereabouts, you'll recall: and like a brick-bat within a snow-ball a huge Pict hurled himself from what Porrox hastening imagined was but brumous insubstantiality.

But you, Vegetius, what were you doing in that communication way?

We'd finished off the few bastards as one way or another managed to slip within our traverses — all the rest we'd flung from the parapets — and the game seemed over.

Yes, yes, that much I know, at least such was the report I received from y'r own runner. Is not that so? But how came the Pict to be a tidy way within our defences? And how came you to be...

Sir! and here it shall be 'Sir', for I am furnishing my report, not only as an *optio* to a *primus pilus prior*, and one accounted a trusted friend, but to the Commander of our depleted — no, skeletal, garrison.

When the first assault broke without warning of any sort, it was flung from our fire-bays on the extreme right flank. A few, a very few, of the enemy tried a second less determined attempt, a trifle to the left, with even less success. We were, as you know, nowhere near up to requisite strength, but as the raid died down it became evident that the attempt had failed. This I reported to you by runner. But it was inevitable, given the frontage, the lack of manipular strength, the fall of dusk, the drifting mist, that some few should climb, though only to be dealt with severally, in their attempt to regain their abandoned comrades far side the Wall

ΣΥΝΘΟΦΟΛΑΣ
ΑΡΚΤΟΦΟΛΑΣ

But here & there whatever the situation,
some man of singular ability & will find
some means to tied back the chaos
for a while & in some limited terrain,
and here this Island, or part of it,
suggests a possibility — some dux or comes
of the status quo of sufficient influence
to gather to himself a strike-force of
equities, heavy-mailed and heavy horsed —
(that might pose a difficulty in replacement
here) ready at once to move with
with speed where needed most, he might
maintain some order for at least a
lifetime

you still ask, where's the connection between
celestial ⟨ΑΡΚΤΟΦΟΛΑΣ⟩ and my ordinary
hypothetical strategos?

Well, ⟨ΑΡΚΤΟΦΟΛΑΣ⟩ is one with
ΑΡΚΤΟΥΡΟΣ, as guard or warden of
⟨ΑΡΚΤΟΣ⟩ and should: This Director
of Toil a chance to be nominated Artorius as —
Hold on! how may 'ifs'; perhaps so a 'but' chuckle that one?
Not so unlikely as might seem —
Some of our nomina have caught me
as Constantinus or Ambrosius, &
already among some others
may be Kurtonnin and Emrys,
& who would expect to find a man
Æternus by name, as I myself did.
He was a sub-regulus of sorts
to westward of these northern parts of
Upper Britain, just south of Petra Cloitha

It so chances also that when my mob
were in Gallia Lugdunensis or Gaul
of Latin speech said his praenomen
was Artorius and that was because
his brother's mother (you know how
in Gaul the women rule and matters,
as a dear besides) and insisted that
far back there was a cult-figure
Artorius of name who
to whom offerings
were made for the soil to ... yield
good harvesting, but
but, just like our Mars, he
suffered the metamorphosis
of ceasing to be tutelar of
the brine plough-shares a'furrowed
and sustaining line and 579
became the tutelar of men.
formed'; clines of battle, not to

7ᵗʰ DEC

NOV — 14/15

formal C

II

THE KENSINGTON MASS
CAILLECH
THE GRAIL MASS

— 7 A —   ✗   ✗   ✗

This one fetches mine light.
This ~~you're~~ junveos with the ~~[crossed]~~ — withdraws.
the coverlet bord ~~and~~ cloth shimmers pale now.
~~[crossed out line]~~

Dont unsheaf that thing here! apart
from the shaven ministers in file of
three the gallery is filled with gleemen
& the warden's daughter, Jor Bgurnod.
& Corbels, hangings, ambo-moueding
the ~~[crossed]~~ toe of the prince of ~~[crossed]~~.
Maureon Jane Roker's grail gonfalon,
~~the~~ Knights of the Sacred Head, & the
sea-guides, Hyacyth, Joy & Fay
at prayer in echelon, daughters of
the mayor of the Sacred palace & ~~[crossed]~~
mayor Moleneux himself, obscure
almost everything for Mr Todd who
knells in the atrium gentium ~~[crossed]~~ twenty
fine pews back for the Carmine baize
reserve. His ~~[crossed]~~ neck cranes
an inch free of his holy-day ~~collar~~
~~[crossed]~~. the would see the workman's hands,
the ~~[crossed]~~ hands of the
workman in the gold tissue — he's
got a thing about seeing the work
done there lifted up. He loaths Min—
~~[crossed]~~ hat — thats capital
he's a fair sield now between & plume
& ~~[crossed]~~ s toe. ~~[crossed]~~ toe, tich lub
The eyes of the testy man in cloth
of ~~[crossed]~~ gilt-edged, seem to be

to wide laundry.
~~[crossed]~~
of ~~[crossed]~~ Serraphin
~~[crossed]~~

THE KENSINGTON MASS

in affectionate recalling of
J. O'C.
sacerdos

that han cure vnder criste
and crounyng in tokne
of the Antistitium of
Loidis regio in
Lower Britain.

clara voce dicit: OREMVS
    et ascendens ad altare
        dicit secreto: AVFER A NOBIS...
and in lowly accents
    he says the rest
should you be elbow-close him
    you may catch his
soft-breathed-out
    PER CHRISTVM DOMINVM NOSTRVM.
Light as air
    the Goidelic vowels of
Maedb's own Munster
    intermingle with
that vocalic pulchritude
he first had heard
    long since
in Alban hill-ways
    in Latium
loved at first hearing
    and now

as though innate in him
indelibly marking him
an unconscious part of him
but far from unconscious
the deliberate cultivation
            in the years long fled.
He for whom the vestal fire
on the Hill Capitoline
was one with the points of flame
            tended with care
within the lime-whited bangor, where
the vestals of **Brigit**
            had trimmed the februal lights
of a long, long since
            asperged and crux-signed
Brigantia of the Fires
            sacred to half Celtica,
as here in green Kildare.

His hands conjoined
            super altare
his full chin crumpled
            to the pectoral folds of
his newly washed focale
he begins the suffrage:
            ORAMVS TE, DOMINE
pleading that the merits of
            the Blessed departed
the veterani in their celestial castrum
& colonia 'in hevyn on hicht'
might assist him at the work
he is about to make

but in especial he asks the adjuvance of
            these athletes of God
tokens of whom are cisted
            immediately beneath
& central to
            the Stone of Oblation
at which he now stands.

He inclines lower yet
          and with a gravitas & pietas
that can be felt
          lightly & swiftly his lips
press, in medio, the uppermost of the
three-fold, fine abbed fair cloths
          of Eblana flax
that must pall
          the mensa Domini
these are indeed 'his own raiment'.
As he says the words: sanctorum tuorum, quorum reliquiae
HIC SVNT his apparelled amice hunches a little with the
thrust forward & more downward head of him. He has no
need of the rubric's nudge: *osculatur altare in medio.*
for what bodily act other
          would serve here?
Creaturely of necessity
          for we are creatures
Our own salutation
          were it possible
could be no other than the rubrics *osculatur*
          were it Argive Helen's chiton hem
or the hem of the garment
          of gilt interthreaded green
          wide laticlaved of murex
the long tunica of
          our own Elen of the Army-paths
whose outward splendour of form
was informed by an instress
          of great noblesse.

She for whom the Imperator
          could not eat nor sleep
nor ride out with his comites & duces
in their coats of grey
          in the forest rides
to track the green paths
where the gentle-eyed quarry
desiderate of the water-brooks
is like to be, nor could he

find solace of his most loved falcon
nor from any venery
            which formerly
had been some respite from
the tedium of affairs of state.

Yet, was it on one such day of tedium, plea & counterplea
— had the Agrimensores demarked the *limes* in question in
accord with our late rescript or did the disputed boundary
rest on no more than the word of bumpkin georges who'd
had from their baldhead forebears that such was the
boundary from before the She-Wolf on the faunine slope
sustained the Twins...

With scarce a third of that day's affairs yet dealt with, he
signified the session was terminated and stepping down from
his curial chair the marbled walls of the aula echoed the
imperial mandatum:

'Tomorrow it is our desire to follow the chase and take
whatever fortune the numina of the groves may grant us.'

Three of the four vigiliae slipped away
his pridie had put on today.

The meet was within the pomoerium
            of the City
that sacred unseen defence
            the augurs plot
clockwise, the sure-binding wall
without which the mortared walls of
            squared, dressed stone
crenellate and turreted
            were contrived in vain.

As they moved off toward & through
            the high-arched wide gateway
the hallooing of brass-throated cornus
slung from gay-worked baldrics
            lifted to the lips of virile
                        proudly saddled

gay vénators
      as a dawn salute
to the Supreme Vénatrix on High
her gleam-white crescent moon
all but faded-out and wan.

Brazen-faced Phoebus
      had not as yet
in his quadriga
climbed to the horizon rim
his gleaming axle-tree
      still unseen.

But to harbinger his sure approach
the brumous half-light
infiltrated here, now there
rather as assault-groups
      probe in column
to coalesce in line
so did the green dawn
      slowly gain the field.

But the red cock and the grey
      had crowed but twice
the Fisherman with the Keys
      had yet a brief respite, but
brief indeed.

His unwiped gladius
      well hid within the ample folds
      of his closely weft, stout-fabric'd
      wide paenula, stained of
      wave-fret and wind-borne cloud drench.

His hands wide-fisted
hands and whole frame built to
haul & reef & steer

His steer-tree more than most
      could manage

Why had he still one mauler
        at the weapon's hilt-grip
(Well, after all there might be
        a further chance
and who should say what turn the pattern
next might take?)

He's scarce got within the warmth the brazier's fire of
coals built by escort details pending further orders, nor had
he found any armament but cursing and denials against the
barbed & knowing questioning of door-keeping sluts
        when, on the instant
the Gallic rooster
        his scraggy neck stretched high
let give, without restraint
        his third high determinate-cry
crowed out in harsh cacophony.

Down the meander and crooked labyrinth of time and maze
of history, or historia intermeddled with potent and light-
giving, life-giving, cult-making mythos
we hear as yet that third crow
dawn crow of dolour
as clear as we hear
        the echoing blast
from Roncesvalles
        and with it, of necessity
the straight, exact, rational and true
'Sirs, you are set for sorrow'.

[*Continuation of* THE KENSINGTON MASS][1]

But what then
        of the FISHERMAN
what of him?

---

[1] [The continuation of the Mass is printed here as it appears in
The Kensington Mass (Agenda Editions, 1975), but without the
notes and commentary on the 14 sheets of David's MS, re-
produced in that edition, from which it has been assembled.]

when from near and by
          perched high on ill-woolded spar
          that served for fallen slat
          of pent-house lid
(Why, I'ld wager
          my good woman's aged mother
but scarce ris from
          dire fevered bed
would, if needs be
learn 'em to woold a fished spar
firm enough to serve sufficient
— a jury-spar you might say
nor bungle the job neither)
     Must these lubbers of southland folk hereabouts
as for the most part live life-long
          within, or nigh as dammit
the sacral temenos of
          the Lord Yahweh's megara'd
Ariel height
must they be taught
          in all & every matter
the Galilaean runes?

Up in Tetrarchate
          you get all sorts of every sort
and the intermixt lingo
          and differing tongued talings of
half the peoples and nations & kin-gens
          from under the bent arc of heaven

Not so long back
          by a lading-hoist
on the new wharfe
          of Magdala quay-side
was a gang labouring with heavy baulks of timber
and such like weighty gear
          and among them
and bent hard to his task
          was one whose toil-sweat
dulled somewhat
          the crines-tangle

some lank strands of which
fell forward
            (as when a fray'd length of dank cordage
dangles inutile the out-board timbers of her)
Yet this could not disguise
            the glint-bright of
            his native hue

No drift of acrid smoulder-weft
            sensed of the nostrils
the old wives will have it
            without a kindling
            of flame-brands

The Tetrarchate is not nominate
            Galilaea gentium
for nawt, for not no place named
            but what there be no cause
nor no occasion

The lettered of our people
            scribae & doctors
masters and law-men
exegetes and canonists
            learned from their young-time
these varying disciplinae
            in schola & seminary
taught of elders of competence
in all that pertains to the
            levitic deposits
the binding mandates
            the sacerdotal code
the five-fifths of the Law together with
            the Second Law et Prophetae
the textual codices
            glossed and redacted of
many generations.
what's writ in membraned
  χρονικά and the fierce words of
            tractates for that time

yet foretellings of things
         yet to be
near four on four centuries back
within the second Olympiad
         as they say in the Ten Towns
already our Tetrarchate was
         known to men
as Galilaea Nationibus.

And these lettered doctors
scribes & exegetes do say

with no less certainty
         indeed more
than my mate judges how the sudden veer of wind
requires a further taking in of
the larboard sheet,

         that what us such, do hear from [what] our fathers'
fathers have told of their time and of the marvels of the old
times before them, in the main, apart from borrowed and
local deviations here and there, do tally with what they
trace out in these written texts some very ancient others
redacted by more recent hands and in either case giving
substance and sure record of what to us, unlettered, was
but lore handed on among our folk and, no doubt, loaned
in parts from the tales current among the mixt kin of the
land.

         How so ever that may be, one such tale was of this
young man of singular beauty of princely blood loved by
all the people, fair of aspect and his golden tresses excelling
his sister's whom he greatly loved. His sword-arm strong
and all his members built to serve what we expect in princes.
Third as heir presumptive to the Royal Seat on Flail-floor
Hill site, Jebus height, above the conduit, the West-most
rise of ground of twin-hilled Hierosolyma.

This much the lettered men, scribes and exegetes find writ
in sacral membrana, the historia of our kings, sayings of

our prophets, and τὰ χρονικά and we that be unlettered, hear what is handed down in tellings told by baldheads to their beardless kin.

But be that as it may, if that vast oak had not the bright-berried growth intwined upon it, which flowering, so I've heard tell, the *filid*, *vates* or druidae (a kind of Levitic priesthood among the Galactic people) do cut with a golden sickle at certain sacred times in their year of Luna months.

That great lignum arbor una nobilis within the inmost *nemeton* of this wild Ephraim holt, had for Golden Bough the pierced & hanging son of the Lord of Salem.

CAILLECH

But as the preacher's tirade yet continued, Caillech the sharp of ear and eye was sharper still of memory and though the clarity of the voice at the ford that had come upon her while she drowsed had now faded out, the very tedium of the continued unabated ambo-flow started from its covert another creature of her memory-hoard — a fourth figure who, when the large church was most like to be empty and (so she was inclined to imagine, when the monsignor was least like to be about) this fourth figure came soft-footed to that same spiked harrow where Phryne, Biddy and Thais had come (singly of course) to say a swift decade or swiftly put up a votive flame and swift away into the gathering fall of Eblana's nearing night.

But no, recall what she was called at all, she could not, though daylight clear the slender, shapely ungloved dexterous fingers of her dexter hand as she kissed the white percher, then flicking off as best those fingers could sufficient of the coagulated grease to impale firmly and upright on the dark-spiked iron hearse her fresh-lit votive flame, bright among the dying *munera*... Then with the same naked hand, grease-mirked now its bright-white palm and tapering fingers, she made the crux-sign down from her gleaming forehead, wide from her left shoulder to the right, without haste — with a *gravitas* — born of unconscious grace. Then and only then, with her still gloved left hand she gloved again her right. That pair could but have been stitched by some artifex of those other Scotti in Pictland's Perthland to grace the highborn of the Scotti of virid Iverna, Eitu of the Marvel Cycles, of the síd-folk.

But still in Caillech's brain the name escaped her — but by

a complex of associations, the Perth gloves brought to her mind one line of verse she's heard from God knows where — yes, from the air from over the border when she'd gone to see [a] relative near the Holy Columba's Derry — all she heard on soft breath was something about a girl who'd to church gone

      'wid gloves upon her hands'.

That unseen and unknown stranger and English officer's voice on the wind set memory's meander on the right track ... *Blanches mains* daughter of Hywl *ri* of Armorica (she knew of her sad tale from an old 'rememberer' in her native Connacht) — he was now long dead, but he had been as the old *felid* were, by heart he had the book of the Four Masters, and could retale a thousand tales other, not only of the great ones of Eire but of the Brittanyest and Gaul and of east lands, so from him she had by heart the woeful tale of the two Isolts, and more clearly the prototype of the theme in Diarma[i]d and Gráinne, and how much of the feats in the Welsh saga of Arthur's raid into the domain of Annwn re-echoed the deeds of Finn mac Cumaill ... but of 'Mary Hamilton to the kirk's gane, wid gloves upon her hand' she had never heard, yet that chance line brought to her mind the *blanches mains* of Isolt, and that immediately turned the key on what was clear in her memory's eye, the ungloved right hand now gloved again, and taut as a sailcloth of darkest hue (as if belayed for some significance), the contours of her hop-sack bodice, the white cambric kerchief at her white neck's turn, a frilled inch of it at right wrist.

It was she for sure, who else? unless nothing in Caillech's memory-store was become any longer certain, but a ragbag of intermeddled fragments.

But no, she it was for certain, who else? In all Eblana, whether in the spacious places of Georgian elegance or by the 'empties' outside Mulligan's in Walker St where lodged poor Finnegan who to rise in the world had carried the hod, or in the quiet museum she not infrequently could be seen gazing intently into a page from the miracle from Kells, or far without the orbit of the City, perhaps south where Liffey's banks meandered the fields toward Kildare, or perhaps by the 'blackguard Hill of Howth'... in all this area she was, if seldom seen, known by name: The Honourable Patricia Shiela Gráinne Isolt Filgate-Flood, relict at eight on twenty of Lieutenant-Colonel Gerald, Montgomery, Breakspeare, Sylvester, Barri Filgate-Flood, R.F.A. retired on half-pay. After that unfortunate affair in Ladysmith year, was it not? Well yes, I've heard that too, some say the old man ought to have been cashiered, but he'd friends at court, not excluding the Old Lady Her regnant self, who for some reason took a personal interest in the case and urged his age and rank as incompatible with anything more severe, indeed saw no reason for the demand for imposed retirement of any sort, but the Jock commander, with considerable support, did not take kindly to having a whole half-company wiped out by shrapnel from Filgate-Flood's eighteen-pounder battery, and minded still more that they'd been mistaken for bloody Boers — which was the main defence.

That's a good few years back now, Charlie. Anyway he didn't do so badly, slipped quietly off to a small property in Ireland and managed, God knows how, to snap up a wife half his age, titled but without a bean, but of incredible beauty.

Well that's he at seventy-eight years of age they sodded but three years back on St Finbarr's eve.

And what of her? — She can be but thirty or so now. Well, certainly he left her neither property or cash, but I hear she's sometimes seen and as beautiful as ever and is known by name but elusive and remote and brief of speech — anyway her bearing once seen is not forgot.

It was she for certain — but that would have sideways knocked his reverence's triune form — though half of the Town of the Hurdles knew of Patricia Gráinne's fond association with the unnamed interdicted three, but that was not of consequence at all [?] since his Reverence Monsignor Aloysius Celestine Ignatius Patrick McGrath ('Aloysay go easy' for the lads of the village) in a pulpit oration had placed his *verboten* on all the three (no names of course) — his term, to be exact, was 'The Trinity of Pariahs'. His theme, in the main, the chastity in general of Holy Ireland, but for some erosion nearer to hand than he had deemed possible, within the confines, indeed, of his own parish. Thus those only of his flock for whom it was intended would, without a second guess, know to a nicety his target. For the remainder in the packed pews it was but the generalized formulae that might be heard in any of the Five Divisions of Eira.

May be some element in Celticity found an unconscious distaste in grafting to his triune stem a further form — for to be fair to Aloysius McGrath he would by no means go easy in this matter of ambo-grease — what is a pulpit stepped-up for if not that such as he, of the *Ecclesia Docens*, should be elevated somewhat the better to be heard of people with words that rouse the unattending ears of those come to their Mass of Obligation.

As the hard rhetoric lengthened it became more evident that the brogued-out citations of the grace of chastity and its reverse were but to camouflage the precise alignment of his battery on its selected target.

The continued tedium of it flowed like a half-heard water in Caillech's head. Strange was the metamorphosis: for though the tirade from the pulpit rose higher still, more deep still the drowse upon her — and a vivid memory, clear as light, actual and defined, but still of something past, held her alert. The preacher's voice was not blacked out, but its flow was of the present and totally unheeded, for though she still half-dozed, a new alertness came in upon her from a voice remembered:

Why yes, for certain, the Lord God, His Blessed Mother, Saint Kieran the first-born of the holy ones — long before Padraig, long long anterior, let these be my witnesses that I speak no lie, those three of whom you ask me brought me their bundled wash for me to launder by this upper water — but scant it was, all told, but onto this damp palm they never failed to pay my due and somewhat more. Kieran, the first-born of the holy ones, bless them. 'Tis my trade to lave what's brought me to this ford and pommel on the green launder-bank above, where my help-mate Morrigu bends to her task — the pair of us slaving all day, and she already womb-burdened since the Lord Dagda rode this way at a night's fall.[1] May the White Christ avenge what Kieran the holy one had no power to avert.

Well, my darling, I've answered y'r question as far as in me lay. — Now in some small recompense would I ask of you if may be you chance to know a matter that weighs heavy upon me. No, no, indeed not on m' conscience, but 'tis a thing of great puzzlement of mystery beyond the strange interweavings of the wonder-tales our *felid* conserved for us of Maelduin, of Bran son of Febal, but of a wholly other labyrinth or marvel.

Yes, for sure I've asked a few, but all I get from any is scoffings and scorn-edged bitter laughter. Yes, worst of all from them — not laughter may be, but straight, strict warnings of mortal sin, for spreading devil-invented tellings an' a fine dose of decades into the bargain.

'Go to Rome for money' I've heard some say — that's no concern of mine, that's souper's talk, but this I know, that little comes my way.

This then is my question: of those three of whom you asked me, one as you must know was called by men, Thais. I've laved and laundered her shift and maybe dressed with special care the gores and gathered pleats and seams of her outer gown — sometimes she wore a skirt of scarlet-threaded weave hemmed with a four-inch hem of plum-hued velvet, such as I scarce had seen on the young fair-limbed fair ones since what time I walked by Shannon bank, for in Limerick town was I born and 'twas the accustomed wear thereabouts — but no matter what graced her sweet limbs, never a time no matter what gear of hers I laved and laundered, there fell to m' labours bright grains of punic sand (whatever that might mean). Next week the same and the next again. And once in the februal octave of the holy man Antony (the weather was soft for the time of year) she stood awhile when she brought her small bundle and I

---

[1] Morrigu, pronounce Mor-reé-goo, accent on middle syllable. One of the 'Washers at the Ford' in Celtic myth, 'raped' by Dagda. See Rachel Bromwich, *Trioedd Ynys Prydain*, 459.

101

could but notice — and here Morrigu will bear me out — for she too in lateral rays of evening light saw those same microscopic grains that made more gilt yet the golden fall of her riverain tresses.

— and she in a sheen of glory, as remote and above me fairer than all the loves of a Tara Ardri, more of wonder than Branwen, daughter of Lir and wife of Maelschecblainn King of all Ireland, she whose beauty, by inadvertence, caused the death of the Blessed Bran her brother, Lord of all Britain, and brought devastation to all Ireland and death to all her warmen and, apart from seven, death to the warriors of Britain also, for grief of which she herself died. They digged for her a quadrilateral grave on Alaw bank, in Ynys Fon, the lesser Innis Manannán.

More then of splendour than any, other than she whose total pulchritude, so I have heard a sacerdos of Melchisedec declare from the Holy Book, is of a beauty terrible as a war-host of Erin, their lime-whited shields in battle-formation and banners deployed, she of whom I was told by an ancient and much travelled White Father that in the hot, parched, arid, desert lands they call her 'the stem that bore our Eucharist'.

No, no, hold y'r gab, child, and list to my taling — 'twas not of the Holy Muire I spoke, but by comparison with the wonder I saw in Thais. Have some sense, woman. Am I like to be vouchsafed visions of Blessed Mother? Get clear in whatever little's in y'r sweet brain-pan that she of whom I speak was Thais and none other. I tell of no vision but of solid actuality — a thing seen with these eyes of flesh.

Anyway, she stood for a while, handed me her wash, paid what was due to me and somewhat over as I've already said the three of them usually did, smiled as was her habit, and was away beyond that hurdle-stake where you yourself now stand, turned for a moment to wave her soft white hand before she turned where the broken shaft of that ogam stone by the wind-felled ash baulks further sight and so was gone with no word more.

No more could Caillech recall except her own embarrassed silence, for her inability to lift at all the deep perplexity — indeed she was aware that her failure had destroyed the half-hope of her questioner, who turned in the gathering dusk to little Morrigu, who called out from the green launder-bank, 'Come now, didn't I tell ye it were to no purpose to enquire of Finn's Caillech or any other mortal, of Thais and her Thebaid sand. I'm off now till tomorrow's dawn-light becomes broad day. Mortal dread I already feel upon me at this water ford as the dusk deepens into night.'

The Monsignor too was still at it but nearing the end.

At all events the Triad of the Pariahs must suffer no loss by hurried rounding-off. My monsignorial office demands a pastoral care, I'm no Chrysostom or such-like, nor suffer no illusions on that score, but yet within this Archdiocese I can think of no man of my cloth I'ld not take on at a straight-hitting bout of pulpit-delivery.

He glances at his watch — the notices for the week and other parish matters had been a little on the long side, hence his carefully prepared sermon, though timed to a nicety, had somewhat overstepped his calculations, but yet but little and on no account must the terminating paragraphs be hurried, still less cut.

The Omnipotent, by whose uncreate Word, *Deum verum de Deo vero*, by whom all things are that are could wait awhile his *Credo*.

Now he was done and not without a measure of satisfaction proceeded at a slight angle to the right across some contractor's hideous marbled flooring of the sanctuary: was re-vested in the sacred planeta and had replaced on his left arm the maniple

and then standing *in medio altaris* began to intone the first four words of the *Credo*, to retire to sit in the sedilia of the sanctuary.

The choir are of not much quality, but at least they chant after a fashion, the rest. But Aloysius, though by nature no Liturgist, carefully observes what the rubrics prescribe, his biretta is off and his head is inclined toward the crucifix at the words *in unum Dominum Jesum Christum*, he kneels at *et incarnatus est* to *et homo factus est*. Cum dicit *simul adoratur* caput cruci [inclinat], and when they sing *et vitam venturi saeculi* with his right hand he makes the Crux sign.

The time is short, already haec ✠ dona,[2] haec ✠ munera, haec ✠ sancta sacrificia illibata has been said over the oblation.

In the North Porch West-wave Launcelot, his long, straight, heavy, well-tempered iron sword-blade drawn ready in his fist-grip held just below the quillons — he assessed the ageing timber as requiring no hilt-work, no great sword-play, — of course any man can err in judging to a nicety even in affairs within his own competence and here I'm on familiar ground — let's see, in any case I have further ways, God knows, but time is now short indeed and I must be within ... His Aryan pommel at the first stroke gapes the aged timber. It chances to fracture the pine-wood panel to which has been tacked the Notices for the Week, this parchment is ripped, so that what does not fall with its nails to the flooring, floats in dusty air. This he regrets, due to the violence of his advent, but the splendour he saw within gave not a second's time but for instant action. Three strides through the rising mirk of dust and falling splinters, and the altar lights that had burned straight and still as spear-points wavered and acrid smoke from the blackened wicks, and the sweet incense directed from the thurible drifted in meaningless wreaths as the across draught from the fallen door let in an enfilade of cross draught.

But he would be and was within that chamber door. Three strides (or one leap at a pinch) and he would be where the Cyrenean deacon leaned forward and inward to relieve the weight. He too would aid the venerable man of that weight.

Rex tremendae majestatis yet *fons pietatis*, all I ask is but the brief space of one leap of a mailed man, for I a *miles* would be not worth my mailed coat did I not aid the venerable man surcharged with that great weight.

[3] [That the transition from the Credo to the Canon is deliberate is shown by another sheet of David's MS on which the preacher glances at his watch and decides that the remainder of his sermon must not be hurried. 'The Omnipotent... must wait awhile his *Credo*.' R.H.]

Holy and Eternal Lord, Gwledig Nef, I ask but that one microscopic fraction of this world's time of you, who within the vast Wheel of Eternity created time as not illusory but of *realitas*. No more I ask but that, not any amelioration of what is adjudged me, on the *in favilla* day, as David and the Sibyl have it. *Nil inultum remanebit* — but I too would aid the venerable man surcharged with that great weight, and it is but for that brief moment I ask it.

It is for time-space of one leap that I ask it.
Gwenhwyfar pray, no, not for
no cancellation of what's adjudged me
but for a stay of sentence, of
exceeding brevity . . .
    No, I see it may not be,
not even though the gladius-pierced
Mother of Mercy,
besought her Eternal Son, the
Fount of Pity, the Gwledig Nef,
(*per quem omnia*)
for not for all the dire and piteous necessity of one moment's grace can I extend my charity to that bastard Mordred, not to Morcant, who, given the passing space of a few centuries will slay at Traeth Mercawt the Lord Urien, the stay of Rheged, and the last hope of the Brythinaunt. Not dissimilar in name, separate

THE GRAIL MASS

Inclined in the midst of the instruments
and invoking the life-giving persons
and in honour of the former witnesses
et istorum, dusty in the cist
he kisses the place of sepulture.

He turns to ask of the living.
Those round about answer him.
He turns again and immediately
            toward the tokens.

He continues and in silence
inclined over the waiting creatures
of tillage and of shower.

Ceres and Liber and
the dancing naiad
have heard his: Come who makes holy
and now and so still
            between the horns of the *mensa*
they wait awhile
his: ratify, accept, approve.

You are his special signs
and you'll be doubly *signa*
before he's at the *Unde et memores*.

            O no, not flee away
but wait his word
not to th'infernal jail
            (as blind makers

in harmonic numbers tell)
not troop off, not you, nor
Peor's baalim
            but wait on him.
Yes, brutish you
            but you his forerunners
each of you, his *figura*.

Need peculiar powers forgo their stalls?
He's no douser of dim tapers
and why should Anubis hasten
except to glast the freeing of the waters.
So stay
            but when they sing
            QUI VENIT
here all of you
            kneel
every Lar of you
            numen or tutelar
from *terra*, *pontus* and the air
or from the strait bathysphere.
            Now constellate
are all your brights
            of this lifted Lode.
What light else
            brighted you ever?

He stands upright now in the weeds
of the young-time, of the sap-years.
            Under his fair-worked apparels
the tubular blacks of the mean years
of the dead time.
            In file of two
the patrician tunicas
move up in support.
            (They've stitched the laticlave so
since the year that measures all the years.)

He hunches free of wrist
            the gothic folds

(O, give us a Roman planet any day!)
Loudly he clears his throat
brother ass must neigh for all his May Day rosette
the belly murmurs though it serve Melchisedec.

Full and clear he rounds his vowels
when he says *Per omnia*
but his full chin crumples to the pectoral folds
at *Gratias agamus.*

And now he sings out
          and alone
the gleemen and the Powers take the cue
he has the Nine Bright Shiners at his beck
when he stands substitute
to the Man in the Mock.

        (you, dark-membraned
awned in sanctus-pent
softly flit, *cum angelis* exult
and with clerestory concelebrants
mix your shadowy webs
they sometimes make you
        signa of the evil thing
but laugh at them
        and stretch again your fragile pinions
high up and over the meal spread
tumbling our Faustian spaces
        where the stone creatures grin.
        You are the proper image
and very figure
        of us all
purblind, yet, somewhat winged.)
He thumbs a page or so
        smooths the violet marker out
swift on, professionally
        minding his Roman step.
Seems to search for what mislaid
tilts this ever so little
        with a sensitive deliberation.

Backhands Miss Weston's leaning lily
clear of the instruments.

You can hear her penny stop
or a beads dropped or rope-chafe
            in sacring-loft
above the table spread
            or cat-call
from pleasure-go-round outside
otherside urbs.

His recollected fingers now
his supports close in
            each to his proper station.
He lifts *ad caelum* his lit-grey Goidelic eyes
            (*non solum corporales sed etiam spirituales*).
Madelene in fox
lets her hair-net bide
and in her pew
deep calls to Miss Calypso Fortesque.

The movements peculiar to the transfigured man
cause bells to be rung.

You can hear now the whine
            from the south porch
where Mrs Fripps has
            chained the dog
            for a thousand quarantines.

The worn bronze toe
            of the Capitoline Fisher
(who holds the troia keys)
you can just avoid, and
            between
the Miss Bodkin's equinoctial hat
and the devout shoulders of Colonel Cornelius
            you can see the work
done at The Tumulus.

And does the sacristan
            fetch out the jackal's head?
He does well
            for all must die
who would eat the Bread
            and where is he who said
I AM BARLEY?
            In the north porch
Lake-wave Lawnslot
            beats against that
varnished pine
            his quillon'd *cleddyf*-hilt
fractures the notices for the week
he would see
            right through that chamber door
he would be
            where the Cyrenean deacon
leans inward
            to relieve the weight
he too would aid the venerable man
            surcharged with that great weight.
In the south porch
            Argos the dog
howls outright.

III

THE OLD QUARRY
Part One

THE AGENT

THE OLD QUARRY
Part Two

a spectacle in the wind for tart's mate
to come weeping to see.
My Ned he offered the reed
iter ~~little~~ Larry was tarragon boy with
his dope.
Nell's Jerry won his tunicle, she says
it's a gran' bit o' ~~little~~ weave. Was high
stakes, an he called Mudhook in the
nick o' time. She says he says ~~that~~
he's luck's on at lune fête.
Three on sm yes — two were nowt.
A cock-shy for a priests' deliberate ~~x~~ lob.
A ~~Sally~~ without the alters & ~~came of~~
he redans from the stark host.
A guy for a pronged plot to put all
in a fine dilemma, hang each on
a nice fork # that's the crux of it
how the hell can you tell, it's a pretty
burden for a white man — after all
he held most extreem views, but as
Virginia
~~twus~~ says, the method's inexcusable.
you'ed hardly credit it in our days
it's positivs Carthagenian, sweetheart,
& I dont care what you say right's right
bond or free, it's all on in me, jaisis
us all the years over.

NB
*
Begin

∅

Wee

Section
XIV

THE OLD QUARRY
Part One

This one fetches more light.
This young one fumbles with the ewer — withdraws.
The coverlet board cloth shimmers pale now.
Paleface folds the spread napkin.
Don't unsheaf that thing here! Apart from the shaven
ministers in file of three the gallery is filled with gleemen
and the warden's daughter, for Gounod... Corbels, hang-
ings, sacristy lizards, the master of the robes, gold-sticks,
gildings, beadsmen, commissionaires, carriers, runners,
exorcists, signallers, doorkeepers auxiliaries, bell-ringers,
Knights of the Sacred Head, Moreen Jane Roper's Garil
Gonfalon, sea-scouts, and she-guides, ambo-mouldings,
aumbries, the Carrara toe of the Prince of the Apostles,
Hyacinth, Joy and Fay at prayer in echelon daughters of the
Mayor of the Sacred Palace and Mayor Molyneux himself,
obscure almost everything for Mr Tod, kneeling six pine pens
back from the carmine baize reserve. His corrugated neck
cranes an inch free of celluloid holy-day gear. He would see
the workman's hands; the hands of the workman in gold tissue
— he's got a thing about seeing the work done there lifted up.
He loathes Miss Briscoe's hat— that's capital — he's got a fair
field between feather and jowl and the Apostolic toe. The
eyes of the testy man in cloth of Reins gilt-edged seem to
be regarding intently No. 6 switch — that's on the onion
stone in the south aisle: General Gandolf late of this parish
and all his men drowned at Passchendaele in a very dark sea.
 He hunches free of wrist with testy twitch the Gothic
folds. (O give us a fiddle-back any day.)
 (You can hear a penny stop, or beads dropt, or cat-call

from pleasure-go-round other side Tiber, or bat-wing brush rope-fray in sanctus-pent high up and over the table spread.) The lumpish man clears his throat; Brother Ass must belch for all May Day hat; the belly murmurs though it serve Melchisedec. He makes bold with the initial vowels. Thumbs a page or so, smooths the violet marker out, swift on professionally to mind his Roman step, seems to search for what mislaid, tilt this ever so little with curious deliberation, back-hand Miss Naylor's leaning lily clear of the instruments. His recollected fingers now. His supports close in. Each to his proper station. He stands upright now in the midst of the traverse, his cuisses on his thighs, his feet shod, girt about the paps. The Cyrenean deacon leans inward to relieve the weight.

(You can hear the whine now in the south porch, where Mrs Fipps has chained Argos the dog for a thousand quarantines.) The venerable man stands in Aaron's hauberk, the rod flowers, the lance stands upright in the cup.

The king of Salem holds his desert food *sine patre, sine matre, sine genealogia, neque initium dierum neque finem vitae habens.*

The maimed king waits. The two fish gleam

The venerable man would prepare his household their bread.

The anointed man (adorned to have access ceremonially with attendants and divers washings, this spread and that held up, canopied, lute-men paid, garlands hung, him tunicled for the solemn entry as bride-day or prodigal's glad return) knows now at this turn the way deepens here — after this latchet, at this vault's narrowing — as sea-change, or snow-line reached; as one who in night saphead-shift crouches alone, after the convolution in column — the drummed assemblies and the trappings of those about to die: as prothalamion finery and proud walking give place at her time's turn — she leans now aproned, her special beauties humbled and work-a-day, who (but now) stood bolt up before them all on the morning of her opportunity and glad appointment — now with careful hands — the matter's intimate, she doth him wash and doth thee wring at sour waters and sink-drift, by gruel given and green faggots fanned and antique songs whispered and magic rockings, she tends her making before she gives him for the Reich.

So he crouches kindly and with attention, careful of the saving formulas, precise in the work of his hands. The gold tissue crumples, the transfigured man contracts over his work.

It's a lover's work here.

Here a maker turns a hard corner.

He's at the frontier and place of situations. There's struggle here: the march means demarcation, graphed and agreed to have or hold down, removed — white wattles and pents recede, dykes west bound farer dole like magician's wall of wove brume or a portable hedge for ap Erbin as rainbow seekers find the way far... as contra-punctal and variously set the mazy barrier seems to be.

Ninth choir's sweet mode (you'd listened long for) jars over this zone like night's whoop on night gust. The fair proportions crook themselves that you thought your chiefest joy. The unknowable baulk runs this nearly that that was this when I looked with my flesh-eye. You've a leg in both. There is opposition in depth for passage to [*several words so struck out as to be illegible*] by mountain way and all hills of Hermon and help-heights. Sally-ports open for the anointed leaders of the raid. There's struggle here and unsalvaged tokens of struggle.

King Hurlame's[1] stroke tumbles with singular resonance for Ezekiel's crackling gully. The spiral tumuli patterns out from New Grange to Hinnôm drift. Wady Sitti Maryam troubles her waters because of that stroke in the two marches, rings hollow back from standing stone — the young man stirs that oak-sprites gibbeted. His white memorial plinth leans toward half-waking Zachary.

Soon will be the fracture of the BRANCH[2]
the silver's told already

[1] Cf. *Morte Darthur*, Bk. xvii, ch. 3 (Everyman edn. p. 240, vol. II).

[2] Cf. Zechariah, chs. 3 and 11 (A.V.).

already the forest of the vintage is come down
already the voice of the howling of the shepherds
(in the beginning of the Sabbath he will walk in the
  slums of Ophel seen at some)
And he too — she'll bite her veil close to see
his gilté tresses clere
the younger one that was pierced
whose white sockets the oak-boughs bruised
whose ivory belly they blemished with iron
so that you wouldn't regard him.

This sone of myn he was perished and is foundun pricks
his fairy mule with bells on her nose, up steeps and down,
easily he passes through:
  Asmonean mortar and Jotham's middle-work
  Ionian courses³ unbind
  flint-faced, square-knit, dressed and adamant
  the Latin wall disperses
  like Pontine fog-gap, lifts a low arch
  (where old hags say the Jebusite wicket stood)
  for the comely Lord. He rides a-phantom
  to Sion mountain for all the guile
  in Ephraim grove.

His wraith-beast treads the dust of west hill with delicate
hooves, nor is any excrement disturbed in the parched,
stepped corridors, in the twisting narrows between the
slits, darkt for arch here and stenching vault — or here,
leprous-bright where the burning ray sickens you. His
tincture of cassia and the aloes of his balming freshes heavy
airs that hang for rancid tripes in offal-gutter by Kosher
Alley and Street-called-Straight. The spawning barrage
lifts for him, the septic and Semitic fly avoids his ointments.
Surely a bundle of myrrh is under his forelock, in the secret
places of his loins the valerian and the nard, his smell is

³ Asmonaean (Maccabean period). Jotham (2 Chron. 27:3,
A.V.). Ionian, later wall — Jebusite wicket. Indicative of the
various runs of wall subsequent to the original Jebusite city
known to David and Absalom.

lilac blome in his tunicle of yaller[4] when he comes riding
on his mule colt. *Primavera* of the showers he is, distillations
of calamus his night-locks drop for charnel-sewer and of
cheese-vendors[5] passage. And look at his cock horse! She's
a beauty. Four white trefoils spring where her gay stepping
is. The stones cry out, the subterranean conduits brim for
her light striking — the dumb beast called from faëry to
carry him. And who is he? That pre-applied grace should
furbish him so fine, to deck him like the elect, who rides
between our walls, who looks in at the lattices
the marble of his shins the latins broke at the ninth hour,
the marks of his just award are upon him though he ride
however so incorruptible, though he drink so soon the new
wine this day in the new commonwealth. Yet his gilt
favours show the oak-bough wrench, his sweet limbs the
felon's-fracture, though his fingers drop spices yet his palms
are grimed for bruising of husks, for chivvying of hogs
in fer countree.

She bites her veil closer who hears from over the Tyropoeon
gully the Shepherd King cry above the gate:
  Is the young man safe?
  My son my son
She would throw off the veil except for fear of Moses,
who hears the spectral rider in his pride
  but what does he seem to cry for
  who is she?
Open to me, my sister, *columba mea, immaculata mea*, what
is he who calls *Thamar soror mea*, we'll purge that brother
o' mine, he stands in his enchanted girths, he speaks
violently of cakes of rye, he feels for his dauphin's sword
(that crumbles in Kedron barrow) he's not yet learned the
implication of the new syllabus.

But what does the aged man cry, who leaps the degrees of
his high seat — he knows him yit whanne he was far that
proud walker at the horse-gate.

[4] Cf. 'The Lady-killing Cowboy', 'shirt of yaller'.

[5] The Tyropoeon Valley, the valley of the cheese-makers.

117

She would make the sign *tau* if any man had taught her
who hears above the commotion (this menial hurries to, and
that supervisor chivvying from) the maimed king cry:
Bring me my cloak of Miniver
Fetch me the twisted torque
Bringe ye forth the firsté stolé[6]
get the ring and leave the book.
Where did we put the variegated shoes
the Duke of Cordova spoiled from the blackamoors.
Convey Scone stone.
Ear-mark the White Tower hoard for the finer gems.
Crown him with the crown of Aix.
Bring me von der Vogelweide sitting on his rock.
He must have music all the way.
Get from the far isles the harp of Trietu and the
 inexhaustible chalice.
Get me the thirteen valuable vessels that are in the west,
especially the accommodating dish of Rhagenydd and the
name-bearing weapons.[7]
Obtain the golden comb of Arthur together with the
silver-looped scissors to groom his chief beauty. Bribe the
Hair-dresser to the King of France, for he barbours in the
best mode (for whether he poll or comb fair or jet, his
civility and mastery are such that he can make of equal
length, narded and garnished, any lank clot or tousle or
matted-mop by sweat or taggle of far journey
 or any disorder by desperate fingers or moon-straws
 stuck
 or disarray by jack-apes tumble or rueful
 chance
 or cruel wrenching by malice or by

---

[6] Cf. Wyclif version of Luke's Prodigal Son.

[7] Cf. T. Gwynne Jones, *Welsh Folk-lore and Folk-Custom*
(1930), 121. Dish of Rhagenydd is one of the thirteen vessels
known to Welsh folklore that have the quality of inexhaust-
ibility. Name-bearing weapons are common to the literature
of the [*incomplete*]. Spears and swords of special virtue.

the blessed and impetuous spirit (when he roots you
    suddenly to set you far)[8]
or by thorn-hedge arsewise or iron boundary mark
or by hot fly-burdened airs, or rain gust
shrill or cauld for swaying transom

or by carrion neb
or corbie-pinion spread
or plaited mock that draws the saving flood
or gnarled bough-boat nine nights on the
windy tree[9] or by that unguessed quickening[10] that
tangles unkempt in consuming mound or eyeless
    sarcophagi.)

The French king will demand securities. The queen of the
french isle will devise a plan. The nine shining courtesans
will not part with him easily, nor their nine maids neither,
nor yet will the Queen-huntress of Poictiers — though she
come from her porphyry piscine as damp as an eel and
leave her towels behind her (this she will do lightly to
circumvent you), though she cause Seine to flood, ministry
to fall, the defenestration of the deputies; by manifesto and
partial mobilization, if mob burn and sluts run bare, though
the twelve notable families be impeached, and the legate
swing, she will regard it as a small thing so that she may
keep him — the chief barbour-surgeon of the French nation,
his unguents, his pole, and his barbour's boy. For there is
none that can tire her hair when the waters have laundered
it but himself. Though the committee of six support her,
though the check-arsed goddams bolt Calais gate for her
asking — yet you must obtain him. Though she close
montes-route (and this she can easily effect, for the Alpine
Margrave winks when she arks her naked bow); the count
of the South March knows her too well — that rules out the

---

[8] Cf. Bel and the Dragon, Daniel 14 : 35 (Vulgate).

[9] Cf. Havámál. Odin hung nine nights on the cross at Uppsala.

[10] No one, I suppose, knows how fast or slow hair grows in
the tomb.

Roland gap. In which case, come by the *Maunche* in a coracle (this you will find tethered, pitched, and sound under Isoud's sea-fence, where her white wattles groin the Armorican fret, southward of the Pagus Constantinus).

Enquire shallows, care Nicht swell, get wind-gauge of the horse-king's black sail (for he keeps an evil custom), set steer-bord south be south be Suevi-shore and come

Come with him over the bitter sea, to dress the hair of this my son, against his living again.

And you

You will need bulls sealed and sight-drafts to be level with 'em.

For this: kiss the toe of Linus.

For this: square Fugger — write off fifty.

Pay compliment to the Little Horn and his body-men of equal armour.

And you, your journey's far.

With your baggage and flasks and sawn-off pieces to-do-as-rome-does. Speak foolishly in Westland both banks the waterspout, in the rectagonal divisions, in gods' darned wasteland.

Tell them tales of Pelasgian comfort. Presuppose inevitable perfectibility. Open a list of subscribers. Repeat often and at large laudable words, and especially be kind. Square the police.

Wear green in your bonnets. Carry gold

for not otherwise will they yield up to you the last great musk ox of the plain and the solitary pampas bull (whose horns and ears are of equal length) for the blood of beasts will I require at your hands, nor the three red men of all my red men that have survived their kindness. Also I require of them a quilted coverlet and a cotton-field song — these I must have for my son's appearing, to rejoice him.

She dropt her veil who heard the wailing on Sion mountain.

Then she heard him say:

I demand it of northfolk and southkind, of fishers in their sea-baskets who drag traeth Metcaut for the Yarl of Bebbanburgh. I demand it of Towy and Teiny and Garry and Ling, Ness and Clyst and Yare and Honddu and all the confluences of the Out Isles, of them I demand the silver beast, for it must be broiled and eaten fresh — it is his special sign.

I demand the Gwyddyl stone of the holy man Pyrus and the ringed stone of Olicana in *Britannia Secunda* (for devoted-men-of-old cut these stones with care)

I demand his tropical bear and his arctic pard,[11] muzzled and chained from the Prince of Rosh (together with his carton of sturgeon paste) though he be five years in planning their transport.

I demand his bough of Baldur, and the lighted tree. I demand a man and a woman of equal fairness whose parts are equal according to their several natures. This I demand of the führer of the north — my exasperated son, who handles my hammer — he is my rod (as were the kings of the nations in the old time before you, as was Nabuchodonosor king of Babylon). I have made him my acid against your corrosion whether you like it or not.

*　　*　　*

Fetch me his harp, his rug and his pot, for his innate status demands them as an elementary right. Marta serve the kittle on, fit the trivet square. Bake it boy as fast as you can, fat calf with rosemary ringed, hyssop the fore-quarters, boil, broil, nod crowders, nod at the merry cleft (for he is more ruddy than any bridal rose when he steps in my hall). This my son was deed and is quykened agen, then eté we and fedé us[12] of his new cup here.

Fetch me the long seneschal[13] and bind him for a thousand years — I would take vengeance on the tall man.

[11] Arctic bears and Tropical Turnspits. Lear, *Nonsense Songs and Stories*: 'The Four Little Children'.

[12] Cf. Wyclif version of Luke's Prodigal Son.

[13] I identify Joab the slayer of Absalom, the efficient man, with Sir Kai, Arthur's seneschal, who was called the 'tall man'. He too was an efficient, over-zealous, unpleasing person. This beastliness, and block-headed loyalty, assert themselves in many of the Romances. Satan, bound for a thousand years, was in my mind also.

* * *

Not so fast
go slow — the unveiling of the skein is in sevens and times
and half-times. In sundry times diversely he speaks, and by
types prefiguring.

The appointed man moves beyond, the last flares peter out,
the ringing stroke of Hurlame[14] tells on dark objects and
the rattling undulations. The venerable man sees no grass
nor well-nigh no fruit nor in the water no fish.

(In the north porch Launcelot beats that varnished pine
— he would see right through that hardwood door — his
pommel fractures the notices for the week.[15] In the south
porch, Argos the dog howls outright.)

* * *

The hymn is sung, the memorial crumbs are gathered. The
heavy file circuits Ophel by-ways, out water-gate, by horse-
gate, to garden-gate, to known copse. The ascertained
place, the place of ill-vassalage, the shameful thicket.
The wormwood cup won't pass.
The twelve legions remain in their quarters, or if they
have stood-to there's no rumour of it. It is necessary that
he should tread in the saphead alone, without his accoutre-
ments, and all lines phut.
The rivals nod[16] sound enough.
Night-drops tarnish their two swords.

* * *

Under the tree these things are done, in a corner of the
enclosure. The grove's the place for meeting and the fresh
wood sees sights. You'll meet me in the garden of our

[14] See n. 1.

[15] It will be remembered that Launcelot attempted with some
violence to get to within the place where the Grail was.

[16] The three disciples, Peter, James and John, asleep in the
Garden. 'Three, three for the rivals' is said of the Trinity in
the English folksong 'Green grow the rushes O'.

122

appointment under her ascendant influence whose light's enough for the tying of knots or the disclosure of the plan. You will know me by my hat and the way I walk, all our friends know the place, we often resort to it, comrade.

I'll galloon and plait your dark stray.

Back from my lune-brow as you like it?

As we did openly, in the suburbs and toward the world, before them all.

That will be nice.

We'll give us the night-fruit, your dear, when we meet ours.

Dingle-way you'll come by the ford of the brook, should the sharp stones afflict you,

I have remembered the remedies.

At the angle of the wall?

Against the potting-shed?

No, where the seedlings wait, I'll be. You can't miss it, by the alignment of skeps where I suppose the gardener learns the sweetness of order, from bees who people their kingdom with contrarious bells.

At what o'clock. Can't you make it — not sooner. I see. It's expensive to deny my part.[17]

Can you keep our soul when it is heavy?

Tell me, gentle friend, ride you on Barbary?[18]

*　　*　　*

D'you mean be me. Or me. O sir it was not I. I vow I've nothing digged in lover's copse. If keel row foul I'm weal of it.[19] Why do you look at me. I too! I do! on the flat or ought you cross, on book or attested fragment, I honest do, by each sacred and especially intimate tie we've trothed often. Haven't I said it over so often, and ever again. They'll all tell you that, the junta of twelve are aware of that.

You might at least try to understand, you know how

---

[17] Cf. 'It is expensive to deny the *filioque*', J. Maritain.

[18] Cf. *Richard II*, Act V, sc. 5.

[19] Cf. Somersetshire song, 'The cruel ship's carpenter'.

difficult it all is, there may be delay. I can't go into all that now.

It's for the Party anyway, I've done my best by the Party. I'd turn all my cheeks for the Party. And not for the first time neither. Well, get someone other. Such kind deeds and kindness should be remembered. You're forgetting the March purge, stone cold you'ld be, if we hadn't manipulated that bend.

Who wants a thank you, but who tightened the string? Well, you sounded like it. I'll layne it no longer. That's one thing I can't stomach, you know that. O, no dissentients, I notice. Well, speak up! Daedalean? That's as may be. O easily, but now, no. That's my affair. Time slips — nor zero nor neaping wait no plea now. There's no ninth stitch for treason's gradual chafe. The adjusted domino is perceptibly awry. Dark fissues [fissures?] spider.

Yet still the set enamel holds, still yet she masks her fashion of forsaking. (Fair day, sweet friend, how like you this guise?)

Time slips, the livid spread darkens under careful wrappings, should you dare to look.

Times turn, it's no help now, the baleful shiners on the night she cried: man child! — they determine my way.

Was written in the twisted caul, and birthday charts they burn, or like you find in midwife's horrid files, should you care to read.

I might have known.

But I too, would have some part.

* * *

Why's he elect between his paps. Are we not all illumined, is the gnosis his prerogative. He's the first who's ever last, despite the Manifesto.

It's always Benjamin's sop. Whose hand he fondles, whose right hand is under his head. I lay he'll put it in a book some day with a fine Hellenic twist.

I could well! I well could do with half that.

I'll be there, dear heart. Come to me soon after supper. But surely, you know I do. How stupid you are. To whom other should I go? O that. You didn't. O but you did. What you say — yes you did.

Think again?

I'm suggesting nothing, but sometimes your fox has pinions, while noodle shepherds smoke holes, lamb's in hawk-fist. Stint now. Who. Unhap? Every time. Will ye not? Will ye so? Not by my counsel. If only on account of many sweet dreads. Once in especial.

To untie each knot will raw y'r fingers certainly. Cut then! Cauterize the separate weeping stumps. Your valley will be pocked with calcined baulks for tender shins when you traipse memory's imaged waste. Lay to root then the severing axe, or better still, get mechanisms that can drill and blast, can hawser your anchored fibres, drag they never so deep. You've half yourself laid bare? Cement the craters then! At least your surface will be proof against the quickening showers.

You must be brief this journey. Plug them well: Lark's song is not your cue. Hood them close: twitch of Tim's tail, or him sleeping may unnerve you yet. Beware of pelicans and flower bells. Ask magpies what they do with ailing mates. Should you look at hedgerows, look very close, and then you'll see how cared-for sparrows fare. Bessemer your heart. Look to our natural mother, be her son, she never learned you any rune other.

The kiss bringer, the smiler with a knife under his coat,
for his silver gain (who knows the place)
treads them the ford
a hemped loop and a forked stick, a decoy-tackle
and a felon's net.
A butty's snout to smell him out
a halter and chain to take him quick
a billet and goad should he be truculent
a gentile file to take no chances
for those who are come to trap the hart on the mountain,
who is white for the dun herd, whose branching antlers
crutch, to bright the ride, as Eustace saw.

For me, Mordred's among the helot pikes, Agravaine laughs under the uncertain flares, where they toss. But you, you can mark out your own. The longer you like, the more various you list. The twisters that sell the pass. The guttering link this one holds shows you his rodent profile.

You will see there also the exploited children of God. Grievance flutters their poles. The common will throng that slope. It is, as ever, illusioned, and up to no good. The loose pack swerves, the figure they cut in the grove is irresolute. Pallid masks shift and duck for the hung boughs. They shape ill.

The informer walks delicately, whose right hand is filled with gifts, but the laminated half-section is aligned, moves drest, compactly to the latin job.

The naked torso flees the grove.

It's difficult to say in the confusion, but this fisher king bellows: Treason! The monsignor's boy, he's caught a fine packet. At all events that were done like a good vassal, whatever you think of the ten.

Acknowledging flares climb the Antonia:[20]

Thank you. Received. Operation complete. End of message. Ready. Communicate X and Y. Party will withdraw on Totem Zone. Please correct. For Totem read Taboo. Counter-sign is Goat's-Lemescos-him. End of message. Please repeat. Thank you.

The venerable man sinks under this deepening of sorrows —the fierce images will beat themselves into the ubblye fast now.

The dedicated silk is rent, the sacred conclave is placed in an impossible predicament. Dampt coals flicker at the raw dawn to light the architrave above the gusty porch.

Dunghill throat and spry sluts gibe in yokel chorus.

Swiftly now the situation deteriorates.

Blindfold buffet, Tyrian cope and stained tessellations.

---

[20] The garrison fortress of the legion stationed in Jerusalem. I suppose them to have been in communication with the party operating on the Mount of Olives.

It's ugly now, the latest developments follow very fast, there can be only one end to this.

The sahib eagle sweats on his judicial perch, hoods his level iris, but he's got an eyeful none the less.
(The Lady Procla has seen her clairvoyant, sir, and is most disturbed.)
The senate and people of Rome wash their hands among the fellaheen.

O popule meus! Three days and nights draw to a single point in the venerable man's hands. His flexed limbs support:
the brass similitude, the horned male entangled, full-moon meals in haste, acacia boxes lifted up, the bread rained down for parched anabasis, the multifold types and signs set — all this for Jacob his darling, sealed and easily interpreted, written in a book.
These for you and me, by wayward Testament
by marvel of lifting water-hole for serf-girl's son-in-the-
shrub.
By gilt of the fleece and dew of the Clough
for Esau the parfitt knighte
Elon a stranger had a fair daughter
she of antlered Hearn had joy
who bore
the six fisher dukes
the nine lords in green
the twelve cantors[21] for the rogations
who is our mother.

By Hagar's incomprehensible penalty and Esau's reason-able grievance, reserve for us some place.
For peoples and nations and kith and *Volk* consanguine by the water and the wood, and spoken the land's tongue. For a clan of the mere and free of the moor, innate and by tribe, for a *Thing* for a *wic* for sud isles and Manau. For kin of the *cynydd* or a *llys* with a wattle for the nine

---

[21] The twelve Arval brethren who chanted over the crops.

degrees. By writ of lynchet, or alluvial *feld* or riding or *tref* or parcelled or common, by twelve poles holt and perched to include the green run where the forked rod[22] bends. By Angle borough or Frank *demesne* or broch for laird or rath for a kern, in betwixt stick or out between stane under which wood or down on what farm her townee's my batty because we were lily-white by the same brake.

For the multifold divisions and this fenced inscape.

For the sweet demarcations.

For *Gentes*, negrin or combed gilt a signification in erd and flud or star-traced or observed at wheat-harvest, or induced from the behaviour of hare o' the hill, or parley of fowls, or by parturient cords drawn to some dark awareness, or half-guessed and fevered out betwixt your last dolorous packet and sung *In Paradisum*.

Or by flax-flames dying that cresset silver poles — they sing high and low to bid him recollect that though the bridge prevail, each several hinge suffers a common change.

Or by some few elect, sawney, tough or fly, who sit solitary martingaled and brother goat well cribbed, who nose out the ineffable plan when shadows creep their bunk-holes in stucco suburb or parched Thebaid.

But for the herd and hand-thrusters, for me and you, it's this cupped and that erect to get some inkling, patch and piece the tangle as best we may.

If he is unknown he is like to be in March leveret lope or brock's hole.

Stocks we call to, pay to sticks *latria*:

How other? since when Elen under the wall digged the transom they dressed that pole with great solemnity and instituted feasts of invention. They carry standing-stone and square stones of Luz[23] and anoint them for the round apses, for surely he was on that hill?

---

[22] [A small sketch shows that David had in mind the water-diviner's rod. R.H.]

[23] The original name of Bethel. Cf. Genesis 28 : 19.

128

And in lands west and outer *Thule,* by Sabrina flood, Ebro, Nidd or soft Thames run, who will be our witness?

Arthur with Baldur, Bran of the river-town, Brons of the net and fisher hauls, each potent lord bruised for the furrow's garner. What vestals clip in effigy, corn-cats and carried besoms and curious sacraments of holt and holding.

Dux he is and maimed for the land's yield; twine him barley beard to nourish the womb-gift. Lord of the cranes and childermass *Yarl.* Pomona leans at south wall, fecunds the fall for his iron hooks.

Liber with Libera dance the sap for his harrowed sides.

If laundes teem, and kine to foal lift their rucked chines and calf-kind[24] truckle warm in t'byre, if from her April purge, Silvi Pales, milch-and-fay, straw-girdled, gads her bounty as a mocked quean would, her cut sark conveniently high like a lenten deacon,[25] fonds her flooers o' the forest, stoops to show her strange increase to whooping shepherd-boy, by storrith-fence over-tump or in-under cot-pent or shippen thatch, by fence by Agnes fountain.

Or calls:

Hut Hoy!

Come yallercup, stay Mell

Come Mulican, Molican, Malen and Mair[26]

Slue back Ringstrake, Ma'n't calf foal

int'gutter, Speckle nor Grisle.[27]

'Ware pilled stick, shoo! shoo!

Shoo Wynebwen!

Come little frecked one.

Come Bella come

---

[24] *kind* pronounced to rhyme with *sinned.*

[25] The folded chasuble worn by the deacon during Lent [and also Advent and at other penitential times].

[26] Cattle-call associated with Llyn Arennig (between Bala and Festiniog): 'Mulican Molican Malen y Mair/Dowch adre[?] ruan ar fy ngair' (Eng. Come home now at my command). For further information on this subject see T. Gwynne Jones, *Welsh Folk-lore and Folk-Custom,* 64.

[27] Cf. Genesis, chs. 30 and 31.

Proo, Proo, Prooshey moo[28]
Come and kick on my pail
in praesepio
I'll show what I've ches[29]
lapped in hay.

If dark-fall leas hear the slow-lowing herd, his olifant it is,
when he winds it,[30] that musters snare-tackle and cat-party.
His temples burst at boundary, keep plow-hand's team
secure afield, his hill-watch their vale nod and nap.
    Cider-jug and ribboned pole depend upon
his dance, his dole on hill-site.
He lets for her heaped belly.
This largesse he faints for at the
aesc-wall, his linden splint renews
his fallow garth, his spilled stream
the thacked grain hives.
Scare-hawk, he is, on high stick for
the yeanlings, rook-boy on brown
orchard perch to keep her cherry ripe.

You could not bunch the various anemone to bid her good
day, nor wish it with violets neither except he be lift up.
    Perhaps you would not wish him well with whom-she-
goes, except the riven sticks had split for you, or make
fanatical decisions to fend the folk, or keep some single
eye that's yours to keep a spectacle in the wind for a tart's
mate to come weeping to see.
    My Ned he offered the reed.
    Her Larry was tarragon boy with his dope.
    Nell's Jerry won his tunicle, she says it's a gran' bit o'
weave. Was high stakes, an' he called *Mudhook* in the
nick o' time. She says he says he's luck's on at lune fête.

[28] Scots cattle-call. Probably derived from the French *appro-
chez-moi.*

[29] Cf. carol, 'I sing of a Maiden', line 2: 'King of all kings for
her son she ches.'

[30] Cf. Gray's *Elegy* and *Song of Roland.*

Three on 'em yes — two were naut.

A cock-shy for a priest's deliberate lob.

A Sally without the alleys and lanes of our city he reigns from the stark post.

A guy for a pronged plot to put all in a fine dilemma, hang each on a nice fork.

THE AGENT

I

What lags you now?
      They're pious men
that hand the wages bright;
who sits in Moses' seat traffics aright.
They're elect of the nation
      and learned men also.
To question Jacob's senate
      who are you?
See prevenient Yahve
      guiding this expedience —
what's from you
      but strait obedience?

In any case the bargain's struck, and ordinary contract now
compels deliverance of the goods — and honour itself would
have you do what is to do.

Moreover,
      the counted silver waits you.
Up! Praise of **Kerioth**:
Up! Zimri's greater son:
steady the articulations —
      do what must be done.

                *   *   *

O how they'll be put to it
down the history maze!
O Ariadne, lend your guiding thread

to sacred doctors and to exegetes
who'll seek to worry out how love
could seem to speak so harsh.

Ah! truth and fact — are you wedded
in the night I tread?

But come, my soul, all this is overdrawn and far too
flustered. If Israel's senate, Yahve's Gerousia, yes, and He,
himself, would leave no retreat, I'll go to Greeks for
argument. Bless their subtle minds, they're gentlemen and
trace the matter out with some give and take.

From what I've heard 'em say
                in the Ten Towns,
Zeus and Prometheus change attributes,
                and so are one.
So still, perhaps, I've part with him,
some part,
                the other half
to work the drama out.
Perhaps? — Why, must be!
How other?
Bride Ishtar!
                Hamans don't hang on every tree.
They're key men
and most integral to the pattern:
                so would I be.
If not with the eleven
                that make the haven[1]
...if not to drink his cup,
new, at supper on Olympus
I'll drain whatever vintage

---

[1] Cf. the accumulative song, 'I'll sing you one-o'.
          I'll sing you twelve-O:
          Twelve for the twelve Apostles,
          Eleven for the eleven who went to heaven,
          Ten for the ten commandments, etc.

this lamb's wrath
        permits in Tartarus.

More: we'll take a rise
out of the Morning Star
and learn the covering Cherub
        his own trade.
I'll sell him as well,
        and lead a faction-war in hell.[2]

But no — won't do — we're still on the dramatic tack; heroics, leapfrog fantasies — we've each a fancy for the crucial role. These chancy speculations fever us — what are the probabilities? What has dull likelihood to offer?

After all, more than one opinion is received, and exegesis knows more than one way.

Let's fetch our precepts from the Sadducees and fur our tippets in the Zadoc school, let's go to college with the sacred swells and hear what comfortable words these cynic doctors tell who've made a job of eschatology, who leave imagined angels to waken Shammai's dead, stiff as their texts of needlework, and bid 'em blow improbable trumps in Hillel's noodledom.

That's goodish sense — they're men of fact and dress our antique dogmas up to date.[3]

---

[2] It will be remembered that the commentators equate the 'king of Tyre', 'the cherub that covereth' (Ezekiel 28 : 12–15), and also 'the king of Babylon', 'the son of the morning' (Isaias 14 : 12), with Satan himself.

[3] 'Zadoc the priest', familiar to us from a recurring phrase in a famous O.T. passage, was the founder of the intruded Sadocite line of high priests from whom, some say, the Sadducees derived both their name and tradition. Their criterion was the earlier deposits and it is by these that their rejection of bodily resurrection, angelology, etc., must be judged.

They adhered to the common Semitic belief in an underworld of darkness and silence (Sheol) and rejected the newer eschatological doctrines which, since the Maccabean revival, had gained credence under the auspices of their opponents, the Pharisees. In addition to this, as influential and wealthy

Shall the God of the living burn among the tumuli for
wanted debtors?

Do not the under-silences keep interminable jubilee?

Beyond the eyeless sarcophagi they know perpetual
sabbath, and all their emancipated years are sevens of
cancellation.[4]

That smells more factual, and suits me well.

Let sweet oblivion lull me, where acts no longer generate
their opposites.

We'll take our cue from canon and deutero-canon: what
says our chrism'd Daphnis — supposing he'd a finger in *In
exitu*,[5] and what old Baruch in his jeremiad?[6]

I'll be their man when they sing
of those gone down to silence:
> *these praise thee not*

Why then!
> nor curse thee not,

because they *are* not.
That suits me best,
where Sheol's hollow synthesis
sets final term to all antithesis.

---

men of affairs, they were inclined toward the manners and
ideas of the dominating gentile class.

So that the party most representative of the primitive racial
conceptions was, paradoxically, the party most susceptible to
the sophisticated rationalism of the contemporary cosmopolitan
world. Politically they were objective and opposed to the
popular aspirations which were inconsistent with the actualities
of Caesar's world-order. Caiaphas was of this school. The
Rabbis, Shammai and Hillel, represented two schools of
Pharasaic thought, the latter being more liberal.

[4] Cf. Lev. 25 (Holy Years, Sabbatical and Jubilee).

[5] Cf. the Psalm *In exitu Israel* (115 : 17, 'the dead praise thee
not'). 'Chrism'd Daphnis' = David. How many of the so-called
'Psalms of David' are, in fact, attributable to him, is a matter
for specialists to discuss.

[6] Cf. Baruch 2 : 17 ('For the dead that are in hell, whose spirit
is taken away from their bowels, shall not give glory and
justice to the Lord').

2

The son of Didymus tries the shutter; if it be firm, he says, against the wolf-wind from the potter's flats, if it be firm, he thinks, against the eye without, against the hooded eye against the chink: the eye that guides the hand that jots the dossier.

* * *

Why's he elect between his paps, are we not all illumined, is the gnosis his prerogative, he's first whoever's least, despite the manifesto. It's always Benjamin's sop.[7] Whose right hand he fondles, whose left hand is under his head. I'll layn he'll put it in a book, some day, with a fine Hellenic twist.

* * *

> Then up stepped one:[8] O indeed it's not I;
> then leaned across another
>   in rivalry:
> d'you mean by me, or me?
> O sir, it's not me.
> Nor me, that I declare:
>   on aught you cross,
> on book or attested fragment,
> by each specially sacred tie we've trothed often.
> Haven't I said it over so often,
> and ever again?
> I've done my best by the Party.
> I'ld turn all my cheeks for the Party.
> Stint that — less now of that, [peace]

[7] Genesis 43 : 44. 'Portions were taken to them' — Joseph's brothers, in Egypt — 'but Benjamin's portion was five times as much as theirs.'

[8] Cf. 'The Cruel Ship's Carpenter':
  Then up step-ped one: O indeed it's not I;
  Then up stepped another, and made the same reply.
  Then up stepped young William, and he did stamp and swear,
  Indeed it's not me, that I vow and declare.
(Sharp and Marson, *Folk Songs from Somerset*, Part 4, p. 12).

ever to all contention, brother,
would you grant.

Is now the fellowship wholly mischiefed:[9]
is this the wounding
            at the love-board
in the house of the friend.

                    *   *   *

The steer-board lord eyes the twin sons of thunder, eyes,
in the plastered recess behind the low entry, where the salt-
tackle hangs and the troia keys, bundled in shadow under
the duffle coat the two sword-hilts.

Eyes again the vacated place that mischiefs the pattern; the
napkin fallen, the spilled concomitants, the seat-board left
askew — just like a bloody landsman — the festive petal
bruised that felt his turning heel, the little cat to corner
gone that hates commotion.

All from the Tetrarchate now, and best part wharf-side[10]
bred — I never could bide his Juda looks.
    I wonder who'll benefit from common purse tonight,
and, here's a marvel:
    where he'll buy with shutters up 'gainst passage o' the
God?[11]

Refolds and folds again a linen cloth. Sees within the dish's
pentagon, under the storm-light that sways from central
thwart
            his tribal manna
            and the sweet flesh of quails.
            Sees the green lettuce
            and sniffs the spring;
            sees the two fish gleam.

[9] Malory, Bk. xx, ch. 1.

[10] There were nine towns and wharves on the lake of Tiberias.

[11] Cf. John 13 : 26, 30. In the opinion of some writers this
passage of St John is puzzling because no shops would be open
during the Passover.

Looks to his feet that garboard-strake had hardened, that
are so clean from Maundy flood
        that on a contrary flood
        had chanced it
        for a pace or so
        but, not for long.
Shifts this half a turn, takes up, puts down, handles this,
now that, regards again the wrapped weapons that thrust
from weathered copes:
        doubts if they be sufficient.[12]

    Remembers what on hilly Thabor
        once he saw:
    that was the hour — the bright hour:
    to see the tribal lords
        and him between.
    O happy would we be
        to wattle the green booths there
        for the metamorphosed three,
    and his between, extra high and garnished
        between mound and cloud.
    It was good for us to be on that hill
        under the mound,
        sleeping or sentinel.
    The lights were uncreate
        on all that mountain;
    the voice rang very clear
        on that hill.
    O these brief hours — then the **valley-way**
    down to demoniac dell.

    Looks to his horny dukes
    splayed awkward on the fair cloth:
        as the white feet
        so these are brighted
        every whit.[13]

[12] Luke 22 : 38 ('Lord, here are two swords...').
[13] John 13 : 6–9 (the washing of the feet).

Looks to his board-mates:
  each looks every one from
one to other, and either to other seems
   more fair-bodied than ever they saw.[14]

    * * *

But now they look, every man, dumb —
and him already, so heavy.[15]
Now the shadow — here the storm-way —
the dark meander now,
  the way deepens here.

Under the faltering wick
this one folds the used napkins;
here the side-light is put out.
Now the concluding ablutions;
he sets the book convenient
for the post-oblation chapter —
the routine drags out,
the fourth libation drained,
the terminating rubrics are
obeyed — the final versicles
somehow got through.
Must be the eighth night hour — close on.[16]
Soon then: go, you are dismissed.[17]
And then without,
  by night-way.
Night now — what meander now?
Is it gutter-way — if it's brook-way
  where is Achitophel?

[14] Malory, Bk. xiii, ch. 7.

[15] Matthew 26 : 37.

[16] The Paschal meal had to be over before 2 a.m.

[17] Cf. ending of the Mass, concluding versicle, *Ite missa est.*

3

By Ophel byes,
out Water Gate, then dingle-way
he'll come, by ford of the brook
to garden-gate,
to known copse: the ascertained place.
A bit below, by where the hanged prince
has his monolith — not far from
sleeping Zachary.[18]
That's where I'll wait for the gentile file, and then lead
on — it's safer than a rendezvous within the wall.

My son, little Kerioth shall be blessed in you and enter
history; we give you Yahve's peace and ours.

Perhaps out Dung Gate, y'r Grace,
and so detour between
      Baal-fire Gully and the wall:
round right of the conduit — facing Queen's Bower,
striking torrent-way b' storm-ditch:
      but, more like
by Stair Street he'll come
through Ophel back-ways, out Water Gate,
up Great Mother's Wady — she who guards the steps
      down past the buried lords — tomb-way;
footing jackal brook-bed right o' the
      shard-tilt that lizard brights.
But, may be,
      you can't tell with him,
y'r Grace, may be he'll take
high-path to turn o' the wall,
close in under the run of the wall, past great
Golden Gate, 'cross Lady-bridge,
up far-stepped way, straight to

[18] The supposed tombs both of Absalom and of the prophet
Zechariah are in the Kedron valley, with many other burial
places.

garden fence,
to known copse, the ascertained place.
But I'll wait below at fork of tomb-way —
that tapes him both ways.
That's where I'll be,
in sight of sleeping Zachary
that foretold the silver.[19]

— By y'r Grace's leave, the bargained silver's in exchange
for facts, and, in a humble way, y'r Grace, I'm fond of
facts — dreams are my bugbear. That's why I'm here.
Begging y'r Grace's pardon —
if you think good, give me my price:
if not, forbear.
Though I sell him for y'r coin bright,
        I'll not paint black
        what's lily-white.

Soon, may be, his beauties too we'll tangle; he's in the
duke's collateral line, as his gilt tresses tell — that's great
David's mark — he's very fair to look upon, y'r Grace, in
all his members . . . he's shining fair, y'r Grace . . . he's alto-
gether lovely — that's what gets you . . . he's strong as the
cedars when he takes off his coat — O m' lord Pontiff,
that's the bugger of it!

Man, so was the Prince of Tyre fair[20]
that walked the aboriginal hill, sealing
up the sum of beauty, the first-born of morning
        who made himself equal with Yahve.
Bar Simon,[21] what says your beauty of himself?
        'As Yahve is, I am.'
So we are credibly informed by our more reliable agents.

[19] Zechariah 11 : 12–13: 'so they weighed for my price thirty
pieces of silver' etc.

[20] For Tyre and the claim to perfect beauty, see Ezekiel,
ch. 26 and 27 : 28.

[21] See John 6 : 71 ('Judas the son of Simon Iscariot').

The cap fits both, my son: these two are as like as Janus-
heads, and so indeed are one.

> She that bore you named you the Praised
> and how rightly: the praise of you
> shall redound to Jacob wherever this
> Good News is told.

> Why! here's chance to make of
> neo-Judas a greater than his noised namesake,
> a Judas to cock a snook at Judas:
> For Simon the plummet drops
> to crucial and chthonic myth;
> the shallows of mere history
> he leaves to Judas Maccabee.
> Here's a role with some recession to it!
> Our score has promise of undertones:
> > let's play it.

Ah ah my son, you see in me no Pharisee with Messianic
Beulahs[22] on his chart where mirage is, but one who loving
our nation would camp it to the inclinations of that rod
which registers where actual water is — actuality is our
lode. Her light is chilly, and we confess to ague.

> I would not intermeddle seeming fantasy with fact, but
we who sit in office, seeing and seeming in detail — and
that uncommon close — the present shape, not being blind,
foresee in part, and as God wills, the shapeless future — nor
is it pleasant, no, no, it's hideous.

> What night is this that Israel's pontiff maximus should
see the forbidden beast who
> > chewing no cud divides the hoof,
> > sculptured above South Gate?
> > Why! Jeremy's gloom is bright and

---

[22] See Isaias 62 : 4: 'Thou shalt no more be called Forsaken...
but thou shalt be called Hepzibah ("my delight") and thy land
Beulah ("Wedded").'

142

what I see uncovers dooms more
final than ever Joel told.
They've closed the canon down too soon
and shall need to add a Caiaphas
to Malachi — if I should prophesy
and, strange enough, prophesy a clean oblation,
      who surely net the thicketed ram
      that is for immolation.[23]

There's some would strain a pamphleteer's
muse, and scribble of neo-Deborahs:[24]
What issues?
Stuff as poor in form as inflammatory in content:
      not bringing the land
      rest forty years,
      but bringing to Skull Hill
four, forty or fourscore
      (one can't gauge to a nicety
      in matters of reprisal);
and, of course
      bringing to as many Rachels
      the accustomed role of Rachel

---

[23] Cf. Malachi 1 : 2 'In every place ... a pure offering', a prophecy often taken as referring to the Mass as perpetuating 'in every place' the offering on Calvary.

The thicket from which Abraham's ram was taken (Genesis 22) is here associated with the Kedron valley and the ram with Our Lord.

What was done at the Supper on Thursday evening placed the offerant himself in the state of a victim and *bound* him to Friday's events. So to say, the 'first movement' of the Passion was already played before Judas left Caiaphas to go to the arrest.

[24] In recalling one of the most moving of the world's poems, 'The Song of Deborah', we recall the event which evoked its composition: when Heber the Kenite's wife welcomed the battle-weary soldiers with all the tokens of tribal protection, roof, drink, food, bed, and with the words 'Turn in, my lord, turn in to me', there was peace between Jabin king of Hazor and the house of Heber the Kenite, and her murder of Sisera was done under cloak of that tribal peace-pledge.

also — a small matter no doubt — bringing to us ourselves as many hours of tedium as our exercise of tact can run to — lest worse accrue.

But why all this?
          Because, Iscariot, few 've the wit
          to perceive
that a greater than Sisera is here!
The chariot? the phalanx
as outdated as the Maccabean tactic,
what can we do against
the triplex acies that's caused
          Caesar's sun to shine from the Caspian
          to the magic hills of the Cymry?

When we, Iscariot, prophesy, as it is required by our office that we should do so, making few pretensions and none as to form — we are not a poet, Iscariot — don't speak of poetry — no, not since the ducal son of Amoz[25] — try us — between ourselves — they can have too much of the real.

Do you, Iscariot, read? — Why yes, of course — all literate nowadays. We read only the great authors — not all the great authors are ours, Iscariot — that was no part of the promises, I warn you — or Yahve lies — but he was ours, one of us — one of our order, of the Society so to say. It takes a bit of a priest, Iscariot, to make the best prophet — and, as we see, the best poet. Turn that over, in that anti-clerical head of yours — you'll find it sober if unfamiliar truth — O I know well these offices are made to be antipathetic — that's typical, that's the cant of the age.

Poetry?
          'Woe to Ariel to Ariel
          the city where David dwelt:
          add year to year,
          let them immolate what is oblated,
          yet will I distress Ariel.
          There shall be heaviness and sorrow,

[25] i.e., Isaiah.

144

and it shall be to me
as with Ariel.'

Mark the changed fact-world! for, to be sure, its change
will demand and determine what is possible in deeds, and
so what is formally possible in songs of deeds.
    Have you, Iscariot, a sense of history?
    I wonder — little of humour, from the looks of you.
    You'll need both tonight — and more.

*   *   *

For now I see new-angled courses rise and dress them-
selves at once on new and squared alignments — they've
three vaults already soaring. Not Nehemias returned nor
no neo-Ezra restores to this tune — a practised *restitutor*,[26]
it seems, one who from dealing in logistics can bring,
position and maintain —

But who's this larking plough-hand,
tunicled like a rogation boy,
            his share-beam's bladed antique bronze
            and pitiless and all.
His team's but two, but white and chosen:
she garland-horned, and his bull-neck gay
— they circle the cumbered slope.
            Must be heavy going:
he'd do better on Cisalpine wheels.
Yet he's plenty breath for bawling
as if this were his Latin spring,
this calcined waste his lapsed *vervactum*.

But do I catch the burden of this Georgie's song:
For Athene to gain
Quirinus must till.
Let's plough their palladia
into their hill.
We'll turn the fossa deep
            for farmer Rufus,

---

[25] Cf. the 'province coins' of Hadrian: *restitutor orbis terrarum.*

he bids them reap
not almond-fronded rods, but fasces.[27]

[27] Cf. Adolf Hitler's aphorism, 'The sword must gain what the plough must till.' Aaron's rod that budded almonds, together with the tables of the covenant and the pot of manna (both 'came down from heaven'), was once kept in the Holy Place where Yahve's sacred fire burned, just as the shields and the palladium (which 'fell from heaven') were kept in the shrine of the Vestal fire in Rome (cf. Heb. 9 : 4).

In the case of ritual ploughing, the furrow was called *fossa* and the turned sod *murus,* to indicate that the future city had a ditch and wall from the first moment of its ceremonial founding. A passage in one of the Talmuds and in Jerome attributes the ploughing-up of the Temple site to 'Rufus the tyrant', i.e. Procurator under Hadrian.

Vervactum was land to be ploughed in early spring after being left fallow the previous year or years. The mould-boards were not fixed until the seed-ploughing at the autumnal equinox. Traditionally, at the ritual ploughing of city-sites, the team was a white bull and a white heifer; the share was bronze.

As we read in Jeremias 52 : 12–14, the captain of the king of Babylon destroyed Jerusalem with fire on the tenth day of the fifth month (i.e. counting from March). Of an event many centuries later the Mishna says that on the ninth day of the same month of Ab (August) in the year that brought Hadrian's suppression of Bar-Kochba's Judean revolt to a close, the ruins were run over with the plough. The Rabbis and the Fathers dwelt on this event. Subsequently the notion became accepted that as a special mark of finality and indignity the old city was 'given over to the plough'. What occasioned the tradition was most likely the usual Latin ceremonial ploughing of the limits of the site at any city's founding. Hadrian, called *restitutor* in so many provinces, had planned (and perhaps commenced) a new town on the site (in ruins since the Great Jewish War under Titus) before the rebellion occurred, to be called Colonia Aelia Capitolina, after his own family name (Aelius) and the Roman Jove.

We see that, as usual, the tradition has its own symbolic validity, though built upon a dramatized interpretation of events which (again as usual) were in themselves of a casual and routine kind, presenting no difficulties of a factual nature. But had the tradition been content with a scrupulously accurate foundation, then again (and again as usual) the symbolic content would have lost nothing. That the Latin inauguration rites whether deriving from the Etruscans or from prehistoric pile-dwellers in the Po valley, should have been employed on

Yet's no March-tilling,
          no mould-board fixed?
then not last.
But's gillyflower month,
    and round the hot nones of it —
near on when General Nabuzardan
lent these nones in these same parts
          a fiercer heat.

And who is this?[28]
So we're within doors and very still — yet through his
narrow lattice I think I recognize, without, a shape or so:
that terraced contour's not forgot, once seen from the Ain
Karim side — whoever he is, he's come to find it in the
fields of Ephrata, and he looks to have stalled himself well —
    our Elohists and rabbins shelved convenient, at hand-
reach; yet, from his hat on peg, I'ld suppose him wrangler
of an idolatrous *collegium* —

----

this Semite holy place is both more significant as symbol and
more credible as event than any supposed literal ploughing-up
of a ruined city out of spite to a particular people. We are
in the position, however, of having to keep in mind the
traditional interpretation and the more likely actuality — for
we are the inheritors of both.

[28] The reader will remember Jerome's reputed ill-temper; his
stone that he used as a pillow (of which Pio Nono is supposed
to have said that without it he would never have achieved
canonization); his companionship with the lion; his sojourn in
the neighbourhood of Ephrata (Bethlehem); his devotion to the
classics; his imagining, during an attack of fever, that Our
Lord said to him, 'You are not a Christian but a Ciceronian;
your heart is where your treasure is'; his being flogged, in his
dream, by angels, and his resolution to turn from his favourite
authors, Vergil and Cicero; his being depicted by Dürer and
other masters in the habit of Cardinal, and by Antonello da
Messina in a large well-appointed scriptorium. It is necessary
and inevitable that our Jerome-conception should be con-
ditioned by the late interpretations of Western Christian art-
works along with 'the documents' and the hard-lived and
tormented existence of the actual man in alien Syria —
necessary because meaningful within our tradition, and in-
evitable because that tradition is part of ourselves.

why yes, and there's his lucid first loves — well dog's-
eared, thumbed, now pushed aside as he writes — that gets
his goat — hot tears for Tully wet our Pentateuch. God
save us, but I like him! He's of an Arya, as are we, and
with bad grace endures the changing needs; yet he must
to his contemporary task.

His most unlikely companion from the Hebron bush
looks less irascible than he — yet he himself looks less
hard-eyed as he makes joy of that beast.

His pillow's hard enough, but what he now begins to
transcribe is hardest:
AELIA AB AELIO HADRIANO CONDITA.[29]

But ah — now we tread more familiar contours — and the
time-terrain shifts, too — our foreseeing angel turns very
recorder and orders back as well as fro:
> very far times: and of anabasis, of genesis.
> What meander? whose beginnings?

Out of Sumer has he called our sire!
One of us, then — very much so — the pair of them.
O blessed sight, how my blood calls now to the prince
of soil-finders — the twice-named lord and his Sarah's boy,
with carried fire in his old fist.
Surely the gaffer of us all —
> the bagman-dux
> from the intersected land,
> where the Mother sits in the
> midst of the fertile grid,
> she of the *kultur*-dispersal *urbes*:
> no wonder for this multitude of horns!

I see the tumulus and the
claved wood laid trim:
this same black rock,

---

[29] Jerome, speaking of Aelia Capitolina: 'Aelia founded by
Aelius Hadrianus, and in front of the gate which leads to
Bethlehem a pig sculptured in marble, signifying that the
Jews are subject to Roman power.'

this same Moriah hill-site[30] — and
'cross wady, the provided anathema.

I see five fresh briary roses
          bright the strong members,
and the spiked briary-bough
          forces the meek head askew —
          nor not so meek —
Old man — it's by his
permit that you use him so.
          God save us this he-lamb's
          horns of wrath!

But let's not tire our privileged eyes more than need were.
Let's focus on the workaday and immediate — there, too,
the lines narrow to the same mark.

But here, necessarily and first, we're faced with Caesar's
interests: accommodate we must — or, be what no man
can effectively be — Caesar's enemy. Such farce, being men
concerned only with the effectual, we need not entertain:
did others not, then *our* purview might, happily, be as
much fantasy as is their present policy.

Yet, in spite of all and for a while we keep the thing
quiescent: but elimination there must be.

We start with all irritants, and make a good start tonight.

Therefore tonight is terminal: this night, this pasch, is
terminal. Not that he's of consequence — but an irritant.
          This skin of Juda suffers ichthyosis enough:
          ours is a physician's work
We have long been credited with an opinion — received
by but few, but now by man seen to be opportune:
          we need an *azazel*.[31]

---

[30] See Genesis 21 : 33–22 : 13. In Genesis 22 : 2, for the A.V.'s
'land of Moriah' the Vulgate gives 'terram visionis'; and com-
pare v. 14, 'in the mount of the Lord it may be seen', and,
further, the Vulgate's 'monte Moria' in 2 Para. 3 : 1. (A.V.
2 Chron. 3 : 1).

[31] Lev. 16 : 7–8 — scapegoat.

A goat's a goat,
the lot's on him.

You see, Iscariot, we're both fond of facts — let's face our facts together and our remembered names shall together tell of this night's rememorable act —
memorable yes, commemorative — yes,
and, immemorial, too.

Come, come, when We, God's elected and chief offerant, choose as his and our instrument a marked delinquent who comes unasked, begging to turn despair to some account, we'd have him greet his turned and unique good fortune with a smile.

Instead of cells, pending enquiry, we raise you up from vagrancy to state employ — obliquely you serve Caesar; for the apprehension we envisage is for the quiet of Caesar — but more, for the quiet of Israel. Yours is a double role granted to few. To few? to few indeed but you, to none so wholly as to you — and you wholly of Juda.

Not so sour-mouthed then!
As the silver, so the prospect's bright,
and this shall prove through you
our new deliverance-night.

Obscure Kerioth shall be blessed
in you and enter history.
Come near, my son:
we give you our peace,
Yahve's peace, of course.
See you be shadowed by
Duke Absalom's plinth under her
ascendant influence whose light's
enough for the tying of knots.
God knows his own
Amen.
May he reward you
as do we, and handsomely.

Go then:
here's not all night to spare.
Get doing what is to do.
See that you're there.

4

Captain, a word.
What's now — the rendezvous is fixed,
what more, get forward.
The first vigilia's all but through;
there's work to do — and
        little asked of you
        for ample pay.
You bring your butty's kiss.
We'll do the rest
        to number.
Get forward.

            *   *   *

Sir!
Corporal? another chit?
Let's see:
        Full half-section, patrol order.
        Side-arms and staves, one coil, a manacles
          (should he be truculent).
        Carried lights.

One half-section, sir.
Side-arms and staves.
One length of rope
        should he be truculent.
Carried lights.

By your Jews' Christ!
a half-section!
Is this the Asses or the
Skaian Gate?
Do we chase Hector round

the wall, or is the new Mars come,
or do we chase the old Mars out,
as Spring by Spring in Latium is done
at these Ides of the first month?[32]
Is he a potentate with twelve dukes
for bodyguard that he must have flamboys?
Is he a robber[33] well digged in?
Do his picked threes watch the approaches?
I'll wager they're asleep — I've posted many picquets.
But has he lorica'd shiners in reserve?[34]

Best wait the Greek calends
and bide till absent Aelius
can dock 'em their passes to Laodicea-on-Sea
and march a toughened Ferrata from Pella
or, draft us the Jovian Twelfth,
or post from Cyrrhus the equivalent:
    a single cohort of the Dandy Tenth:
    (they'll fetch their washing
    from Dubris beach-head —
  what's seventy-five years back for the Tenth —
  if Julius' virtue there was somewhat wounded —
  the whole island is ours forever.)[35]
They'ld take on six of his dozen legions,
though marshalled by the Heavenly Pair.
But let's be actual:
    let's S.O.S. the Gallica —
    they've the hang of

---

[32] On the 14th day of the first month of the old Roman calendar (March) a man was ceremonially beaten and driven from the City. He represented the Mars (as agricultural god) of the old year, and was called 'the old Mars'.

[33] Cf. Mark 14 : 48.

[34] Cf. Matt. 26 : 53.

[35] [These three lines, of which the reading is uncertain, are in a much later hand of D.'s.]

mopping-up in groves,
and know the tactics of a war of conjurors.[36]

A full half-section! a windy *cornicularius*[37] with a scratch
squad of batmen and chitties were ample.

But, carried lights
      for the god o' the grove!
Who'll be his censer-boy
      to go before?
Who'll sing his introit hymn
      when we fetch him in,
Who'll respond to his *Judica*
when we drag him bound
to the steps of the Gabbatha,
who'll lend his issue sagulum
      when we vest him
      Jack o' the Bean?
Who'll garland his skewered limbs with flower of may
      for the solemn entry,
who'll chant his trisagion
      but the Cock of Gaul?
Last Sol's noon he came to town
      cum floribus et palmis:
On Jove's night
      we'll stick a feather in his crown
      and call him Purpuratus!

[36] The allusion is to Lucius Aelius Lamia, nominated as legate
of Syria but never posted. The Syrian command included:
Legio X, Fretensis, stationed at Cyrrhus (the famous 'Tenth'
of Caesar's Kentish expedition); Legio VII, Ferrata, at Pella
near the seaside town of Laodicea; Legio XII, Fulminata
(station unknown); and Legio III, Gallica. This last regiment
may naturally be supposed to have had somehow an association
with a Celtic land — the place of 'druid groves'. The modern
Welsh word *consuviur*, lit. conjurer, is used in the 'medicine
man' sense, and goes back in idea to the druidic 'mystagogues'.

[37] In charge of a unit's clerical staff; a kind of Orderly Room
sergeant.

But let's away:
this pantomime must be advanced
before the light of Venus-day.

THE OLD QUARRY
Part Two

That's the crux of it how the hell can you tell, it's a pretty
burden for a white man — after all he held most extreme
views, but as Lavinia says, the method's inexcusable. You'ld
hardly credit it in our days. It's positively Carthaginian,
sweetheart, and I don't care what you say — right's right,
bond or free, it's all one to me, fair's fair all the years over.

It can't be defended — I could run out and scream. I
always said he was without piety. I'm sorry for her, poor
darling — she's really cultured, you know.

I'm certain she's psychic.

I'm sure she suffers — you don't know what it's like to
get a hunch from upstairs.

You know nothing, nor understand what is expedient. I've
been in these parts upward, should say, well, let's put it at
thirty, and thirty falls is a fairish slice. Some of you, well,
I'll not speak of that, it's all one now, but undoubtedly,
I don't think — no one will dispute me, I hope — we were
stayers — in those days we were what I should call stayers
— could take a knock and give one.

The administration first, number one last, that's how
it was.

You enjoy the fruits of — I won't say — I don't speak of
myself, nor of my own generation only, but you enjoy,
the whole empire enjoys that large measure of:

it is well sometimes to quickly, to quite dispassionately
note carefully what positive, constructive goods
follow the *signa*.

This is an exercise especially necessary to a generation which affects to disparage the very virtues required of a formative age. I say the wide measure of:

the decencies the
amenities

the number and sequence — radial in extension from our centred omphalos (the diagonals and strict-angles we plot, the geometry of which in one night piles up a squared and revetted work on however meandering a broken contour), all this we bring — out to the *limes* our equation plots itself, *agger*'s run is south wall when stall-booths lean where once the rear mortar-team stacked their flanged dark cylinders. Where the forward traverse angled, Juventas plays; the mound that grows for little Julian, the daisy diadem he plucks for Jill, yielded on its dim parapet the bright *corona muralis* for the foremost lance-jack of the Third Maniple when he obtained the glittering prize. Pero steps lightly the Pentelic stair where Marius stubbed the fire-step in his issue boots. When Io, in her confirmation frock, offers her doll, she genuflects on the swept tessellations within the precincts — this is where Crixus helped tidy the night furze for the *extraordinarii*[1] to square their bivvies in the forward place. In her lower chapel the city's mediatrix leans among the penny tapers and the faithful tenderly put up the suffrage; it was precisely at this strata that you couldn't see our backsides for dust when he put up the counter-mine in Gallery Four.

The crux-formed interior lines the sappers establish on the night of 'Z' day, at the consolidation — it is this digging that determines your pavements. The circumscribing tapes our field companies peg out, the incised figures our trenching tools describe in the earth at the first conquest, remain for all time the ground-plan of the places we inhabit. Yes, even in the protectorates and mandatory areas — beyond the pillars even, the pharos shines to some extent.

[1] *extraordinarii:* [i.e. *pedites extraordinarii*] position forward of the praetorium in that section of the camp nearest to the enemy. Cf. diagram in Seyffert's *Dict. of Class. Ant.*, trans. Nettleship and Sandys, 117.

I will not venture on prophecy, but I would certainly suggest that within the lifetime of some of you our surveyors will find employment for their plane-tables beyond the Straits. It will indeed appear the eighth wonder to square with civic geometry those circular tumps which our cartographers have remarked upon. The mind of the insular peoples is essentially asymmetric.

The indeterminate wilderness that is their natural habitat reflects itself alike in their attempts at fortification, their fibulae, their ceramics, their loosely co-ordinated attack formation, in short the thing is all [of] a piece — of number and measurement they know less than nothing. It will be a new thing indeed for them to observe (at those rare intervals when the drifting vapours of that zone permit them vision) how it is possible to establish contact between two points other than by proceeding in spirals. Yes, even the breeched Cattavallauni may know that much within a decade or so — in tentative Britannia also we will establish an arbitrary line and how to intersect that line accurately that they will learn — the crux-form they will certainly learn that form — and the parabola of the weighted thong, it is true they will learn about that also, before they shape themselves into the shape our pontiffs have divinely determined.

It may be long before it is permitted to any one of them, or indeed possible to any of them to articulate with any ease *civis romanus sum* . . . O no by no means. That is by no means established. They're a mixed bag — it seems certain that in each of their dialects there is evidence of pre-Aryan influence, at least syntactically — but damn me I'm no academic.

The pax we bring is frequently
misunderstood and constantly
misrepresented
perhaps I may put it in this fashion (it's a little way I have of expressing it to myself sometimes). It is in a manner of speaking as if we said to the backward peoples, Our halter, you say, chafes yr neck, pray think of it as the fending bulla for the adolescent — times will tell of you to come to the adult toga. Virility through the putting on of our garment — that's what it amounts to. Of course, there's

rough and smooth in attaining to world citizenship. But all this conception has only been implemented by the firm disinterested behaviour of what is now, alas, a passing generation. I am afraid their qualities are passing with them. I must say, I conceive it incumbent upon me to say, I don't like the look of things. I hesitate to use the term degenerate, but a squeamishness, certainly. A most misdirected concern — noses poke and questions are asked from here to the Province. Allow me, please allow me, permit me some understanding of the working of their minds — the issue is a simple one.

He's all right — take the pipe line, a sound enough scheme — yes, there have been moments when more tact and less mingling of the blood of goats and devotees would have served — I grant you that. But in the main — he's done well — it's a ticklish appointment.

Religion? Why certainly, that's at the bone of it — same as everywhere, what I call the unhappy fallacy.

Perhaps, yes — but here we are concerned not with metaphysical conceptions but with the ordering of a protectorate. O I agree, very likely, very nice, but if every inverted gnostic coming eating and drinking to break their nonsensical taboos is to be protected at Caesar's, that is to say *our*, expense — no he did the only thing — the fellow had to swing. O no, no question of that — the administration is clear of all that. The thing wasn't done in a corner — took towels — it was a formal act: Everybody saw it — whole policy demanded it. Can't afford to offend them, that's the length of it. Tentacles everywhere — give 'em a dish of sow's ears in Pontus — nothing between the pay-sheets for the Ebro garrisons as like as not, you'ld feel the pinch on the Palatine next perhaps.

You laugh — their wires are well earthed I can tell you. How? You're asking me. Enquire of Pharaoh king of Egypt, but don't mention frogs nor the health of his first-born son — he fears death by water. You remember Marcus Tullius? No, I'm forgetting — well, he'll live, I'll lay long odds on that — they sealed his lips all right, more than once — admitted it. The stock-market — why of course. Why yes, every time. The pound sterling. Why certainly.

O Moses, for Remus and his sacred bitch don't get on to
that that's a topic I can't abide. Everything's economic now
that isn't class. Yes come off it that's a good [? chap]
and in either case the problem is Jewry — it's really too
much. The fellow's half negroid however comely — any-
way the matter's through, or will be by chotadown.

You're wrong there, I've known them . . .

No I'm not. I know the ropes, and the peculiar circum-
stances, they'll insist on sundown — it's one of their
Doubles, Extra grave. The instruments of execution must
be buried by sundown. There is at least no question of
their exact observance — you must grant them that.

As a matter of fact you're all too Jew-conscious, that's
what's the matter with you.
   Their pantomimes who show the victim and the sub-
stitute the mockings and reeds held and hood-man blind for
kings of misrule crowned with greenery and donkey rides
and strewn juniper and howling women with their mani-
ples to wipe the poor bastard at the sixth halt — this is no
more Judean than my foot — we did all that at my garrison
up country at this time of year — at least within a matter
of weeks, and so I've heard they do the same at Alex — it's
probably common to all these half-breeds this side our sea.
Now let's forget that barley baals must die, and hear about
the Gallic exploration. Come on Julia my heart let's hear
about your Western trip. Tell us everything about your
tow-headed fancy in his speckled trews, Dux Vintogeterex
Nodens filius Lugobelinos the gay boy of the Goidel world
the pride of Lutetia. Tell us more about woad. Do they
bathe in it, or are they tattooed. I'm interested in all the
details. Let's have all about the Moon Goddess and her
potent son, grottoed and sung in your crypted Autricum
— skip the mouldings, we've had all that from auntie
Agrippina. Come on, leave out the sunrise at Massilia and
the Phoenician sailor — I want to hear about the Cave in
the Rock. We all love goddesses, Frog or Ephesian, extra-
vagantly multiple for the Artemisia, or simply trimmed

like yours, my latin norm — Hey ho the Julian line! Go to Rome for morality, what do you say, gaffer?

I say it confirms what I'm saying. It's confirmation all right, a little nearer home than I'd bargained for — you've all got the bug. First it was the paltry Greeks then the Mauretanians, now I suppose we shall have a society for the preservation of the Celtic *numina* — peroxide for the high Belgic modes, a wattled hut for yr town garden on Esquiline — that's the way! A tin torque and checked *bracae* for little Quintus, and a mistletoe sprig on a miniature oak and a clockwork druid for baby Lucia — I know!

Venus Genetrix, let us pray, let's have the more venerable hocus pocus if we indulge at all.

Venus Verticordia, a penny in her box wouldn't do any of you harm, but for my part I would like to see appointed a commission of cults — only a root and branch reformation will meet the case — we know what the primitive use was — there is our genuine indigenous deposit: Picus, Pilumnus, Picumnus, now . . .

I say — sir — you know — you spoke just now of paltry Greeks, it wouldn't do to enquire too closely into the sacred genesis of our aboriginal Picus.

I repeat, Picus, Consus, Volumnus[2] — we know our native gods — you observe the gender, that is, of itself, significant. It is a question of recognition, not of enquiring into pre-history nor of comparative religion.

We know the Roman deities because in them we perceive those virtues which have made us — how much we fail in that recognition demonstrates to what degree we are non-Roman. Those only understand the myth of the Roman centuries who are themselves true Romans. Picus not a Roman! is that what they figure out nowadays. Claudia

[2] Cf. Minucius Felix, *Trans. of Xtian Lit.* (S.P.C.K.), 73 [better: *Octavius* xxv. 8, Loeb edn., pp. 390–1]. Cf. Jackson Knight, *Cumaean Gates* (1936), 169.

Quinta, I presume, was a Euxine tart, we scuttled our ships
at Antium, Lake Regillus was a notable defeat, a Punic
drill-sergeant taught us the manipulation of the *pilum*, a
Macedonian tactician our characteristic assault-formations —
is that how it runs at the Academy? Everything to detract
— ransack any pedants' data — any pettifogging tale serves,
any contribution toward the contemporary jape of
Rag the Old Lady
anything welcome which defames the
res publica
Let them all come
who can knock a pile or two from under the
Pons Sublicius
make any slave free who will help block the
Via Latina, at the Appian fork[3] whereby to sever those
    arteries
which vitalize
the world
The poltroons will perhaps be satisfied when the bough
which alone affords them support, crashes, to the disarray
of all that is, and all the world run in fruitless Lupercalia,
and Spartacus will astonish the shades with his merriment
to see so universal a crucifixion of privilege. The ex-
patriation from among us of all that has made us, pietas,
gravitas, dignitas, each on a slave's gibbet.
Then the bear-garden will be free
to proletarian hysteria
those use atonement cults who are conscious of a very
actual depravity.
The high-flying *logos* mewed and brailed at the paps
of a Memphian *theotokos*, those blends of sensuality and
otherness that get our dear young ladies on a tender spot —
and fill the Serapeum at all hours to enquire after last night's
interesting fantasies — and what it psychologically connotes.

O it's well enough while the thing holds, while the axle-pin

---

[3] The Via Latina and the Via Appia forked 500 yards or so
from the Porta Appia, within the city.

somehow keeps in position. For instance — the periodic alertness of the consuls checks this corrosion to some extent — but wait till all the barriers are down.

Why, young man, I'm not an old fool. I know that as well as you. Should you care to acquaint yourself with my record you will discover that I have publicly spoken in favour of
some measure of
at all events locally
toleration toward, and even, in some instances, the protection of, indigenous cults. It is true I have confined my observations in this particular to the procuratorship — which I know intimately, none better — but obviously the same principles, in varying degrees, would apply to all the provinces, indeed to all the provinces, senatorial or more remote — however, I make a reservation — I'd be sorry to commit myself as to any Celt or ... Ah yes! I feared that association would draw you — the obsession of the age — the *Teutones*. You know as well as I what the Curia has determined — good — if the Curial considered policy is to be one of extermination — if the cry in the lobbies as among the permanent officials, as in the gutter, is to be: *Delendi sunt Teutones* — we had better begin where beginnings are. I am not persuaded of the new dialectic which inverts causes and effects, nor do I imagine we can destroy the teuton economy without proscribing their metaphysic, which alone makes durable their sublime autarchy.

Yes, you hear me correctly, quite accurately. You are accredited to the second cohort of the XII under the new dispositions, not to a department of the propaganda. We can, then, admit and enlarge upon virtue, as we think fit at least, at this table — and we shall. But if the Hercynian is to go up in smoke — have no illusions, the blond deities are for it — and naturally the Ist Minervia, and the VIII Augusta will have work repugnant to their regimental tradition, if I know anything about the senior officers. Why yes, why not — half again, careful now. I'm delighted you find it so — to me it's a little on the sharp side — but it does something and one needs something. These sudden turns find one out as one gets on.

O, I should say a few points over — it's somehow raw, in spite of this curious oppressiveness — some freakish stuff comes up from the Bozra gap — you know that these fella'hin have a rigmarole — the only bit I recall runs somewhat:

The wind from Edom brings
  a stained tunic

metrical? — sort of — rather the kind of thing you might hear among our own land-workers — especially in the south, at the turn of the year.

Not the least — no idea — don't suppose they have either — the oral style, you know — local additions — parrot-stuff — transpositioning of obsolete words — syntax all to bits — and a 'Q' text that never was — but what intrigued me was: brings a stained tunic — finds one's liver that I do know — slap through the laminations of any lorica ever riveted — makes you feel really dicky you know — or will by the time you're my years — I'm not sure this stuff improves matters — however it does take the edge off things — one can't

tread the wine-press
        alone
without some dope
don't you try.
Any more?

I don't know — I believe something to this effect, if my memory serves.

... stained garment — *tunica* I suppose — by cause of his toil at the vallum — hill-fort — he resembles, or seems to be ... one who has scoured vats in Helbon[4] — that's interesting in a kind of way — I believe the stuff was actually barrelled at Damascus ... stinking of must. If he is solitary he is swift and his terribleness is in himself — that's how it seems to go ... Who is he, ... the lovely one in his dappled stola ...

[4] Cf. Ezekiel 22 : 18.

O, but I like it frightfully — there's something really to it
— can't you say it — all — consecutively?

I've never been the kind of fellow to redact, collate, tran-
scribe, let alone translate this latro Aramaic — Saturnian
rigmaroles and the like — quantitative, or accented — it's
poor stuff you know for all the high-born antiquarian
patronage. Let me see — how it might shape to our ears —
it's hardly my province. But anyway let's [?] be the bard
for once. Yes yes another tot, why not, after all the stuff
isn't physic.
 From Edom the wine-red avenger
 From the wilderness he comes
 Alone in his anger . . .

No no — you've got the cat out of that rabbit all right. No,
no, no, no, no, honestly — you dear pet — there's yr clas-
sical education for you — can't bite on real poetry, even
when it's served you hot on a dish and
 sweet-Isis-give-me-a-boy!
 it's garnished swell enough, already. But no, you must
 — you
 can't you
 can't
 leave well alone
bring out the academic cruets — smooth everything with yr
[*word missing*] brought tepid from the school kitchen —
form indeed — you poor sweet — I'm ashamed of you.
 O, but I do mind — it's not
 a-matter-of-taste
wine-red avenger — really. No, I'm not being impertinent,
nor provocative — it matters — can't you see it matters —
it's the only thing one can
 speak of
 with any conviction
 with any certainty
 I don't know about the
 splendor veri
 It's all very well but says little. I do know the thing has

164

to be
felt and
to feel one has to strip, to
peel off
a-lot-off
— all perhaps.
Anarkhos you say? That's because you will think politically, and even in that contingent realm I can't see we've made a shape which, being recognized, pleases — anyone — except perhaps, the usurers.

We, yes us precious Romans have done more harm and been more oblivious to our harm-doing than all the trousered-men put together.

I am going on and yr both to listen however much it [*breaks off*]

Thank God — I was — actually — born — outside the world — by your reckoning — for all daddy's hundred per cent patrician loins — and mummy — well of course, she's as guaranteed Roman as a bad frieze. Anyway, I do believe it affects something . . . gives one more chance.

As a matter of fact — you — might of — assimilated something — in Galatia. I've always adored Galatians — their foolishness has a real sensitivity. They're subject to enchantment in some way — they're rather like cats on a windy day.

they are aware — that's it.

What you've done with your awareness I can't imagine. But still — perhaps all your perceptions are cramped in that — battle-dress. Do you really have to wear that hideous attire — off parade.

Standing orders? What *do* they think
can
happen in
a-place-like-this.
They've not thrown a straight brick since the second Maccabean war.

Anyway, I — think — it's — necessary to get one's early contacts outside our thing.

Well, I'm sorry, but it's the only sort of idiom I use.

If you have the civility to listen and aren't too far gone you may glean something. That's better, unbuckle that unsuitable gear — the dying Gaul isn't about to make a last spring and I'm no Amazon. Standing orders! O God, you're as hopeless as daddy. Very different from my other young man — he captured half a hill in Africa wearing slippers — he says one can't be agile in the *caliga* — he's furious with this new set-up of making everyone wear legionary dress. Says it's bad from any point of view. He's awfully good about it being falsely utilitarian — yes I know — when you leave the vallum they spot your gentleman's contour — well, he's quite right — one can't be panoplied as a leader and have the freedom of idiosyncrasy proper to leadership and essential to it and still be safe — that's where a bureaucratic plan always comes a cropper. That's what he always says, he's as intelligent as he's beautiful — you must meet.

Always were a ragtime mob — at least the Fulminata is a regiment. [*Sheet of MS missing*]

As for last night — I was — of course, in — my bed. Where else, do you suppose. I'm not the A.P.M. of this village, you know. I'm attached, supernumerary, pending allocation to unit — I believe — that's what I am as far as I can discover.

Sorry, I thought the whole complement of the Antonia with all its details, clerks, cooks, sanitary men, optiones — gentlemen and others — together with all the personnel of all the garrisons in Syria stood-to last night — from the sound of things — what will our dear Tiberius say to such slack ways. Haec nox est and you hogging it. O beata nox! and you sleeping on. If you want to know about the dispositions for the policing of this zone I think I can help — I'm almost word perfect: *senior N.C.O. of half-maniple furnishing town-picket for the 48 hrs terminating at midnight* — well, you see that means they clicked for a bit extra and doubtless took it out of the prisoner — it's an ordinary routine duty — unless of course the *Chiliarch* of Reserve, Temple Area, Post — your friend — was detailed for special escort — but how unlikely in this case. The occasion would hardly warrant his being disturbed.

Not as though a potentate and his armed suite of twelve had to be secured with some appearance of respect. In any case I'm not remotely involved.

O surely, come — at least a tribune (why you lapsed into Greek I can't imagine)
    at least a gentleman
    to
    fetch him away
           [Two sheets of MS missing]

I mean simply that.

Before Aeneas was, he is; before Ilia was chosen another was forechosen. It's as simple as that, I mean

It's round the bend of the road where things happen, and Roman roads never bend.

You look for the goods on the roads — it is rather in the spaces between the roads you should look, by by-way and on hill-site. There will germinate the nova vita — everything is taped on the via IX and on all the numbered arteries where the standards shadow the speculator. The immaculate walk *in via*, in the tangled ways between our efficient grid — that's where the surprise is — and no Roman ever cared much for surprise. One's flanks are in the air. One can't guard one's flanks from the perfection coming up from the *terra informis*.

It is these men will be sworn to the new *sacramentum* maniple by maniple in the secret places.

Don't be childish, do you think I've lived twenty-eight years in our society not to know that all perfections come to a sticky end.

I'm quite immune from getting involved. I'm a vestal to the personal comforts and I intend to persevere in that vow but I do think one ought to realize what kind of outfit this is. No need to scuttle one's intelligence as well as one's conscience. There isn't a major war on, although one would suppose so to look at you. Keep the eyes of the mind skinned for heaven's sake — you'll see some pretty frightening sights — but I — don't — know — I think — it's — all —

one can do situated as we are. Anyway what I won't have is *ersatz* consolation of any kind.

Sometimes I wish they'd take away the river that runs by my door, but what I never wish is that I was taken in by this organized deception whereby we make an emporium and call it a Commonwealth. Jove shield me from that, that's this virgin's last prayer.

O yes — I — do — I'm not a little piece from the *Suburra*, I'm an educated girl, for all my attractive appearance. Well, all right, only do remember which — you see — quite different.

Now look here — we're back on this boring subject. For God's sake let's forget the activities of the Police for a bit — it's perfectly absurd. It's back-page news for the *Acta*, if that.

Well it was your unhappy fault. If you come in looking like a pantomime Mars — I thought some Olympian — and what with all the racket I naturally think that a new Rex Judaeorum attempts to disturb our universal pax. I know that the pathetic tetrarch is as touchy as [?]

But to get back to — about ourselves — well, I don't know, but the cultures we liquidate for the good of the liquidated — But it's not at that level I mean. I'm not talking politics and I'm certainly not talking ethics — as to the latter we can call it quits — so you can cut that once and for ever. There are values below all that and it's the intricate design of those values which interests me.

No not all — because I think they're realler. That's why — more real and antecedent to, first in importance as in reality — so then first absolutely and every time.

It's this tentative thing we need
so much
to not to
know — is
vital
    no perfected Roman, turned out correctly — can —
      understand — that
  Do you suppose that

for all the years
anno urbis conditae will be the year from which
to measure all the years
that measure
the stature of man?
Yes, I suppose you do on the whole.

But when you come to shades of underground, and there,
in that muted and static illumination that's well devised
for the judicial observation of objects-as-they-are-in-them-
selves (Lord, how you'll loathe no high lights, won't you. —
I'm too fond of you to wish for you this necessary elimina-
tion of all the kind of overstatement — the cut and dried so
dear to your precious hearts. However, we are up against
the real and must be objective.)

When you have eaten dog's meat and so come to from
the forgetful river[5] there they will expose for your un-
wonted consideration, for a specified number of quaran-
tines, two objects
no turning to where the candid Iope
nor roving when
Helen leans
to out-do Kallipygos,[6] to bring down the nether Troy, as
that of our mortal world was, by those same guiles, easily.
It's eyes front the *Manes* will demand and you as sober and
as sick as cats. Their statutory orders will be: Compare the
objects and in Roman manner, furnish an accurate report.

I wish for you that you like me would pray to the
powers tutelary: give us our purgatory now, for although
to know the truth when almighty propaganda is prevalent

[5] It will be remembered that consciousness was only regained
other side Lethe by eating animal blood.

[6] Venus originally a Latin goddess of the spring. First equated
with Aphrodite after the defeat of Lake Trasimene — a temple
was dedicated to Venus of Mount Eryx (Sicily) on the Capitol.
This place had long been sacred to Aphrodite Urania.
    Aphrodite Kallipygos (eupygia). The hetaerae — olisbos —
baubon — sexual goods (largely manufactured in the town of
Miletus). Phryne — Hypereides (her counsel). Symbols of A.K.:
the myrtle, rose, apple: the dove, hare, sparrow, he-goat, ram.
As sea-goddess, the swan, mussels, dolphins. As Urania, the
tortoise. She was guardian deity of Thebes.

has disadvantages, yet to be auxiliary to what will prevail is, in itself, pleasant — that should appeal to yr Roman minds, to say the least.

I say it — I believe it makes a difference.

O — I — know — all — about — that haven't I heard it — all — since — so high. I've known it all since I've known I was a girl, and that was early on.

Even my nanny saw herself as the administratrix of the *ius gentium* I do believe. Almost a sort of Dea Roma putting the truant world across her knee. It's intriguing to contemplate the spinster having vented her inhibited desires — should rationalize her outburst to her own satisfaction by supposing herself to be within her diocese as much an upholder of the Roman thing as any praetor — one gets the same thing in the kitchen — you know one is shown one's own baize door as though the garnishing of Roman larks for a Roman oven must be as much *in camera* as shady sessions of the cabinet. Jill's as good as her mistress at this top nation complex. Of gardeners I will not speak. The raw-boned Pict captured by a Phoenician syndicate sold by a Jew bought at Alex the bill of lading checked by an Ethiopian, freighted to Ostia finds himself in our happy home. Takes his master's name and bless him his very leeks dress by the right and each cry out: We flavour only the Roman broth. How it's managed I can't think but I do know that our genius to govern is absolutely astounding. Talk about divide and exploit, the very subjects of our exploitation fancy themselves no end once we give them a Roman rig, relax their taut cognomina agreeably to a civil ear.

Touch the *nomen* and destroy the *gens*, for names have power to activate or make impotent, collectively, as privately — we all know that — we understand the matter when we suffer it.

The topography of Clodia, whose meandering margin rucks a quilted sea — the lie of her, the several undulations, this wide asylum, this gradual recess — each are named of

Clodia's name by Clodia's friend — call herself Claudia —
and, on his chart (still the Fair Isle), each shelving beach,
this promontory place (he's navigated often from the
wheel-house of the mind), all his derivative nomenclature
must know the blight and shadow of alteration. He's quite
put to it. A vowel change defeats him — association's all
— strike at the word and suffer the metamorphosis *in carne*.
    Young gentlemen in Gaul have told me how that among
the insular Belgae, the best people, at all events, affect our
ways in everything (hypocausts that foul their flues — no
doubt — just when the nones of March are apt to find one)
but still, they do their best. Mint a coinage — the Divine
Augustus, become interestingly abstract in the die and
strangely wild in the dented green gilt, inscribed: Verica
— Rex, with a victory reverse, or, Eppillus (these gentle-
men wear the toga, as I'm told, but — keep their trousers on
— can you beat that one?)
    Amminus with a Pegasus (he's our creature) all of them
with polite terminations for the Camulodunum Romano-
phile.
    Caratácus, the growing lad
    it may be, but
    Carátauc, the leader, it
    will be
    when there's total war.
Why yes — on the cards for years — of course.
    Caelo tonantem credidimus Iovem
    regnare; praesens divus habebitur
        Augustus adiectis Britannis
            imperio gravibusque Persis.

When poets sing our universal peace they do but grease
the diplomatic elbow with the unction of Mars. So — sell
out Olives and — buy in Iron. That's my tip. But for the
Dalmatian separatists and that nice packet from Germany,
the advanced young Belgic notables would, long since, have
had their belly-full of our refinements. Cunebelinus-Rex,
for the die-sinkers with the malleable gold. Cynfelin Bren-
hin, for the harder matrix of the tribal memory.
    Caratácus for the communiqué — yes, but Carátauc for

the war-throats [at the contested ford. Caratauc! harsh and
trumpeted, to counter-point, to lift up hearts above, the
ponderous and registering fro and thud of the Mk. IX
medium Petraria. C'ratauc!, broken and contracted: Crixus
says to No. Four: the bastards call on Nike. Let be — let's
see, let her deliver them, if she will have them.]
    In short, there's everything in a name.
    Not interested? Aren't you. You may find yourself,
within a few years, under the pharos, O.C. embarkation
supply train — or something equally cushy — waiting on
the prevailing Channel swell — anxious to see the last of
'em and so back to the mess at Bononia for a strong one,
complaining of the saturating vapours that drift all day from
that most intolerable of islands. So don't be so superior.
A little information as to the political and cultural con-
ditions of those parts may yet serve you. But leave that —
I was only pointing out that we are awfully clever at this
business of assimilation. I don't think for a moment that
we've worked it out — our craftiness is simply intuitional
— not rationalized — we are very clever but far from in-
telligent. But as cleverness wins every time — it's grand for
us, but not quite so grand for the assimilated. But, as I say,
in a quite baffling kind of way they simply long to be
considered absolutely part of our racket. It makes one
inclined to think that after all the human species is more
dog-like than cat-like, a depressing conclusion.

This is where we return to nanny — a fine lot she ever
got out of:
    her highly referenced and
    absolutely reliable
    genteel and, perfect for
    the children of — gentlewomen whose —
    husbands — are — stationed — abroad
    (senatorial provinces preferred)
    What's her end — after
    patiently balancing the
    silver spoon that you
    find in the mouth of
    ev-er-ry brat

delivered out-of-due-time
inbred and querulous
in all the best nurseries of
the
gens Cornelia
mind you, she so served three generations of us, to my
knowledge — she found employment in our ménage at that
time when: 'I'll fetch Arminius to you' was sufficient to
sober any Roman child, and any Roman grown-up too.
That is to say she got me at the peak of my beastliness
— how I — loathe — all children — especially at the in-
between period — impossible as companions and yet too
aware to be regarded as merely automatic — with all the
savagery of a grown-up and with none of the camouflaging
conventions — for manners cloak the whole hatefulness of
man — and if persevered in — really make a new creature
— but don't talk to me about sweet little Lucia — I re-
member: bloody little Julia — all too well — but what did
nanny get — last week — what did she — pardon me —
last Wednesday. Socia's false ringlet — a shade on the low
side for this season. Don't pretend to mind — aggravating
circumstances! pour me a stiff one!

Poor bourgeois nanny whose sole conception of right
behaviour was not to disturb the *numina* of privilege —
and the *manes* of the people of Rome, whose whole care
has been for yours and mine — our like — whose supreme
moment was, to wear, on the bund at Ostia, cousin Pom-
ponia's cast-offs, who feared more than anything else re-
buke, from her adored persons of quality, who was paralysed
at the thought of being done violence as a stoat-run rabbit.
When I survey the unredemptive cross on which, in such
bewilderment, the clownish victim dies — I need some-
thing stronger than this — I want something that gets to
the spot — want a corpse-reviver if ever a girl did.

You — indeed — you — do — anything! why it's all one
with your day's routine — day by day — each day — and
I suppose — if more obliquely so — with mine — each day
— I can see you risking all that good that hangs on Socia's
favour because an octogenarian slave has passed out under
the cat.

But as for this man there's nothing amiss with his like condemnation.

He's all [of] a piece as an artist should be, and to great artists all things serve a turn — whether amicable or inimical — if life or here death — no swing so take a roundabout and show you're fly to turn all things to beauty for beauty's sake — and so make hares of them all. This so-called Jew at least has had his say has sabotaged convention has put a few over on the men in black has tilted at the windmills of both the bugbears — is sublimely conscious of his mission is without fear or has overcome it — believes his derivation to be uncommon — doesn't give a damn for anything because he so offers himself to all as to make the dark weal on either smitten cheek feel like that infusion that lips give when lovers bruise each other — is master of the labyrinth and indeed, as I gather he has hinted, its original engineer, by whom all things are, who would guide all men safe in the meander, is invulnerable because without armour — took flesh either in a Bedlam or was begotten on Olympus — I can't say. When they delivered sentence: *Ibis ad crucem* — I guarantee he heard it as groom in a world other from ours might be expected to hear his banns. He would step up like a young man to his nuptials to embrace the wood — he leans against the parados of shame to look on the city and the world as one of your *teutones* might lean from the revetment of his ditch over the *limes* with eyes of ice. Or as Cocles alone on a swaying pile commended his spirit to the fathering river.

Or as Cloelia who breasted the torrent-in-the-way, who held her chin above the sewage, and who, beyond the spray, saw on the aboriginal hill the white lintels, and heard the welcome over the drag and suck.

Like her so his, incomparable limbs are wide, like him so she against an evil tide unloosed her girdle Beauty, short-shifted for the Games casts all at the final handicap. The weighted quincunx indicates the odds — the thumbs are up.

(The dowagers fan their sagging paps and hope for more. Anastasia sits very still and wonders for the weight of her body and to what divers ends the fruits of copulation come.

The quietly-dressed Levantine Jew leaves by Gangway VII, marking his tablets as he goes. They fetch sand for the next turn.)

Did you suppose to see the blossoms displayed?

This hard war has weaved him his *Kredemnon*, which, though the warp be crimson the gutters yield its weft.

Insulate, in the viscid habiliments of struggle — behold him —

The salutary spectacle is, in the first instance, seen of the soldiers, as is proper.

Beggar man,
thief,
rich man, and if
priests dare look, for them also beauty on five hooks discovers herself, the sum of Aphrodite and the wounded Eros, the pierced Hermaphrodite.

If the intolerable waters have passed over him his draggled plume is up. He's freed the conduits whom they laved in the excrement of the town — and what's more he knew it — I have no particular misery on his account, but respectable, provincial, well-intentioned, blockheaded sweet nanny — that's another tale — unless, *she with nothing has got something*.

I wonder if, behind that mask of yes mam no mam delighted mam she really, when she regards the Roman sword says to herself

Lord take me away from that river
sword sever my bonds and deliver.

(I can't believe they all believe about the bunk about Dominion status — honestly.)

Perhaps she knew, maybe too she saw, as clearly as our Jew, the acres of asphodel. But still that leaves us with 89 per cent of the raw material right here, you can't get away from that.

*   *   *

Well my dear that's a long interpolation and damn me you seem to feel it — it's always said that whatever else is bad in this town the water is capital — suggest you — take more of it have it brought to the table — there's plenty of it since

175

Ponty did his job at all events and damn well managed and little thanks.

But really — I barely followed you — but —

Don't mind her sir — look — you were saying — just now — about the weather —

Yes — yes — I never knew anything comparable to this and I've seen a few March hares in these parts. But we were on another matter — my dear you've really put me out — why —

I think you sir were saying sir something about the barbarians —

O that — O was I — well as one who knew the *limes Germanicus* fairly well if locally and long since, their prisoner in fact and damned unpleasant. I have a soft feeling for them and could say more — but it was that question of the toleration of rites that I wanted to make clear. It is a matter I've argued often time and time again and blackballed for me pains. — Now listen, if Julia is in any mood to listen to one of her own class — and blood. It is well enough that the Phrygians should revere the great mother, the Epidaurians, Aesculapius, the Syrians, Astarte, it is unexceptionable also to say that the Romans worship all the gods — in the sense that we permit the religious rites, cannibalism and such-like apart, of those committed by history to our protection. It is important in any nursery to be patient with the various whims of childhood and what does our *Imperium* necessitate, if not that we should be the nurse and mother of the peoples — the **Bona Dea** in very operation.

To all she offers her august breasts — to these she leans and stoops to guide, this little one she persuades with confectionery, these two mewlers at the table-end will discover all in good time her agility, and the length, both of her patience and of her reach, and as for this hussy, for her the rods are untied and she must take it — to what degree the lictors feel disposed.

It was a great labour and contention that gained her the remedial place.

She, the Channel.

The iron phallus that brought
life-in-death to Ilia.

The necessary and fierce concomitance the beasts communicated under the fig-tree. The venerated objects which for us latins and for the world's health, came down from heaven, which we guard — look upon her and understand what these things designate.

I'd like to hear sometime what sustains you and your set — for every age has its illusions [...] it will be no illusion to see some beggars-on-muleback and illumined slaves — these will be the supposed purveyors of divine life. Those essentially sane virtues which our philosophers have remarked upon and our soldiers have made actual will be half-guessed at, feminized, glossed. These will presume themselves able to pluck the immortal flower by this mumbo-jumbo or that initiation. How should such mystic inheritors do other than misconstrue the documents even though they claim to be our assigns. Doubtless they will carry our signum (crested, I dare say, with a new-fangled device) and style their hirsute magnates *Imperator* — but what will it avail? Scratch their togas and find their torques. Tattooed they are under their *tunica* and barbarian they will remain. I see a thousand years of it and more. Those may well screech to the gods who have destroyed the vicar of the gods. They perforce tread the tortuous ford when the bridge of the bridge builder is down.

Cheer up gaffer they'll never break the squares never not in the field ever. It'll pass sir take heart — no cause. It's a phase — we're all initiate now — everybody does it on the stations — there's damn all else to do.

Phase it may be, but when men have arrived at a rational attitude and then fall back upon mystery-mongering, it is, for them, the last phase. I see clearly how this corrosion creeps. I've watched it for forty years or more. I'll not mention names. I've already remarked his good sense but she gave him most serious jitters. Dreams mind you — obtruding the occult into the actual machinery of government — spooks mark you, to rattle him at his morning routine — that's what it's come to. I'm sorry for him — I know her type — very sorry.

But I leave you to it — my way's not yours my day's not now — times turn, and anyway it's past my hour.

At least we can preserve reasonable order and normal sequence while yet we may — at all events in our private lives.

A man's ninth-hour sleep is good for him no matter what hanging witch-doctors raise a dark cloud to give their inconspicuous deaths a kind of notoriety — I offer you an old man's suggestion. You will do well to notice that what is bogus is always disruptive — the affected and the abnormal alike in life as in art always seeks a sign — a stimulation — it's easier to darken the sun at noon and to raise the dead than to quietly sort the documents, check the evidence — be tolerant here, and firm there — expand the privileges of citizenship gradually — deal with ascertained facts realize the relativity of things — the ordinary civil servant attentive to his office hours is more beneficial to mankind than all the fanatics, who, unable to endure the ordinariness — the trivialities which determine even the things of great moment — the contradictions — leap like suicides over the cliff with some salvation formulae on their lips — and half the world goes leaping after them — generation on generation of them — it's the demand for the short-cut — to what is other — I advise you both my dears to attend, rather, to what day by day actually is. What is other can well look after itself.

Sleep well sir.
    The old bore's gone.
    Now I can resume my advice to the young. Come closer. I suggest you set up shop — take a little place off the *Fora*: *Madame Julia, consultant in comparative cultures. Today*

at 3.30 in the smaller atrium. Subject: What's wrong with the Twins?

It'ld draw you know.

I think that's damn funny I must say.

You're not going to escape as easily as that — I'm all out — I know I've had a few but I'm talking wisdom. No, yes — no please — try the other amphora — empire vintage you know — this: Buy Roman is the final straw — it's the last disaster if one happens to care for — variety — for perfection — the two civilized necessities. I undervalue no- thing — get that idea from under yr tin hat. It's a question of assessment. We must hold the scales without being blind- fold. That is the supreme function of the sophisticated person — as the most developed so the most difficult, then the most onerous.

There is a common illusion — which I expect you share — about how it is salutary to endure hardship — how that the simple, rough, life is in some way, of itself, nearer to 'reality' (so the insufferable cant runs) — nothing could be further from the truth — it's a pure escapism — of a peculiarly subtle kind and one which all authority whether of the nursery or of the state, is quick to exploit. The real test of virtue — is whether we can be virtuous in the lap of comfort. That's the real rub — any dunderhead can practise heroics given sufficient privation.

O what a dolt for an intelligent girl to have about the place. The point is what's all the organization for — my God, my Tribune of [. . .] may be a cissy but he can at least follow one. The bridge, the road, the postal service, admirable — incidentally, before I forget and before it gets any darker — I do hate this ridiculous gloom — it puts me off — I do detest phenomena. I'm true blue Roman there; anyway incidentally — I wouldn't mind betting our old friend the bridge in certain of its developments will be regarded in future ages by all the most sensitive minds as the one really worth-while thing we've managed — there we achieve real line — singularly moving — something comes through there I grant and of course, the knottier problem for our engineers — naturally — so much the better aesthetically. — Yet what contemporary of yours or mine is aware of this — but, don't spill this particular bean — they'ld be sunk if they knew — as I implied just now — before the old man pushed off — the only hope for a Roman is not to know — that's why our works are so seldom great, for to be a supreme artist one has got to know and yet be as one who knows nothing. At any rate, once and for all don't imagine I don't appreciate our contribution — the bridge, the road, drains, hypocausts, baths — that's grand — soldiers everywhere — lovely — what else — same drinks, same food — asparagus wherever you will — Camelodunum oysters on the Alpine stations — sunned olives at Bononia. I'm all for all that — I'm all for giving Dame Nature one in the pants — what next — she has no idea of distribution — same Hellenic frills — ah that's where we strike bed-rock — a Greek façade won't save us — not, at all events, without Greek imagination. Anyway the Greeks were half-dead when we began to ape them: not that I think personally they were ever much alive, but that's a long story. Plastically we present a kind of death-mask of the Greek thing — only ill done, coarsened at all the articulations — just where you want real refinement in fact. A fine lot of copy-cats we shall appear. — How well I know the pathetic academicians who fetch a tape to this Juno and that Hermes and balance the fatiguing results at every turn of the stair, to relax from a niche in one's *tepidarium* or to clutter, forever unweathered, a perfectly good vista. I'ld forfeit all my charms to be appointed Mistress of Demolition throughout the Empire. I would begin, very literally, at home — you've not seen mama's recent acquisitions — you'ld adore them — they're right up your street. It's unfortunate that our vulgarity is most obtrusive in the most durable of all materials — we obstruct the map with mediocrity of marble.

O dear you have a perfect genius for backing the wrong *quadrigae* — as a matter of fact those straight realistic portrait-busts of the oil-king in pentelic and the like are nearer to our genuine expression — and so, at least, are interesting. There is such a thing as Roman genius, even in the plastics, and it is highly realistic. As a race we can only understand those things that we physically collide with. The Gods never conceived a meaner joke than when [they] suggested to the Roman matron that she would cut a fine figure in the *chiton* — I doubt if the world will ever recover from this jape — its ramifications are likely to be infinite — and the subtlety of it — Greco-Roman — that's the sort of composite they'll coin to fool posterity and fill the academies with plaster.

But the portraiture, characterization, there we are at home. Maura always says that. She always says that after the incised inscriptions the portrait-busts are where we are liveliest plastically. I'd rather overlooked the inscriptions — we are — aristocratic — there. It's an extremely interesting thing — one detects a streak of true refinement there — the spaces *between* the incisions have such significance in the best examples. Our masons seem to have a genuine understanding of the alphabet in a kind of physical way.

As we used to sing in the nursery
With a tingle-tangle titmouse
                    Rome knows Great A,
            B & C & D & E
                F, G, H
                    &
                    I K.
If 'and in them the Word was made stone' is what posterity will say of us, it is some consolation. It may redeem us in [the] opinion of the ages — modify the school-marm prize-fighter impression — for that's about it. Or are we so potent and have so imposed our shape upon the waking minds of men, so insinuated the male principle as to vulgarize and flatten out the subtle maze, so mapped the meander of our intuitive origins (Aphrodite of the oblique approaches, pray for us, who gave us Aeneas) the eye and central keep, that the quincuncial fosse and fretted troia cat's-cradle a defence for, by traverse or horse-dance.

The virile tree is from and to the Delphic cleft. Let us pray that men remember their hidden mother and with tentative feet and appropriate humility trace the twisted lance.

No Lancelot no! you must be lost before you find the cornucopia, the lamb that bleeds beyond the double guard of Guenever within the vaginal traverses the Durotriges fence on their high places, at the navel of the spiral at New Grange, under the seal where the leaning stones deploy to loop the cist for Minoan or Menai Scylla. It's always from chamber to chamber — in and out the creep-way as you have done before. To check at hard pin-head the monoliths stand in diamond deployment, you must get in and get under for the good, the vital wires are earthed and hard to come by, you'll feel like a motherless child before Rhea encloses you a second time, before you revive the maimed king before you find your margarite. You must be lost, and the Roman way is to be certain of one's bearings. In this we have denied our maternal genius. Juno has been quite successfully liquidated in spite of our litanies.

Not everyone that says to her: Lady and Queen, at the Matronalia, enters into her labyrinth, not the incense at Lanuvium, not the goat-skins the sacristans fetch for her, not the careful feeding of her geese avail, for to obey would have been better than ritual and to hearken than to call her Regina Coeli, Empress of the Spear, Mistress of Parturition, patroness of cannon-fodder, and all the rest of it — how the liturgy swells to shape the heavens to Caesar's advantage — shall this city reduce that city magic batterings and impact of total prayer when that city generates and is mistress of, all effective cacophonies and deployments to bind and loose, widdershins or *ex oriente*, coeli et terrae, invisibilium, as in all things in our proximate, plaster and very visible Roma.

Look, you used to be quite a little dabster at the palm, before you took the veil the highbrows weave to mesh nice girls and damp 'em down. What do you make of this anyhow? O well, I mean, you know you know quite well — it's all [of] a piece. I mean, the heavens, and so on, this and that initiation, pull your socks up when you meet a solitary crow — the black cat gone, and the blackamoor met in the narrows, I've heard it at the midnight hour, she said she

distinctly saw it when the old bastard died — over the
moat and like a candle beneath the hill, don't go under the
scaling-ladder go outside the testudo rather, look out for
the Ides and do be careful with the salt, the future in the
quincunx and that's torn it if she's given him gloves. I
mean all the extra-rational felt-in-bones stuff, somehow-
infected-by-nanny-from-Delphi when she powders the
flanks of you and Prudentia on mid-summer eve when the
moon was full — all the phoney stuff, you know — it's all
apiece — that's how I figure it out sweetheart.

I see you're impossible — but anyway let-me-look.
(Let's while away the gathering gloom with trifles, we
will unwind, or let's pretend to, with old hag's lore and
ordinary intuition, the wholly boring, personal coil, of one
conventional, insufferably unaware, upper-class male —
after all most girl children come to a similar employment.)
No, the other paw. That, O that's nothing — that's an
interesting juncture and that looks very jolly for the future
Mrs — what's your name. Now the other one. Hold it so,
no, so, that I can see — more light on the dark science.
I see you're fond of travel, of circumnavigation possibly
— well, the empire is elastic and the water wide and in your
profession I see no reason why the indicative diagram
should do less than plot the inclination of the heart. Did you
ever want a blonde with a gold fibula, who could manage
an osier-boat in a back-water holding a fishing-spear in her
hand and calling below the falls 'giff giff' 'daly daly' to
charm the laminated water-beasts in west-waters before she
casts her net? O no, now come, you can't interrogate the
Sibyl — you know, like that — I can only say that's what
I see in the crystal of your palm — I wish you joy — the
men are savage enough, your bed will be your battlefield
and no mistake if you fall for the queen of the insular
Parisii.
Cumae? — why yes, I learned a lot at Cumae — they've
a fairly continuous tradition there, and taken quite seriously
quite a lot might be unravelled — but don't mistake me,
it's an arduous process — nothing to do with this nonsense,

with the booth in the bazaar, or the select apartment next
the *masseuse* who comes whether a subaltern of the Ful-
minata has the palm of an ape or of a divinity — but
   we all care for
   the Bull that died.
   All want to know
   We all wish to
   snuggle back to the womb, all
   need to find a
   way
   all legitimately desire to know
   why
   the Land is Waste, anyone
   would describe the most complicated
   troia to
   bind and loose
the apparently inconsequent actions of the fates — all batter
at the brass doors, and it is disappointing indeed that even
the initiates emerge from the gate called False Dreams, ivory
or no. Though one rose from among the dead it would be
of no advantage — one can believe nothing on hearsay,
after all, still less on [*torn*] authority. Uncertainty is not
a thing to be rid of — it is a condition of having separate
existence — an Olympian messenger would avail nothing,
his news would fall equally under suspicion — scepticism
is not a pose, it is an inevitable consequence of being Lucy
and not Lavinia — Lavinia and not Lucy. But how dark
it is at this hour's turn — most extraordinarily dark.

IV

THE BOOK OF BALAAM'S ASS

shape of a few lines here.

¶ I have watched the wheels go round.
in case I might see the living
creatures like the appearance of lamps
in case I might see the living god
projected from the machine.
I have said to the perfected steel:
Be my sister, & to the glassy towers:
Bend your beauty to my desire.
Indeed for the glassy towers I
thought I felt some beginning of
his creature. But my hands joined
the glazed-work unrefined & the
terrible crystal a stage mask if
you presume to come to a lovers'
length of her; no love or nearer
acquaintance.

¶ I have howled at the foot of
the glass tower.

I took hold of her glistening rods
& travailed for her adamant
surfaces.

THE BOOK OF BALAAM'S ASS

SHE'S BRIGHT WHERE SHE WALKS SHE
DIGNIFIES THE SPACES OF THE AIR AND MAKES
AN AMPLE SCHEME ACROSS THE TRIVIAL
SHAPES. SHE SHAKES THE PROUD AND ROTTEN
ACCIDENTS; SMALL CONVENIENCES LOOK
SHRUNK SO THAT YOU HARDLY NOTICE
THEM:
like when pale flanks turn to lace with agile stripes the
separating grill — until you quite forget the necessary
impertinence
   the shackling and iron security
   by which and
   in which and
   through which
   you indulge your fine appreciation.
   The sapless trunk set in the corner for her talons in
make-belief of her true domain, the stale urine on the
sterile floor, the one who leans without: his watch chain,
his corporation badge, his blank employee's eyes turned on
the man from Amsterdam who strokes the cougar in the next
cage down. The identification plate: *Ben*, Inner Turkestan,
1923, presented by His Holiness the *Amiral* of Balasquez,
the hieroglyph that tells you she's a male born in captivity.
   or like
when Northumbrian brides make the stucco twiddlings seem
to ring and these Erastian marble piers they overhaul so
carefully seem *almost* to support a proper altar-house for
the moment when she passes. You almost are able to forget
their special voices and the furnishing — even that bloody

187

organ pipes down before her minstrelsy. The Patriarch of
Uz would whistle low, could he see the liquefaction of her
silks.

or when
a living sail turns the headland close in to change the shape
of the small sea, sets free the constricting esplanade and
bends the rigid sea-rail to a native curvature (for space
itself, they say, leans, is kindly, with ourselves, who make
wide deviations to meet ourselves). Even the Hotel
Victoria shouts for joy and nods her vile proportions; the
Bedford finds it easier, for she has anyway a freedom of
her own. Her square-set walls carry, where her windows
bay, a refinement of iron to strut the virid baldachin; her
balconies have leaned out of another century. She's inclined
herself, she's been conditioned, she's felt her proportions
modified by, gained a passing fulness from, each surprising
advent that comes to break the waters and to shake the
town.

These incomings that lend life, blow where they will,
day by day play some new trick to magnify; (who's not
seen antique tea-pots make the clumsy china breathe when
she sets it down)

or
stiff-legged calves who make the gradual fields skip like
imagined hills, play erratic circles to accuse the static adults,
drifting on stubble-sea, or set heavily like islands humped
— who know the business of their kind, who've long since
shaped to the economic requirements, they know the text
and the gloss and that's that. They eat hay all the day long.
Their slow bellies remember one thing perhaps. Their eyes
question you at the field-latchet, they seem to have seen
things like you before. Each man walking they question.
They seem almost to rumble you. They startle when you
come on hind-legs at them; you come fore-paws waved to
shoo them off. You subdue imperiously with fragile man's-
hand, bellowings and forest-might. You scorn crumpled
or bright horn that gored the burning cat with your an-
thropoid gestures. They sheer away and turn to regard you,
their perplexed bull-brain can't untangle, no key to open,

no twitch of tail or hairy ear clears the tormenting buzz of memory — the bovine race-myth not unravel. Short-horn lows to this frustrated Hereford — long-lashed bends her corrugated forehead to the immediately consoling grass.

Pray stone bulls won't make the stone low his name, who toppled his diadem to reach his fodder
between the irrigation ducts.

Should the stone whisper out of Chaldea,

By Christ, drover, you'll wreck a china-shop

Could she blink a thought-maze back, there would be a Dialectical incoming for you!

Lords of Creation, hierarchy of use and delectation, rational souls, convenient syllogistic cornering of memory and will, and dumb beasts perishing as poor brute-bodies must — She'd make a Balaam of you to narrow your path, she'd drag you down on Christmas night into an appropriate attitude till your arse reflected the nine Choirs shining. She'd teach you manners; for she has part in the patrimony, her brindled coat and mild eyes sheafed and pencilled to make your bowels turn like a dark lady, and twice as natural, are His idea of her. He hung the creases round her strong neck turned like you twist amber beads for Agatha and crystal for Lucy and Perpetua. She is a legate in bonds, she bellows loudly as she ought to bellow. But she'd show you a classless society. She'd thrust you on your origins. She'd break down and nozzle to your foundations and toss high for the windy advent day a thousand middle-walls of partition. She'd rend your temple veils, she'd find more than two bugbears for her pronged bright thrust to rive (turned so like to the bifurcated steel that found their flowered groins of the noblesse fair game after the long idiocy of agriculture). She'd hoof-down and shoulder through, she'd make circles round your intelligences and properly box your realm of ideas. She'd make your exploiting governance wither away all right — if she could recall him sweating out his chrism, easing his tailless flank under the burning sun-baked terracing.

Of course there is another possibility, the children-playing-out-of-school might quite unconsciously draw the pin.

189

O but they do — I've heard 'em often — they teach them all that kind of thing nowadays, they've taken over from the old wives. Their professorial two-piece sapphic cut slick between Otto's varnished states and the steam-control, the potted cacti and the incubating tubers you'd think enough to lay the ghost
    still the mumbo-jumbo
    shake the totem
    sweep and garnish
    break up the categories, debunk the long-standing de-
      lusions
— but as a matter of fact they keep up the immemorial formulas as bold as brass — they can say
            Ash when green
            Is fire for a queen
as pat as Belle Berners,
for these being dead, speak.

Our feet are set in the slippery place. We're on an incredibly delicate filament all the time. Any accident might be the contingent cause, you know. How they play with the stuff, they treat it like literature done in 13pt.

They don't give a bugger to have the plagues added nor have their part taken out of the things written nor be without the holy city, but it gives you an uneasy sensation to know how near the knuckle they get, you can't be very comfortable to see quite well-meaning decidedly informed, sensitive types, chinas, home-town peers, liberally minded, of like-fashion, of [?] one-head, known to Tania and Baby, Aunts and sons' wives of Livinia, fellow-citizens of us from the womb up, known to father's pharaoh and of good report, pukka men of their hands, not slanderers dogs, nor sorcerers,[1] regular at the rails, smilers at flag-day corners, blameless, not extortionate, superior to party, not loving their own selves, bird-lovers, and inventors of humane bull-slaying, temperate, fair-spoken, appreciative — all this

---

[1] [Cf. *The Sleeping Lord*, pp. 97–111, for another version of the following pages.]

190

and a great deal more — it arouses complicated emotions to see such intimate friends unawares seated confidently in a ventilated room smiling at superstition on the fifth of November — they'll laugh on the other side of their faces at gunpowdered reason.

I know it bores you, Cicily and you too, Pamela-born-between-the-sirens, but Bertie will corroborate what I'm saying, and you ask poor Clayton. Willy and Captain Varley never use any other analogies and Belle Varley takes it like a lamb, and even asks intelligent questions between her dropped stitches — her nice eyes wide — about all kinds of details about what the 5th did after Sandy Picton left them in the abortive raid east of Hulloch — oh yes I was, I was with Sandy for a time only we differed in glory, but I expect he'd know me. It's all very well to yawn and let the dead bury the 6,000 mental cases still under observation — that's the figures for October 1937 anyway. Yes I know the next packet will make it all seem silly like Spud Bullen's unwearied and graphic account of an assegai's accurate trajectory and penetrating down drive was to us when he told retold and developed his tale in a rocking cubby-hole with a box barrage down. Poor boring old Spud, the tedious old sweat — like Emeritus Nodens of the 2nd Adjutrix who regaled them with tales of the elusive Pict with half his face vermilion that burned through the creeping brume sleuthing white for the native night of that Ultimate Province — they came over he said in front of Borcovicium he said it was perpetual shade as black as the inside of a Capitol wolf further forward in the signal stations — he supposed the Otadini came cat-eyed from birth — for their woaded wombs open onto a connatural gloom — no he couldn't say he had, properly speaking, but he'd met a man from the Victrix whose statement could be relied upon — and after all it was their sector in the normal run of things. He'd keep up this topic whether you liked it or not — you couldn't choose but hear — sometimes he'd borrow his thrills from Pontus in Asia — then you were cooked. I ask you — what can exceed the tedium of twice-told tales from East of Suez
especially when

they come to the phenomenon of levitation, of the solitary and invisible spear that bolts from the meridian sky every third day, the one amphora of sherbet for a month of Sundays for each half-cohort and

O! Cripes — he's commenced on the camels — their hostility to man, their peculiar aversions and perfections, especially when you

are cornered for a thousand and one nights. I've known him keep up this topic till:

with Linus and Cletus their tongues like files and Marcella poor child yawning and twisting her silken maniple.

But it is inevitable and meet:

while there is breath it's only right to bear immemorial witness.

There were breakings of thin ice I can tell you and incomings to transmute the whole dun envelope of this flesh.

We have seen transfiguration on a plain, swiftly and slowing unsheafing slow like beggar-shifts kings' hand unvest to shed bright reality on dusty precedence.

That's what it was like sometimes — a slow discovering — night by night (the slow days raced)

The night: at night the veils were drawn slowly for you to see the limbs there; it was at night they spangled the clods with stars and lit torches for the humble and meek. It was at night I saw the weedy white [ex-]clerk's caul left at the sap-head and he standing between two armed at all points, and he himself, too, crowned with iron and bearing the weight of it, smiling in the brazier-flare, coming and falling gustily with the down-draft play in the windy place.

You, Bertie, Leslie, 'Waladr, Joe, Griffin, Lambkin, Hob, Malkin, Warwick, Talbot — you Hector, whose arse they couldn't see for dust at the circuit of the wall — the bastards got you in the end.

You will be my witness who knew how the leaden clay could flame, you who saw the second hundred thousand shop-keepers in glistening scape-goat hauberks.

Tilly Vally Mr Pistol that's a pretty tale. La! on my body — tell that, sir, below stairs. Gauffer it well and troupe it fine, pad it out to impressive proportions, grace it from the Ancients. Gee! I do like a bloody lie turned gallantly romantical, fantastical, glossed by the old gang from the foundations of the world. Press every allusion into your Ambrosian racket, ransack the sacred canon and have by heart the sweet Tudor magician gather your sanctions and weave your allegories, roseate your lenses, serve up the bitter dregs in silver-gilt, bless it before and behind and swamp it with baptismal and continual dew
and see:
Gentlemen, I will remove the hat. You will observe the golden lily flowers powdered to drape a million and a half disembowelled yeanlings.
There's a sight for you that is in our genuine European tradition.
Lime-wash over the tar-brush there's a dear — cistern the waters of Camelot to lave your lousy linen. Ploegsteert is Broceliande, these twain indeed are oned.
Here we have the windmill. There you see the advancing hero. The structure is of reinforced concrete, the loop holes are of the best pattern and well disposed so as to afford the maximum sweep of fire, the approaches are secured by a treble belt and his trip-wire is as cunningly staked as only he knows how. It's stockaded and aproned and gabioned and flanked, it's as level as Barking and as bare as your palm and as trapped and decoyed as a Bannockburn frontage for 300 yards from below his glacis. All the fine waters in Headquarters' larder won't raise a mole hill for Lieutenant Fairy on that open plain where he's detailed, in the inscrutable counsels, to make a soldier's fall. He can take thought if he likes from now till zero, he won't add a cubit of cover for himself nor all his franks, not for:
his bosom and intimate china
2nd Lieutenant Jack Smart
not a bush, no brick-bat, not any accidental or advantageous fold, no lie of dead ground the length of a body for his trusted prompter and expert in war: C.S.M. Varro

Nor his second, the paid man of fortune — Sgt. Michael Mary Gabriel Aumerle.[2]

Not a rock to cleft for, not a spare drift of soil for the living pounds of all their poor bodies drowned in the dun sea. For:

Corporal Oliver of No. 1, nor for
Corporal Amis and
Lance Corporal Amile of No. 2 nor for Corporal Balin and his incompatible mess-mate Corporal Snout (there was a marriage and there was a balls-up, they tore No. 3 in a faction again and often).

Nor for Lance Corporal Holt nor his sly, insubordinate, most secret, butty Pte Heath, nor for Lance Corporal Bawdock the laughing leader of No. 4 nor for:

'66 Adam and
'66 Bell

nor for '22 Hilton and '55 Rolle who marched without talking, who 'listed from countrysides unknown to each other but of whom Nosey Tupper said:

Two jokers from one womb, I warrant. Nor for Clym and Clough and Gisbourne and Goodfellow who plucked and roasted the Picardy gander on the evening of the show, behind Neuf Barquin; the appurtenances they consumed with fire, the fire they kindled with seasoned wood, the wood they lifted entire was Mademoiselle Milkducks's privy door (and Christ her rage — her sturdy stubbed thighs her dirty kyrtel raised when she ran for the Redcap). They left no trace but a cinder ring for the dew to avoid — but there's no cover for them either, nor for their grease-lined bellies. Nor for '14 Bullcalf that Armourer Sergeant Brackenbury clinked for asking for two dinners on one plate — poor simple sod, he took the gloss literally, but he knew the official definition in front of the Mill, because of Hauptman Bebba's Parabellum.

Nor for
Goater

---

[2] [Cf. *The Sleeping Lord*, pp. 100–1, for an expanded version of this passage.]

Grover
Bunker and
Cobb
the Jutish heavies who murmured into their bivouac sheets
of narrow tillage and divided inheritance.
Nor yet for
Loddington
Weeden or
Grimsdall
who mouthed inarticulate words at the latter end of the
binge at Fleubaix, of Hycga their tall father, who burned
twelve Welshmen with fire in Pigotts garth and had his
oats in Speen.

These three chair-maker's mates moved lightfoot from
Fricourt to Highwood saying: There's nothing like chalk
to dance on. But there was no help for them either.

Maschinengewehrschütze Balder Helige with his little
gun, got them all three at the tail of his traverse.

Nor for Willy Hall, who left his lambs up spout and got
'pressed in parlour at Burnsall together with Masher Willy
Cawdor.

Nor for '16 Nicholay whose branded arse made him a
jape at M.O.'s inspection, nor for his towny '02 Absolam
who laughed up his cardigan sleeve, who kept for his joy
the Sergeant Carpenter's gentle bird, the popinjay of La
Clytte, three days and three nights in the hay-loft above
Snob Springer's shop and fed her on citron and bully, and
white wine and bread.

A few others were in on this scandal and Lieutenant
Lovelace was suspiciously sore for his elevated and disin-
terested status; and when it all came out Corporal Snook
gave his evidence with a wry look — but the tumult of war
stilled their uncharity.

Wig Muckermann's minnie emptied flame and mingled
steel, like grievous hail, like the wounding towers that
dilapidate death alike on cuckold and goat. So it was with
the popinjay's clients — they all went up together in one
burst before the mill; and the other names inscribed on
that particular packet were:

three poor men
bible-punchers
whose souls are with Jesus
Tom Bradshaw
Skinny Bowditch
Ebenezer Wrench who stept from his gospellers' tub in
Tiggy's Fields to join the East Surreys but was subse-
quently transferred, and with them:
Harry Gill, who wore under his service jacket: his issue
cardigan and another he'd stolen, and two waistcoats above
his issue shirt; and under it a woven vest of lambs wool and
next his greasy skin a body-belt twice-tied (Chitty Tuk-
bacon swore he'd seen the poor sin-bearer shiver over his
steaming skilly in a mid-August trench. And Taffy Prosser
whispered: It takes a powerful spell, man, to work such
unnatural ill on a person's body, and Trelawny his con-
fidant said the platoon would come to no good, but ship-
wreck, with so cursed a hand on board; and God damn such
a shaker said Major Thwaite. Jasus! there's bane some
oppression for sartain said Geraldine Purcell). He was parted
from Bradshaw, Bowditch, and Wrench in middle-air by
the separating arm of a woman, carrying faggots, who leaned
from the moon.

Nor yet was there aid or covering wing, or upright,
or linden-hedge or agger or paraduct or mothering skirt for
a frighted last-born or gunnel from the evil swell; or any-
thing drawn to mask or shadow, or brunt-bearing mound
of salvation, nor any sweet water to check the scent, or any
device to stay a ravening pursuer or conduit or sewer for
a felon's joy or blanket for head for dark imagining in an
evil tower, nor his scutum for your trauma, nor any go-
between nor ballast to jettison to rectify the deadly list on
her, nor cool and immediate dock for nettle in that hedge-
less field, nor any reef to take the outer squall, and what
of His sure mercies that he swore in the ancient days —
where is His tempering for our bare back and sides, where
is provided the escape on that open plain? You'd like a
pavise to tortoise you to move with your mates like a wall
against his liquid pitch or the locked shields that determined
the boundaries of western man — or an hare's form for your

kicking hind legs would be something: The foxes have holes but
Tommy Tucker
'02 Snug
John Plowman
have sweet Fanny Adams when Hieronymus Högemann feeds his Big Willie in Aachen Alley and Rembalt the Galician pulls the string. There will be no failing of fuses or charges on their part.

Iselin, too, with his adjustable sights for his cumbrous weapon grinned through his concrete slit to see:

Dai Meyrick and Madoc Sey searching for a mountain. (For it was the property of these men that they would not walk on the level except by compulsion.)

But there was no help for them either on that open plain.

Iselin it was also who accounted for Langland and Rhymer and Byrde because they looked this way and that for a green lane. For it was the property of these men that they would always walk where grass was. There was no help for them either on that open plain because the virtue of the land was perished and there was not grass but only broken earth and low foliage of iron; and from the tangled spread of the iron hedge hung the garments peculiar to the men of Ireland and their accoutrements, and the limbs and carcasses of the Irish were stretched on the iron bushes because the men of Ireland had made an attempt on the Mill in the autumn of '15 and again in the spring by express command of the G.O.C. in C. so that the Mill was named on English trench-maps: Irish Mill, but on enemy maps it was called Aachen Haus. And as there was no help for the men of Ireland so there was no help for the men of Britain.

Further forward and under his very nose were also bleached rags hanging, and with field-glasses it was possible to discern in those cobwebs the checked cloth of the men of Lower Britain because earlier still the men of Lower Britain had occupied for some hours a drain called after them Jock's Folly. But there had been no help for them either because the configuration of the land was such that it had been the simplest thing in the world for the men in Aachen Haus to dislodge them, and make their ditch quite flat with heavy mortars operating from Aachen Alley and Aachen Support. It was by express command of the G.O.C. in C. that the men of Lower Britain had been sent forward to hold their drain in the early summer of '15 and of whom only three returned and by the same command the men of Ireland had made the attempt in the autumn of the same year and again in the following spring and it was by the same command that Mr Fairy and his men from Upper Britain made their diversion. And three men only returned from this diversion and they were called

Private Lucifer
Private Shenkin
Private Austin

and the reason for their invulnerability was this: Pte Lucifer (Squib Lucifer he was called in his section) was possessed of agility subtlety and lightness so that however so often Hans Iselin screwed up his left eye and however so precise his aim and however so accurate his telescopic sights, and with whatever despatch he co-ordinated his movements Pte Lucifer stood upright under his fire the most beauti-fullest of men laughing like anything, so that there seemed to be added to the properties before mentioned that other, against which not sharp steel nor any chemical discharge is of any avail. It seemed to Hans Iselin and to Balder Helige and to Captain Bebba that Pte Lucifer was possessed of the quality of impassibility. So that afterwards, in their reserve billets, they would often say: How should we contend against spirits. That Tommy was no infantryman but an anointed cherub.

And that is the reason why he was called one of the three who escaped from the diversion before the Mill. And as before he was called Squib Lucifer, so afterwards he was called Pussy Lucifer, because he escaped the ninth death.

And the reason for the invulnerability of Pte Shenkin (Pick-em-up Shenkin he was called by his section) is that he was the least sure-footed of men and the most ungainly and the more easily confused of the men of the Island of Britain, and the most slow to make his extremities do what his stomach or brain desired, and the most forgetful of men, and when he slept no one knew at what hour he would awaken; nevertheless he was possessed of a certain guile and there was in his maladroitness a scheme of self-preservation, and his stumbling often saved him from reaching a disastrous goal. And when he stumbled in the morning it was never certain whether he would regain his feet before sunset (for after sunset, he said, a man can walk with more composure) or if he mislaid his knife or his hold-all or his camp-comforter, it was not certain for how long the parade might be left standing, or the Orderly Sergeants blowing and stamping before he would recover them — for it was his ingrained habit not to move without these articles of kit, unless he were compelled by violence or the express command of Sergeant Varro.

Now it so happened that he stumbled half way over into a shallow crater where his intricate equipment easily entangled itself so as to mesh his floundering limbs in a discarded concertina of wire. Now partly because he had no effective interest in the G.O.C. in C.'s diversion before the Mill, and partly because of his inability to deal with any complicated derangement of things and partly because of his very great and continual fear, he remained as quiet as a rodent in his burrow of salvation and over his drawn-back ears and unseen to his deflected eyes the missiles wove this way and that a steel hatch for him. And once the studded heel of Squib Lucifer darkened his snuggery and he heard, above the noise of the weapons, familiar laughter on the plain.

When it was quite dark and there was no sound at all except of a difficult breathing coming up from the earth, and intermittently the half-cries of those who would call strongly from their several and lonely places, on:
that creature of water, or on
some creature of their own kind by name, as on:
gentle Margaret on
Gwenfrewi, on Ermintrude
on Babs or Belisaunt
on Aunt Birch on
Ned
on George on
greasy Joan

or on those Bright ones to whose particular cults they were dedicate, on God the Father of Heaven because with him there is neither wounding nor unwounding, on God the Word because by him we know the wound and the salve, on God the Life Giver because his workings are never according to plan and because of the balm under his wing, and because by him even the G.O.C. in C.'s diversion before the Mill can shine with the splendour of order, the Sanctifier and lord who is glorious in operation, the dispositioner, the effecter of all transubstantiations, who sets the traverse-wall according to the measure of the angel with the reed, who knows best how to gather his epiklesis from that open plain, who transmutes their cheerless blasphemy into a lover's word, who spoke by Balaam and by Balaam's ass, who spoke also by Sgt Bullock.

On the Lamb because he was slain.

On the Word seen by men because he was familiar with the wounding iron.

On the son of man because he could not carry his cross.

On the Son of Mary because he left his mother.

On Mary because of her secret piercing.

On the Angel in skins because the soldiers asked him a question.

On the key-man, the sword-bearer, because he lied to a nosey girl and warmed his hands at a corporal's brazier.

On the chosen three because they slept at their posts.

On the God of the philosophers who is not in the fire, who yet can illumine the nature of fire.

On Enoch's shining companion who walks by your side like an intimate confederate, who chooses suddenly, so that the bearers look in vain for your body, who takes you alive to be his perpetual friend.

On Abraham's God who conditions his vows, who elects his own, who plucks out by tribe and number, or who adopts by grace.[3]

On the Lord of Noe who contracted with all flesh indifferently.

[3] [The Melchisedec passage occurs here in the published version; cf. *The Sleeping Lord*, pp. 108-9.]

200

On all the devices of the peoples, on all anointed stones, on fertile Goddesses, that covering arbours might spring up on that open plain for poor maimed men to make their couches there.

On her that wept for a wounded palm that she got by a mortal spear — that she might salve a gaping groin that the race might not be without generation.

On the unknown God.

Each calling according to what breasts had fed them — for rite follows matriarchate when you're all but done.

That's why he heard Dai Meyrick make his dolorous anaphora, like the cry of a wounded hare, on Magons and Maponus, because his mother was of the line of Caw of North Britain and her love was beyond the Wall with the men of the north (albeit she sat under her husband in his Moravian Bethel, at Drws-y-Coed-Uchaf in Arfon in the apostasy of the latter days).

Pick-em-up Shenkin could stand this no longer. He found that his wire mesh slipped away from him easily. In his covert he had not been altogether ungraced because of the diverse cries coming up from the earth, and because of the baptism by cowardice which is more terrible than that of water or blood. Remembering the Rocky Mountain goat he leapt from shell-hole to shell-hole (and no one could tell whether he leapt because he feared or feared because he leapt) until he regained the security of the assembly trench. And that is why he is called one of the three who escaped from the diversion before the Mill.

The invulnerability of Pte Austin was by reason of the suffrages of his mother who served God hidden in a suburb, and because of her the sons of the women in that suburb were believed to be spared bodily death at that time, because she was believed to be appointed mediatrix there. And it was urged by some that Mrs Austin conditioned and made acceptable in some roundabout way the tomfoolery of the G.O.C. in C. Anyway it was by reason of her suffrages that Private Austin was called one of the three who escaped from the diversion before Mill.

And as before he was named by his section Ducky Austin, so afterwards he was named Austin the dodger.

But for all the rest there was no help on that open plain.[4]

* * *

Well, Mrs Balaam, how do you do? What a mouthful of counted-blessings for a weave-the-woof prophetess. You're a fine one to turn a golden hem on the drab skirt of 'em, if you try a bit longer you'll be all lining and no cloud and talk of Ambrose and his song and categories of things to praise — you'ld laud a dunghill for the children to gain their tributes from its fetid slopes. You've fair danced a jig for all your informed disillusion.

You would to me a tale unfold of this unhouseled and unchrism'd flesh whose end is bare of sweet reason.

In each slow turning of each fold in the miserable garment of our sorrow you would show a mockery and grim futility, where lice for woven beauties crawl. You would show ape-heads for fair princes when they lift their beavers up, and Geraldine's terrible paps for a sweet queen's embroidered bodice, and leprous wood to crumble in our trusting fists — as illusory as that fungus-barter which Gwydion's magic made (when he effected the rising of the south to obtain for his brother the bed he was after).

You would cry wolf, and portray his loping flanks, his hunched malicious twist, his grinning maw, as though he were conceived outside love's covenant. But look! where he stands to mock your anthropomorphic prejudice, see where he regards you, his grey beauty flaming, his strong pelt praising the Lord of all glistening hair on lion, on fox, on tunnelling badger. See him lurching his glory, see his loose limbs stretched familiar on the predella of the throne, with the nine choirs to stroke him. And hear his grim voice that his erect throat trumpets out among the flock of the elect; see him, the ravager of folds, redeemed and fold-keeper.

And look a trifle lower, my dear: observe our impoverished world of shadows — look from archetype to type and see his mate: humbly she gives her teats, with dignity, in the form of a servant, for our sakes, under the

[4] [The section published in *The Sleeping Lord* ends here.]

202

appearance of bronze, she stands on her pillar to nourish the Western world, her tongue unslaked in the heats of the Capitol.

It always comes down on its feet you know. She's got an uncanny balance on her. Do what you will, half a mill-stone of righteous anger won't keep her under, nor the faith of a moralist remove the mountain of her delectability.

Or she can be lithe, she can insinuate, she can creep in. She creeps and enlarges herself and stands upright. She shakes her comely body before your eyes for all your locks and ward.

You can bolt and draw-to, you can double-blanket and shutter, you can treble-batten within and without — there'll be a breakthrough on you. She'll find a crevice, or make one.

There'll be saxifrage for your flint-face, your spittle will make a trefoil spring for some perishing beast to nibble.

Your constricting venom may stay a blood-flow though your malice sought damage however so strongly.

You don't have to be necessarily aware, you may be actively hostile to the precious influence.

He can make your beggarly store-box a cornucopia for his chosen. Nor does he ask the Abyssinian maid if she would care to please us. Nor coax with rewards the starry shoots on March-bank to tangle for us their fragile varieties. Nor urge with bribes the banded cat to sport on narrow sills for our great wonder.

King's-eye is pierced with winged steel and thegnes grieve to make a woven work for queen's pastime. It would be difficult to speak of a just price here.

He is hardy indeed who would allot praise or blame or judge between maids-toil, and the finished beauty that wins enchantment, gathers worship, holds the minds of men, becomes a word to work powerfully, generates makers' marvels, is a star for us, breaks our contingent misery with the noise of its perfection, day by day wins exaltation for us, deprived in our separate prisons where we painfully seek to maze turns of loss and gain, sort tares from grain, winnow justice and mercy with a shadowy flail in the felt darkness of our threshing house. The moping owl would jest at our complaint (she who boasts wings like an angel), nor does she hoot against the moon because day-labour is denied her.

We make her wisdom's sign. We honour her for Minerva's special pet. Does she overthrow the nature of a sign, because she incarnates the thing signified? She receives into her white fist vermin for her sacrament, nor envies the Eagle's wanton marriage with the sun.

If she were a leveller and preached from her stump or barn-rood she might speak against the rich store of first-fruits and unspotted males of the first year; folds impoverished mewling first-borns snatched from unguarded cradles where they take the air, to garnish and nourish eyrie and eyrie-brood — and all this wide-winged damage done in broad light, and warming to her tale of inequality, she might paint a fine picture of her own meagre pilfering, secured at some hazard in her shadow-world of webbed and tendoned toil against whose fragile membranes stretched the night-gusts play, and moth-touch and dark-fays flit and tumble — all to vanish, flee trembling, to hunch and hang in angle or cranny-corner the instant Madame Eglantyne rings the Angel (and,
mother Hob puts out her mouser and Peter takes on for infamies, done in the dark and
Bugler Perry moists his sour night-lip for the first un-welcome blast and you and I blaspheme where we lie).

If she could choose she might make a fair case against the chancy ways of fowl with fowl.

Her owlish wisdom best sits on her while she knows her place in the fantastic hierarchy, whose only order we can seem to figure out is:
this blood for that life
this pain for that wholeness
moon-toil for this ebb
his skin for her grafting
this million years of sea-wash for that pebble for this gilt for her lily.
You give and I gain. That drought and all dead for

peculiar splendour of this one withered tree to eke-out a half-line for this poet in his poverty.

Peacocks and pelicans in pride and piety for licentiates of divinity to draw Lady Bodkin to heaven on strings of analogy.

Your move and he pays.

Berserk raid of no particular significance for two millenniums of copying clerks to redact and gloss a long song for your heart's joy, and a long imposition for Maisie Potter.

A schism and a division and a sociological drift — a donkey's hind leg for masters and doctors.

For me and for you a split inheritance.

Torment by fire and water and devices of iron for prayer-wallahs.

No trouble for the vicar of Croydon.

A fire lit by candle-light for the flesh that houses a true conscience.

Grace abounding for tinkers in dens.

Gain for contractors in lead.

A silver-gilt cup and melted dish for Jack Horner.

The dedicated paraphernalia and the good earth for all the Lords of the Council.

The maculate womb of a soiled font for *Ranter* and *Ringwood* and a sacring-bell for cow *Crombeck*.

The needle's work re-sewn and apparels contrived to caparison a Faery Queen.

For all God's children a consummate prose-style.

And for you, dear reader, a birthday gift of *Lycidas* and sonnets 55, 106, and 130, and so much more besides.

For John Wesley a horse and the opium of the word.

For Emma a wooden wall.

A dark continent for the Unforgettable Salutation.

A green hill and no wall for Chinese Gordon.

For Britannia a fork and a classical hat and a ride on a lion, over seven aquatic hills.

Whichever way you take it, her black's his white — You have to be agile to trace the fleet-foot doubling Influence. The tare is wheat within your pruning fingers. In the twinkling of an eye the leaden echo wakes for shepherds and bar-tenders the

Song: Sela.

Who shall say the measure, and the price? It is extremely difficult to determine if we could have had that store unlocked in praise of lip and eye and brow, known dark companions, sung both high and low, laughed for the very artifice the strict discovering sonnet yields, line by line. Been bound with Amaryllis in the gay woof this lyric weaves to rapture us. Marvelled for her sign set in the sea, and yet not lost beauty's best: the paps that rejoiced the Eternal Son.

Comus is worth a masque — yet that salvific mummery they used day by day (make ditcher's son and Colin Clout parrot their holy rigmaroles or carol:

nay, ivy, nay,
or on her special day
sing
Levedy quene of Paradys
Electa
mayde milde, moder es effecta)

masqued more the delight and depth for us, staged the happy fault, could sing about the Golden Tree, more than blind makers tell in cool translucent numbers.

It seems a little hard our frailty should use us, that if we say: Here is white Iope, let us bind on Eliza her cremosin coronet, lend to blithe Helen permanent marvel by words artfully contrived, or make *Epithalamion* too swell a job, we turn to find Her gone whose types and shadows we served so straitly.

But heap the parti-coloured hedge-yield, weave for hair-twine and for bright limbs bind stars of the field. Compare this fair with that delight, sing a song of journey's-end, extend your praise to the turning worm, take Jack-a-lantern for your nimble star, skip with elfin-sprites by rills and with melodious birds sing of the foison and the sowing. Make harmony your friend and let her witch you with the jocund sights she can discover. She knows where secreted, beneath her sister's mantle. She'll draw back this broidery and you'll agree the mystery is amiably tabernacled. She'll show you deftly God should be pleased with his latest artistry.

You'll be out of grace not to praise waters-meet and the meadows you see between and
buried cunningly
the spines for your green fingers; and the cherry ripe to snap at you; and that shrew, quince, that looks so honey

The worst of it is you want all the Egyptian cakes with all the manna of the exodus for all your sore Anabasis all the time. You would have the silver on the white, and bakers' marvels tier on tier — and yet have the bride with her little knife destroy the sacrifice.

(Rubric: And afterwards she dispenses this fortunate bread first to the elders and to the rest in order and X Y Z and Ampersand all want a piece in hand. Then all depart, and Doris weaves dreams with hers, and chooses Captain Broke
and so it goes on.)

*   *   *

I've known him cut a square stone in Harrogate for the South Wall — for the fifth layer — to shine like the Sardonyx. Others he quarries in Tooting Bec. They say the long fault running: Penge, Norwood, Coulsdon gives him Chalcedony — every now and then. The Zone is his great problem — you can't say much about the Zone. We all know the Zone we all weep in the Zone. It's a great crust runs there about, they beat his messengers in the Zone. It never distils a balmy shower on the heath. He's naked in the Zone. You would perhaps have a good case in the Zone. If you went to the Zone to curse you might manage it. He's unashamed in the Zone. It's always 3 p.m. on the heath, you are always in civvies walking the tired tracks between the cigarette cards, there are discarded contraceptives to drape the fern roots on the heath, the viper's dry belly draws out between the torn late-pass and the Odeon counterfoil, two one and threepennies Block D — that's for bread and circuses and that's for a lot of fun. These trophies of innocent recreation are surely pleasant discoveries to any humane person on the blasted heath. All

207

drill and no relaxation never did any body of men any good. It's true they went too far in Syria and with wise foresight the Divine Pontiff docked the hot baths — but it can hardly be said that our lads are in danger of effeminate tendencies. It makes your bosom swell with proper pride to think of the tempered discipline practised by those who will some day be called up to defend our beautiful country. The Zone is a prepared womb from which they spring, fully conditioned for such a task.

All the doors are shut in the Zone.

All roads intersect in the Zone.

They've swept and garnished the Zone.

It's been a long job for him but he's won.

He's emptied the Zone of Being by an incredibly complicated process. He's found a common denominator for all his devices on the heath. You can hear their teeth clatter against the dark stones he rations them for bread.

They never complain in the Zone.

When their teeth break on the dark stone they say to themselves: We're the boys of the bulldog breed. This is the price of our freedom. We can take it, you can't have jam on everything, there is a price to our enlightenment. After all it's the twentieth century.

O they don't know it's the Zone.

They're as mercifully conditioned as a limbo child.

Yes, some of them no doubt do — yes but there's a lot they can praise and anyway they know it's necessary to the defence of the realm — it's obvious you can't have National Parks everywhere — you must have the works somewhere. We can't all indulge our fine feelings — and think of other nations — they have Zones — there are a lot of Zones up and down Europe — you must have Zones you know. I don't say they are — but I only know this Zone and that's the bugger I'm going to talk about.

But everybody knows that Hampshire is a beautiful district, you can't deny that.

There's a lot of sky, too, of a sort, over the heath. It's a grand place for a healthy young man, it's a far finer and fuller life anyway than being cooped up like the old monks.

I always said there were worse places than the heath — you'll be glad of the heath when the show starts. I admire the way they cheerfully go about their duties. It is the Zone mind that will save us when the time comes, you mark my words. I'm sure it's a pleasure to see their tanned faces and smart deportment — sometimes you see groups of them recreating themselves, having one on each other in the hollow saloons under the lights without shadow.

There is no shadow no shade, no shade to caress, no walls on the heath, no recession; it's all on one plane in the Zone. The durofix plug for the proprietary print of a fine Highland Scottish and soda in trews casts no gradated shade on the bald partition. The Air Arm leans from a functional stool. There is no nonsensical upholstery to the furniture of the heath and quite right too. Let us have the best a streamlined sensibility, modified by the exigencies of the market, can provide in bulk. Art and Industry have kissed each other on the heath. On the heath you can see a free democracy preparing to defend itself. You can examine in detail the component parts of our society and the general level of our culture.

On the heath the issue is apparent.

There you have nature as she presents herself in South England and put down quite frankly on this scrub and undulation the unselfconscious works of early twentieth century European official and domestic construction. On the heath the habitations of Peace and War are discovered and show how they naturally erect themselves when freed from love's constraint. It's a sod in the Zone.

O Mrs Balaam if you want a long thirst to quench after a long burden of prophecy — go to the Zone, you won't be troubled by the sweet influence in the Zone.

Pilkem heath seems fragrant to the memory: her disarray is lovely with the urgent squalor of union — the terrible devastations sing: it would be difficult to think meanly of King Pellam's Launde. But what shall we say of this place?

I said: Ah, what shall I write. I enquired up and down. (He's tricked me before with his manifold lurking places.) I looked for his symbol at the door, I have looked for a long while at the textures and contours. I have run a finger over the trivial intersections and felt with the hand under and between. I have journeyed among the dead forms causation projects from pillar to pylon. I have tired the eyes of the mind regarding the colours and lights.

I have felt for his wounds in nozzles and containers. I have wondered for the automatic diversions that rattle for a dropped coin when she calls for another, when he suggests a soft water. I have tested the inane patterns without prejudice, for it is easy to be blinded by pre-conceived opinions. It is easy to miss him at the turn of a civilization. I have been on my guard not to condemn the unfamiliar. I have refused the tests of theorists who come with manuals. I have opened my heart to sterility when she said: Ain't I nice with me functional flanks — the sockets of my joints go free of your handiworked frills: you can, given the equation, duplicate me any number of times. I'm very clean very good. All the merchants adore me. I'm bought and sold in the whole earth.

There's no trouble, sir, you just turn it so — or so — the light goes up at the ace of clubs — very well thought out isn't it and inexpensive.

We have them of course in Dominion buck with a nailbrush and pull-through and a cast-horoscope, and a list of the Popes of Rome — That runs at a higher figure of course.

O yes our agents follow the Eagles. I don't think that you will have any real difficulty, but in that case I advise our other model ask for *The Odalisque* it's identical with our occidental pattern but sheafed in frosted Caucasian cellophane that no type of arachnida can penetrate nor great heats dissolve.

You can hold it in your hand
You can tie it in a knot
You can swing it to and fro
You can put it into reverse
You can be sure of spun buck, sir, you can't improve on our spun buck, my love.

It is most convenient most adjustable most reliable you see how pliable.

210

It will lie flat in his slicer
You can't do better
Can't we send it sir, to
any address
to cottage or hall
to any shire or commote
across the sleeve or over
blue water.

I have watched the wheels go round in case I might see
the living creatures like the appearance of lamps in case
I might see the Living God projected from the machine.
I have said to the perfected steel: Be my sister, and to the
glassy towers: Bend your beauty to my desire. Indeed for
the glassy towers I thought I felt some beginning of his
creature. But my hands found the glazed-work unrefined
and the terrible crystal a stage paste if you presume to come
to a lover's length of her, no love on nearer acquaintance.

I have howled at the foot of the glass tower. I took
hold of her glistening rods and travailed for her adamant
surfaces.

COMMENTARY

by René Hague

These notes were not intended for publication; they have been assembled from letters and memoranda prepared by R.H. at various stages in the editing and transcribing of David's MSS, and from a running commentary — addressed for the most part to himself — which he wrote as he typed, often several times over, the versions of the poems now published. The notes are printed here in their original form, not only because they illuminate many difficulties in the poems (particularly in those texts for which David himself left no notes), but also because they display R.H.'s great learning and wit as well as his incomparable familiarity with all of David's work.

THE ROMAN QUARRY

Excerpt from a letter of 1 January 1976 to H.J.G.·

'The Roman Quarry': here's a typed copy. I have this time followed the MS line by line, which makes it more convenient if you want to check the typescript with the original: but that the line-arrangement of the MS is not an indication of the way in which David wished the poem to be printed is shown by a comparison of the MS with those parts of it which were printed in *The Sleeping Lord* — 'The Tribune's Visitation' in particular. David was, to my mind, odd and mistaken in the importance he attached to typographic arrangement on the page. He took a good deal of pains over this, and I believe it was wasted on the reader, because printing has not the flexibility he needed.

On the other hand, the short lines he used when writing his MSS seem to me most effective, and a great aid to the reader; and this because the writing (in the literary, not the literal sense) is so close and packed that it is well to have it in short bursts. It makes it much easier to follow, and I believe, too, that it makes it easier to follow the flow of David's thought. Unconsciously, too, his line-arrangement in the MS seems to be dictated by the way in which thoughts occurred to him. It may, of course, be mere coincidence, but it often appears to me that he starts a new line at just the right place — and by no means always because he had reached the edge of the paper; it is surprising, for example, how often a line ends with the definite article 'the', and then the next line, which contains the noun or adjective, comes in with particular force.

This may well be a difficulty for printer and publisher, because it makes every passage that much longer.

I first thought of this piece as 'The Roman Quarry' because it contains so much that re-appears in *The Sleeping Lord,* where a number of Roman pieces are collected. As I went on with the typing I thought Oh Hell this is a Welsh Quarry: we're down in this blasted Pliocene (if that's the word) grit-stone, old red sandstone etc. — I must get Ann Ross's (I think it's Ann) *Pagan Celtic Britain* and T. Gwynne Jones's *Welsh Folk-lore.* But in point of fact, as I went on, I began to see that the whole thing is Roman or rather Romano-Christian. The real point is to bring the pre-Roman, pre-Aryan indeed, myth and religion into line with what we already accept as a foreshadowing of the Christian, through the medium of Rome. It is very cleverly managed by the poet, as a quick summary of the contents shows.

It is comparatively simple piece; that is to say it is easy to follow, even if you need to have read much the same sort of books as D. — and there's no great problem there — and to know or know where to find out about Celtic heroes, gods and myths. Moreover D. himself provides a good deal of annotation. The later, in fact, D.'s writing, the simpler: as a comparison of *The Anathemata* with *The Sleeping Lord* makes evident.

We have a great advantage in 'The Roman Quarry' that we have both a beginning and an end — and practically all that comes in between (there are, unfortunately, 10½ pages missing, one or two of them at places where they are badly missed), but on the whole we have a complete piece: and this in spite of the fact that it purports to be 'Sections VIII–XII' — what sections I to VII were we can only guess; but this hardly matters, for it is becoming increasingly obvious that everything David wrote from the time of and after *The Anathemata* was intended as part of a vast poem which he was never able to put together. The theme of it would have been the same as that of *The Anathemata,* the building up of man's development to his adoption into kinship with Christ in godhead (my theological expression may be a little shaky) in the historical facts of the birth of Christ, his sacrifice in the Upper Room and on Calvary, and the inclusion in that metamorphosis, by pre-application or by retroactive application, of all that has been most precious to men of all times and cultures. It is for this reason that the Mass is central in all this writing. Any mention of the Mass suggests to the poet the circumstances of the sacrifice on Calvary, the Roman administration of Palestine, the extension of Roman imperialism — and commercialism — and the rule of the Roman financier: and similarly any mention of those brings to his mind Calvary and the Mass — with the result, as we have seen before, that at any particular point in his writing the number of alternatives open to him was so great that he had great difficulty in, as you say, organizing the work.

In this MS, for example, we open with the Roman trumpet, and in one of the attempts at continuing *The Kensington Mass* the crowing of the cock suggests to the poet precisely this blare of the bugle. In that case, in fact, he chose a different alternative — the battered condition of the penthouse roof, how Peter's old mother-in-law could have made a better job of mending it — how he had seen men unloading timber (suggested by references to 'spars', 'baulks', etc.) — how one of the men was a *Celt*: and so we're off again. Here we have it the other way round — the Roman bugler is a Celt, and so we can slide into a consideration of the illusive world of the Celt and the factual world of the Roman. And then each of the various roads has any number of bifurcations — the Celt suggests Galatia, and that suggests 'Drunemeton' (oak-grove) and that suggests the Golden Bough, mistletoe, and that golden-haired Absalom, and that Absalom's tomb across the brook Kedron, and so we are back at the time and scene of the Passion...

From a letter of 31 July 1980:

I think I should copy again and draw your attention to a duplicate of the opening page ('There she blows' etc.) [p. 1]. This is marked, as its fellow, '58' at the head and '1' at top right. But it starts off with the following passage in pencil, marked at the side 'N.B. Keep':

They say he is himself both sign and

thing signified.
They say he can raise a gale o' wind and
   still one.
They say no tree can hang him but
   a cabbage tree.*
They say he put a spell in his fierce anger on all trees, because
no tree bears, no grass and no fruit nor in the waters no
fish in urbes throughout orbis.

space — few lines

I left this because 'There she blows' is so good a start: also
because I felt that these were rather a dauntingly theological
opening — with the technicality of the question 'How can some-
thing be both the sign and the thing signified?' — I've written
about that elsewhere, I think — the thing signified, in this
unique case of such an apparent absurdity, being the mystical
body, signified by and identical with the consecrated bread
which is the sign. Moreover, it's a phrase picked up and mis-
used by expounders of D.J.

Might it make an epigraph to the whole book? And it might
be worked to have that page — what's the perishing number
— 56, which starts 'Should ever the men of rule' [p. 43] (where
the reference is again to the mystical body) as a conclusion?
That would mean putting it at the end of 'The Tribune's
Visitation' [p. 58], where the Tribune offers a spurious mystical
body.

p. 43
Should ever the men of rule... This is to me the most im-
   portant passage in this MS so far, and one of the most im-
   portant in David's work.

It is true that we lack the preceding pages, but it is not
difficult to guess what they would have contained, for they
obviously must have re-introduced the 'men of rule', Rome
and their contrast with the 'masters of the covenant', i.e. the
Church which lives by the new covenant sealed by Christ.
We started this MS with Rome, in a Roman guardroom; and

---

* D. wrote a note about 'cabbage tree' which we do not have. Someone
told me the point, but I've lost it.

this led into a discussion of those who live on the borders of the empire; so to Celtic feeling for illusion, fostered by the climate: 'From infancy they feed on illusion — the very elements refract their thoughts' [p. 5]; and the poet develops the theme that as 'myth' (in his sense of the word) is more real than 'fact', more proper to man as a maker rather than a calculator or technician, so 'illusion' is more real than factual assessment and measurement, and the fostering of kindly, localized 'tutelars', of the individual and 'demarcated' is more acceptable than the uniform, standardized and universal. (This is a theme treated more than once in *The Sleeping Lord*, particularly in 'The Tutelar of the Place' and in part of 'The Tribune's Visitation'.) It is presented again, with great force, in the 'Keel, Ram, Stauros' section of *The Anathemata*: there the Ram (taken from the Book of Daniel, 8), used elsewhere, too, as a symbol of Rome (as Daniel used it of the Persians), is, with David's entrancing felicity, given even more appropriateness by being attached to the Roman siege artillery: so that there is an immensely powerful contrast between the two made things which share the same material, so dear to the poet — solid timber — the ship, and the battering ram, or catapult.

At the same time, the other central theme of David's work, the factual historicity of the redemption and the offering of the liberating sacrifice in one place, by one victim, at one particular point of time — and the universality of the body which was brought into being by that sacrifice and the completion of the sacrifice in the Resurrection — had to be reconciled with the love of the 'particular and differentiated'. Here the answer is given. So far from reducing all things to a common level, as the 'men with the groma' seek to do, the 'Lar' 'named of all names and master of them in very flesh', becomes 'lord of each locality'. So the individual is preserved in the universal, the one in the many, through the fact of the mystical body: and not as a philosophical concept, not 'where men of mind clamber the steep concepts'.

The Rome that the poet loves, the 'Roma caput orbis, splendor, spes, aurea Roma', is not imperial Rome, nor even the early Republic, but Christian Rome which held on through the Dark Ages.

UNDER ARCTURUS

From a letter of February 1976:
Two things are immediately apparent about this piece: that chronologically it is very late, and that, as a stage in composition, it is early.

The lateness of the date is suggested by the handwriting, which is much smaller than that of earlier MSS and letters, made with a black ball-point, legible — though at times with some difficulty — but not so legible as earlier work, and very like the writing in his letters during the last years he spent in *hac lacrimarum valle...* And this lateness in date is, most happily, confirmed by a little sum which David works out near the end [p. 83], where he tries to determine what year A.D. 1971 is in years from the foundation of Rome — he nearly gets it right, but spoils it at the last moment. Anyway, it is, I think, conclusive proof that that sheet was written in 1971. I should have said also that the pattern of the writing on the page is typical of his later letters — a blunt-ended wedge, with the wide end at the head of the page (but a good deal over to the right-hand side of the paper), narrowing down to the right-hand bottom corner.

As for the earliness in stage of composition, this is clearly shown by the hastiness of the handwriting, often very much of a scribble, by slips of the pen, sentences that are incomplete or change their construction, and by the great but at times uncontrolled fluency of the writing. On the other hand, it would not have taken David, I believe, so much work had he decided to finish it; and this because the theme and the way in which it is treated is so much simpler than that of *The Anathemata*. It is, in fact, very straightforward, the most straightforward and simplest of the four main MSS ('The Book of Balaam's Ass', 'The Old Quarry', 'The Roman Quarry', and this 'Arcturus').

The way in which the piece originated is typical of David's way of working. We start in the middle of a sentence taken from the printed part (in *The Sleeping Lord*) of 'Balaam's Ass'. I suspect that when D. was looking at 'Balaam' in order to polish a section of it for *The S.L.*, the notion of a Roman legionary called Nodens and his tales about the Picts and the darkness and mists of Scotland, of Lower Britain as he called it, suggested the exploration of the avenue that was thus opened. And once started, new ideas came pouring out. This involved him in his 'blanket-stitch' technique; he writes a passage, and immediately an embroidering of that passage or something new prompted by it proves irresistible; he then goes back, rewrites the passage with alterations and additions, and repeats the process several times; so that progress is made, but always by an initial retracing of his steps. The general effect can be confusing, but it is not at all difficult to follow the main thread.

Although we start in the middle of a sentence, it is a perfectly reasonable start: some Roman legionaries are talking together. The place is not indicated, but I have the feeling that it might be a garrison town anywhere in the empire. The time must be somewhere in the third century A.D. It is after the abandonment of the Antonine Wall from Forth to Clyde (which was around the beginning of the third century) but one of the speakers (Crixus) speaks of serving at Dumbarton; and Britain is already under pressure not only from the Picts and Irish but from Saxons.

The speaker tells us how Nodens (an 'emeritus', time-expired man, reservist, maybe, called up again) describes the perpetual darkness of Caledonia, and the speaker says what nonsense such talk is; that he has served up there and, on the contrary, it often has much more daylight than southern latitudes. He explains this, and goes on to describe the country of Britain in general. He then puts forward a theory of what may happen when the pressure grows greater, when our empire is not 'declined but fallen' (i.e. after Rome's withdrawal in 410), and how a leader such as Arthur might arise, and hold things together for half a century or so; how he would ultimately fall and give rise to a myth; and how in later years, in what we would call the early Middle Age, that myth will be expanded.

This allows David to work out an ingenious variation on his theme of the contrast between the 'utile' and the 'gratuitous', myth and fact. This hypothetical Artorius's work will be 'inutile' but the very failure will create the myth and so allow the 'splendour of the extra-utile' to shine out [p. 70]. This is a most interesting comment on what D. has written more than once about 'myth' in general, Arthur in particular, and the greater realness of the poetic as against the factual. Here I am inclined to feel rather as Huck Finn felt about the Bible. I can't unfortunately remember the precise words, but when asked what he had thought of the Bible he said words to the effect that he had found in it 'some interesting statements — but tall'. David is perfectly right: but you have to be quite sure that you are at one with him in his use of words, and what he says is open to misrepresentation ...

Crixus's intervention is a digression, because Nodens insists on being heard, and so we get down to the real heart of the piece. Nodens starts to tell of an attack on Vercovicium (Housesteads) when he was stationed there. This is very graphic, very realistic, written in that combination of the conversational or colloquial and almost-but-not-quite self-consciously poetical which is peculiar to David. A first assault, in the course of which the General in command is killed, is beaten off: but a much more serious attack is threatening, and when the Senior Centurion takes over the reader is really anxious to know what steps he is going to take (for the General, we are told, has made arrangements against such an event) — and then, just when you want more, the piece ends. I have omitted a couple of by-roads down which David travels — a strongly argued poetic plea for the attachment of Celtic mythology, through Arthur, Artorius, Arctio (a Gaulish goddess), Arcturus (Bearwarden), D.'s 'Bear of the Island', to classical and Christian myth; and a similar connection of the Roman General (through his British wife and his death on behalf of the people) ...

What I am most anxious to do now is to go through the pages and stitch together a continuous version. This will not be difficult, I think, but it calls for some ruthlessness, for when you select one of a number of versions you necessarily sacrifice something you would like to keep. You may, again, wish to keep something which you are forced to omit because it turns out to be a *cul-de-sac*.

It will be an unfinished fragment, of course, but a completed one as far as it goes; and I'm most interested to see how it turns out.

Hadrian's Wall and the country north of it had a special fascination for David: being, I suppose, the one border (or *limes,* as he'd say) of the empire that he knew from staying in Northumberland. You will remember that the long hours of darkness, the mists and the haze of sea meeting mountain and estuary, come into both the Quarry MSS, and in those — I forget which at the moment, perhaps in both — he develops the idea of the connection between the Celtic love of myth and the deceptive illusive contours of their country.

Very much in my mind, too, is ... the matching-up, so to speak, of paintings and the themes in David's writing that correspond to them. I'm familiar only with the most obvious ones: the *Tristan and Iseult* pictures, the *Morte Darthur* ones, *A Latere dextro,* the *Wolf of the West,* ones like (let's see if I can spell it this time) *Manawyddan's Glass Door* (Celtic illusion). — However, that's a different, and a tricky, story ...

Most of the following notes, more detailed than any others left by R.H., were made for a reader puzzled by certain place-names and allusions in the TS of 'Under Arcturus':

p. 64

Emeritus: a man who has served his full time in the army and has been discharged. This man must have signed on again.

Nodens: D. uses the name, I think, to indicate that this man is a Briton. Nodens is the name of a Celtic god, to whom there was a big shrine at Lydney in Glos.

2nd Adjutrix: the Second Legion, raised in the provinces, as we might say 'auxiliary' or 'territorial' as opposed to regular;

or better, like Indian army regiments, Gurkhas, East African Rifles, etc.

Ultimate Province: i.e. Lower Britain — what we would be more inclined, looking at the map, to call Upper (i.e. North) Britain. The reference here is to the part of Britain north of Hadrian's Wall, which ran from South Shields to the Solway Firth.

Vercovicium: Housesteads, some 30 miles east of Newcastle, on the Wall, where a big Roman camp has been excavated.

Votodini (also spelt Otodini, Otadini, Botodini, etc.): those who inhabited the country north of the Wall, in S.E. Scotland, with their centre at Edinburgh (Celts). They are the Goddodin of Welsh literature, who appear in *I.P.*

Phoebus ... quadriga: the sun, in his four-horsed chariot.

leaden Cronos: the dark grey ocean. D. makes use of the legend according to which Cronos (the Roman Saturn) after being supplanted by his son Zeus (Roman Jupiter) lived in an island near Britain, at the end of the known world; he accordingly often speaks of the outer ocean as Cronos.

Bodotria Aestuarium: Forth Estuary, the Firth of Forth.

Arctophylax: also Arcturus, or Arktouros: the constellation we now call Boötes (the Ploughman), using 'Arcturus' for its brightest star. The Greeks called it Arktophylax, the watcher of the bear (*arktos*, bear: *phylax*, guard). The further north you go, the higher Arcturus is in the sky, so that the high northern latitudes may be called 'under Arcturus'. Arktouros, latinized as Arcturus, means the same as Arktophylax (*ouros* = guard).

the Strider: Mars, known as 'Gradivus'. Gradus = pace. That 'gradivus' = striding is rocky etymologically, but D. believes in the Snark (I think?)* maxim, 'What I tell you three times is true.'

passus: the Roman pace, 1,000 to the mile (5,000 feet).

* The Bellman, in fact, in *The Hunting of the Snark*!

caligae: soldiers' boots (singular, *caliga*).

Mythras (more correctly Mithras): Oriental sun-god, whose worship was popular in the empire. There is an altar to him at Housesteads.

milia: thousand paces, mile.

acies ordinata: ordered line of battle.

p. 65

milliarium: milestone.

viae: roads (singular, *via*).

limes: frontier. Here the wall, built by Lollius Urbicus, governor under the emperor Antoninus Pius A.D. i39–42, from Forth to Clyde, abandoned some fifty or sixty years later.

manes: spirits of the dead.

Eboracum: York.

p. 66

Quercus: oak.

Fraxinus: ash.

agger: mound; here the central, cambered part of the Roman road.

ulmus: elm.

frangit per medium: he breaks it through the middle. A Davidic slanting of the language, introducing the rubric which instructs the priest to break the host in half.

optiones: assistant centurions (singular, *optio*).

the Bear of the Island: as you will see later, he is looking forward to the application of the title to Arthur.

De Rerum Natura: on the nature of things — the long poem by Lucretius, about 99–55 B.C. (a little before Vergil), in which he seeks to explain the universe as entirely material.

defected oracles: this, I take it, is an ingenious Davidic twist, borrowing Plutarch's title *De defectu oraculorum* (which attributes the fall in population to the decline of oracles) as one more brick in the myth v. fact structure. What is in the speaker's mind is an odd little piece of dialectic: i.e. the Roman order and uniformity irons out the local, particular, respect for numina associated with one place or people (as with oracular centres) and thereby weakens the resistance, based on spiritual vigour, to pressure from outside. What a master of symbol, in the original sense of sum-bolon, the two halves of a token, which serve for recognition and to guarantee the authenticity of the person who produces the half that matches the half retained by the giver — in this case the reader and the poet.

comes: companion (of the emperor), so delegate commander or governor: later, count.

quondam lux, luxque futura: once light and light to be: a version of what was said to be on Arthur's tomb, *Rex quondam, rexque futurus* — once king, and again to return as king. (The idea of a Roman looking forward to Arthur and, what is more, looking forward to a 'cooking-up' — by Geoffrey of Monmouth, I presume — of a *rexque futurus,* I find brilliant. It so cleverly slides Rome through Arthur into Christianity and the restoration of an order which is not merely Roman but cosmic.)

Lower Britain: the northern part (as above).

Petra Clota: the Clota or Clyde rock, the Rock of Dumbarton, at the head of the firth of Clyde.

Gallia Lugdunensis: one of the three divisions of Roman Gaul or France, from the north-west (Brittany) to the Loire, the present Belgian border, and south to its capital, Lyons (Lugdunum).

Marmor: Mars.

adjutrix: here an adjective, meaning 'helper'.

Lupercalia: the annual festival at Rome in honour of Pan (Lupercus — interpreted as 'wolf-god', and so celebrating the she-wolf's care for the twins Romulus and Remus).

Rhea Silvia: daughter of an early king of Alba Longa (before Rome was built), dedicated as a Vestal virgin. She was raped by Mars, and bore the twins Romulus and Remus. They were thrown into the river Tiber, adopted and suckled by a she-wolf, and later found by a shepherd; grew up, overthrew the wicked uncle who had tried to drown them, and laid the foundations of the new city of Rome. In the course of this they quarrelled, and Romulus killed Remus.

Clio: the muse of history.

Lethe: the river in the underworld from which souls drank (and thereby lost all memory) before returning to this world.

dux bellorum: literally, leader of wars: military commander.

Scotti: the name by which the ancients knew the Irish.

Cumaean Sibyl: the priestess of Apollo at Cumae, near Naples, who was consulted as a prophetess or seer.

Ten Towns: the Decapolis, the part of Palestine which straddles the Jordan south-east of Galilee.

chrism'd Daphnis: i.e. David, the shepherd boy who was anointed as king.

Foundation of the City: B.C. 753.

oppidum: fortified town.

ter-nox ... Hercules ... Alcmena: an example of David's magpie-work. 'Ter-nox' (a word that occurs but once) refers to the night on which Zeus visited Alkmene, during the absence of her husband Amphitryon; he extended the night to three nights in duration. The husband returned later in that ter-nox and Alkmene bore twins, one of which was Hercules (son of Zeus) and the other Iphikles.

p. 73

terribili sonitu ... taratantara: from the old Latin poet Ennius' line, *At tuba terribili sonitu taratantara dixit* (But with a fearsome sound the trumpet said taratantara).

bucinators: trumpeters.

Silurian: south Welshman; the Silures lived in south-eastern Wales.

p. 74

Isca: Caerleon.

Glevum: Gloucester.

Dunsinane: Macbeth's castle, attacked by men carrying boughs from Birnam Wood as camouflage; Macbeth had been told that his castle would not fall until Birnam Wood came to Dunsinane. (An interesting parallel to what David quotes from *King Lear* on the title-page of *The Anathemata*. In each case the poet allows the speaker to look forward to something which the poet and the reader know but the speaker can only know by attributing this particular foreseeing to him.)

libra: balance.

cleddyf fawr: great sword (Scottish claymore).

p. 75

statera: scale or balance. (But I don't follow D.'s reading of the Brennus story (Livy V. 48). The Romans complained that the weights the Gauls were using were over the standard weight. Brennus, with 'Vae victis', tossed his sword into the scales — though surely not on top of the gold, but, as an added insult and injury, on top of the weights? And I don't

228

think, Dai, that we can accept the comparison with the *statera* on which man's ransom was weighed on Calvary: that seems to me rather steep.)

felid: bard.

Desi of Iwerddon: Desi were Pads in S.E. Ireland (Welsh Iwerddon).

Octapitarum Promontorium: St David's Head.

Venta: Caerwent, Mon.

p. 76

paludamentum: General Officer's scarlet cloak.

p. 77

Creiddylad: the same name as Cordelia.

Dalriada: the north-eastern part of Ireland.

pallia: cloaks (singular, *pallium*), but the word was not used of military cloaks.

p. 78

via quintana: ran through the middle of the troops' quarters in the camp.

p. 79

pexa: nap.

Onager: (lit. wild ass — from the machine's kick), catapult, launching a sling of stones.

p. 80

Uriconium: Wroxeter.

Varae: St Asaph.

Deceangli: living in N. Wales, around St Asaph.

Segontium: Caernarvon.

p. 81
primus pilus prior: the senior of the 60 centurions in a legion.

(It's difficult to express Roman military ranks in English terms. The centurions of the first cohort — and a cohort must have been something like a battalion — must have been of the same standing as a Lieutenant-Colonel, and yet there's something N.C.O.ish about them, and still more about their *optiones,* in D.'s writing.)

sacramentum: military oath of allegiance.

p. 82

primi ordines: senior ranks of centurions.

p. 83

manipular strength: the maniple was a subdivision of the centuria, something like a company.

THE D.J. MASS SEQUENCES [Part II]

From a memorandum of 20 June 1979:

After devoting much thought to this confusing matter, and after writing many pages only to destroy them because I was adding to the confusion, I have come to see that I must remember what J.-B. Reeves would so often say (some of my friends will remember, and can even imitate, his accent and intonation) — Let us proceed from the known to the unknown.

To begin, then, with the known. What MS and printed material have we?

We have but one printed piece to record: *The Kensington Mass*, printed in the *Agenda* David Jones special issue, Autumn–Winter 1973–4, and again, with an attempt at a 'continuation', in the Agenda Edition *K.M.* of 1975. D. himself described this as 'an entirely new version of a fragment he first drafted *c.* 1940 but subsequently lost' (Editor's Note, approved by D., in the D.J. special issue). D. was certainly working on this in 1973, although it would be a mistake to think of it as 'the unfinished draft of a poem which David Jones started to write in 1973' (even if D. used those words himself). That would be true only if we took 'which' to refer not to 'poem' but to 'draft'; in other words, D. had been engaged on the poem for many years, and what was printed was one more attempt to finish a new draft. The draft ends with the first line of what was to be a continuation, of which more will be said later in this memorandum.

Turning now to the MSS, they may be listed as follows:

(1) D.'s 'fair copy' of the BBC [Grail] Mass: 7 sheets (f'cap),* clearly written in pencil (except for page 1, which is in red biro). This is headed:

(7 sheets)   *The Mass*   (c. 10 mins)

Note that on the back of the last sheet of this MS D. has pencilled 'Jerusalem in the first cent. A.D.' — a link with 'The Roman Quarry' and 'The Old Quarry'.

(2) The BBC script, obviously made from (1) above. This is not strictly a MS, for it is typed and duplicated, but it contains a number of corrections or changes made by D., and so far as I know it is the only copy in existence. 4 pages of script, but we have 5 sheets because we have two copies of page 3. We also have the folded sheet into which David has roughly sewn or stuck the script... From that wrapper I quote: 'Note. An original version was made round about 1945' ('in 1958' has been crossed out) 'altered in 1958 and that printed here is a revised, corrected and somewhat altered version made in January 1965.'

This shows, I think, that in this script and the fair copy we have the Mass that David (through the editor) speaks of as lost in the note attached to the *Agenda* D.J. issue and the Agenda Editions booklet. 'Round about 1945' fits in with a date we shall later (when we discuss a number of known dates) decide is the date, or approximately the date, of David's first writing such a poem. 1958 is the date of the recording at the BBC. What happened to the 'original version' we do not know. From the way in which he writes in this note it is evident to

---

* Size, quality and colour of paper used are indications, albeit approximate, of date. The disastrous changes in paper sizes, with the consequent disappearance of the respected and even venerable names — crown, foolscap, dble crown, royal, demy etc — and the introduction of the disgusting 'A4', did not become generally accepted as normal until... when?... some ten or a dozen years ago? All D.'s earlier MSS are on good, reasonably heavy, cream wove foolscap folio, 13" by 8". He was often forced in later years to use a vile, harder-textured, much whiter A4: a bond paper, in fact, not a writing. There is a corresponding change in D.'s writing and its disposition on the page. As the years go by, the writing becomes smaller and more difficult to read; and the increase in the width of the left-hand margin as he moves towards the bottom of the sheet becomes more and more exaggerated. In early MSS D. uses a fountain-pen — until the '40s or so, I would say: after that he uses a biro.

me that the 'original version' was not another different Mass, but a draft of this one.

The phrase 'that printed here' is puzzling. Where is 'here'? Wherever it may have been, the poem was certainly not printed anywhere, so far as I know. It may well have been intended for publication in 1965, and I can only conclude that D. lost it: this again confirms the view that here we have the lost Mass.

We may note, too, that David's note on the wrapper proves (by the dates) that it was put around the BBC script at least seven years after the recording in 1958, at a time when he intended that script to be printed. Note, further, that the title 'The Kensington Mass' has not yet appeared.

(3) The intermediate Mass (the first to bear the title 'The Kensington Mass'). After typing it, I now feel that it can be regarded only as an attempt, made probably in 1965, to prepare a version of the BBC Mass for printing: i.e. it may well be the 'somewhat altered version made in January 1965' of which David writes on the wrapper of the BBC script. Or it may be the 'original version' mentioned there — or a draft of it. In any case, it has a page missing, it is more prolix, I am sure, than David would have allowed it finally to be, and may therefore be regarded only as an interesting adjunct to the BBC Mass.

It is certainly intermediate between the BBC Mass and the K.M. in the sense that it is the first piece to be headed 'The Kensington Mass'. This may be an appropriate place at which to say a word about the title, a matter that is connected with the chronology of the Mass poems and of all that David wrote after *In Parenthesis*.

There can be no doubt that David first started seriously to think and write about the Mass theme when or soon before he was living in Sheffield Terrace, off Church Street Kensington, and would frequent the Carmelite church in Church Street.* Several dates recorded below confirm this. The origin of the

* [*December 1979*] This is true if you give full force to 'seriously'. But it is now clear to me that all the 'Mass' writing started (as did the 'Roman' and 'Romano-British or Romano-Celtic' pieces) after D.'s experience of Jerusalem in 1934; that 'The Old Quarry' was an early form, and that it provided a starting-point for the BBC, the intermediate, and the Kensington Masses. The handwriting and the paper also confirm the earlier date for 'The Old Quarry'.

title, then, is plain enough. Why he did not use it for the BBC Mass, we do not know. It may well have been that to do so, at that time and in those circumstances — recording at the BBC — would have needed too much explanation. It may be, also, that it was not until he had moved to Northwick Lodge in 1947 and looked back at the conception of the poem in Sheffield Terrace that he saw the aptness of the title 'Kensington'.

It should be remembered (I am pretty sure that I am right in saying this) that there were not many churches where you could attend a proper High Mass. Most churches did not have sufficient clergy, so that you had a sung Mass (Missa Cantata). You had High Mass (Missa Solemnis), of course, at the Cathedral, at Farm Street, the Oratory — at Our Lady of Victories? — and, I would wager, at the Carmelites. If I am wrong about that last, then (since the BBC Mass and the intermediate Masses are High Masses) I would say that the original scene was the Cathedral, which David certainly attended over a good many years, including the war years. Ultimately, the scene of the Mass was transferred to the Church of Our Lady and St Thomas of Canterbury in Harrow.

Let me put down in correct sequence what we know for certain of dates that concern the Mass sequences:

The early 1900s. James Jones reads at Christmas Milton's 'Nativity Hymn'. I mention this because of the use that David made (his correction, we might say) of the concluding part of the poem, for many years. David's letters — some of them to be printed in *Dai Greatcoat* [pub. 1980] — say a good deal about his interest at this time in the sacramental.

'Long before 1914' (D.'s words in a letter of July 1973) 'when I was at Camberwell Art School — old Solly' (Reginald Savage) ' — my attempts at "figure composition" nearly always of some mediaeval subject introducing a vested priest...'

1916. David's first glimpse of a Mass, in a battered shed behind the lines: described in a letter of July 1973. A great source for the 'new things and old' treasury, still to be drawn on in the last year of his life — the 'points of flame', for example, in the printed *Kensington Mass* of 1974 and 1975.

1919. As a student at the Westminster David goes across to the Cathedral. Through post-Impressionist theory he links liturgy and artefacture. (Crude shorthand, I fear.)

1921. David stays with Fr. John O'Connor in Bradford and, in September, is received by him into the Church. He would have served Father O'C.'s Mass, as he would later at Ditchling and Pigotts. Many mannerisms were stored up: in particular the 'throat-clearing' (noted, too, in Canon Gray) and the 'testiness' — stories like the one about the cushion which David forgot to move at the foot of the altar steps ('he booted the bloody thing across the sanctuary').

1934. David's visit to Jerusalem. Many letters explain how this determined the course of his writing after, or overlapping with, *In Parenthesis*. A good example is the letter printed in the *Agenda* D.J. issue.

1939, January. D. writes to Harman [Grisewood], 'I'm immersed in my Absalom, Mass, part now'. This is, to me, of special interest. We meet in 'The Old Quarry', and again much later in *The Kensington Mass,* the golden-haired Absalom hanging in the tree, the parallel with the Golden Bough, and the (surely rather strained) parallel with the greater son of David who hung on the tree of Calvary. In a passage in 'The Old Quarry' the move from the Upper Room to the Garden of Gethsemane is described, crossing the brook Kedron and passing by the 'tomb' of Absalom. The origin, then, of the Absalom–Mass conjunction is David's visit to Jerusalem and his later reading of Schürer's *History of the Jewish People in the Time of Jesus Christ* and Smith's *Historical Geography of the Holy Land.* It is this perpetual hoarding and maturing of an idea that moves me.

1940, March. Again to Harman, 'I've been continuing my "conversation" at the time of the Passion' — a reference to [Part Two of] 'The Old Quarry', a sequence into which the BBC Mass flows.

1944, Whitsun. A note to Louis Bussell on the back of a sheet of a draft of BBC Mass sources. The date agrees with the editorial notes in the Agenda *Kensington Mass*: and the particular sheet on the back of which the note is found starts with a version of the 'Launcelot' passage in the BBC

Mass, ends with BBC ending 'Argos the Dog howls outright' and then, after three large stars, has an opening of 'The Wall'. 'The Wall', with other *Sleeping Lord* pieces, was extracted from the 'Roman Quarry' MS. Since *The Anathemata*, too, leads into (or was developed from) 'The Old Quarry', all the post-*I.P.* writing is thus seen to be linked — except 'Balaam's Ass', and even that, in a somewhat roundabout way, can be brought into the same net.

1945. Note on the wrapper of the BBC script: 'An original version was made round about 1945.' With this we may take the heading to the intermediate Mass: 'The Kensington Mass, *c.* [cigarette burn]— 48'.

1952, 7 Feb. Death of Father O'C. Dedications to him therefore later than this.

1958. BBC recording of *The Mass.*

1965. Wrapper of BBC Mass: 'that printed here is a revised, corrected and somewhat altered version made in January 1965.'

1968. A sheet accompanying a group of 'Mass' MS sheets has a formally written-out date, 27 and 28 September 1968. This shows that although David had been using the title 'Kensington Mass' for some time, and was using it then, he was until then, i.e. until September 1968 at least, working on a Mass sequence that was not the printed *Kensington Mass.* See group (6) below.

1973–5. The Kensington Mass, printed in *Agenda* D.J. special issue and in Agenda Editions booklet.

There is obviously a break between 1965 and 1973–5. Some time around 1972 David wished to re-write the Mass poem. By that time he was in the nursing home (Calvary) and had 'lost' all the drafts of the earlier Mass poem. They were either in Monksdene or stored, and in any case were not available to him. This explains how it is that while the *Kensington Mass* starts more or less as does the BBC Mass, and has a good deal in common with it, yet it differs greatly and follows a very different course.

Returning to the MSS:

(4) 17 sheets which are all drafts of the opening of the BBC

Mass, 'Inclined in the midst of the instruments'... See also groups (10) and (11) below.

(5) 27 sheets of the same sort as (4): they are drafts, however, of later parts of the BBC Mass — repetitive, interesting, and at times leading into 'The Old Quarry'. Among these, and among other similar sheets that can be attached to or are included in other sequences, may be found a number of evocative oddities — a touching shopping list, for example:

Thursday	12 eggs	
	2 N.Z. butter	
Tuesday	4 Darilea cheese spread	
afternoon	1 Keelher marmalade	(Keiller, I think?)
	1 Digestive biscuits	
	3 Ginger biscuits	
	Nescafe	
	¼ lapsang tea	
	200 Benson & Hedges cigs	

(6) 15 sheets which might be included in (5) above: they are separate only because they emerged later from various other groups of MSS. They follow hares put up earlier, and start a couple of new ones. One sheet is carefully, and usefully, dated 27 and 28 September 1968, which shows us that David was still working on the BBC type Mass at that date.

(7) The Caillech MS. 28 sheets. Although this is a new departure and a new scene (Dublin), all the sheets are headed 'Mass/Ken m J O'C' and we are still in the BBC Mass series. That this is so is shown by Caillech's ending with the same 'Launcelot' sequence as the BBC Mass, and by the Caillech passages on sheets 17A and 18 of the intermediate Mass...

Everything so far, remember, is earlier than, and distinct from (even though with resemblances to) the printed *Kensington Mass* and its continuation, both printed and in MS.

We now come to the printed *Kensington Mass* and the associated MSS. Of the printed version I need say little, except that it was written in (for David) a comparatively short space of time, for as late as September 1968 he was working (see (6) above) on variations of the earlier Mass. He had lost the latter, but he remembered sufficient of it to start the new piece — let us call it the A.K.M. — at the same point in the Mass, as the priest first ascends the altar steps. John O'Connor and his characteristics were still, of course, vivid in the poet's mind. We are taken down a new turning, however [p. 89], at the kissing of the altar: from this comes kissing the hem of Helen's chiton — the British Helen — the Emperor Maximus and his dreams — the hunt — the dawn — cockcrow — Peter and the crowing of the cock. So it is that we are once again back at the starting-point of 1934, Jerusalem at the time of the Passion. And so again we link with the long MS that so often insists on recognition, 'The Old Quarry'.

Let me note, too, another important difference between the BBC Mass and the A.K.M.: the latter is a Low Mass. In the couple of pages on which the priest appears he is observed at close quarters — as it might be by his server: and that server might very well be David himself. So we come to

(8) David's completed MS of the A.K.M., the typescript marked for the printer by William Cookson, and the corrected galley-proofs. (Those last also contain 'The Narrows', which followed the A.K.M. in the *Agenda* special issue.)

The MS is in 12 sheets. A line has been drawn by D. below the text on each sheet of the MS, leaving a space for notes. Only one note has been written, and that has been struck out as being unnecessary.* We can attach an exact date to the last sheet, for on 4 March 1974 D. writes acknowledging my reference to the O.F. original of 'Sirs, you are set for sorrow'.

(9) We come now to the source MSS of the A.K.M. First, we have 35 sheets all of which are variations of the opening lines: (*clara voce dicit: Oremus*). In a sheet, written on both sides, which is pp. 7 and 8 of a letter or a draft of letter— probably to Nancy Sandars, for there is a reference to 'your trail in complex labyrinth of the matter of Ur of the Chaldees & the Mesopotamian lands and the Philistines & the Sea Peoples' — D. explains why he starts the poem with the rubric and 'Oremus'.†

---

* Uncommonly tempting to write notes at great length.

† He is much disturbed because it appears that Orɑmus is being printed instead of Oremus. (There are two prayers at this point of the beginning of the Mass: the first, *Aufer a nobis*, is introduced by *Oremus*, let us

These sheets, again, have room left for notes — but only part of one note is written, 'Such were the rapid twists and turns of J. O'C.'s thoughts'.

(10) Blast! we have 10 sheets included here before the BBC–A.K.M. distinction was clear. I shall leave them here for now. They are all versions of group (4), 'inclined in the midst', the beginning of the BBC Mass.

(11) Blast again! here is another bunch of 15 sheets which also belong to the BBC, because they deal with incensing the altar. I see that when I first went through all these MSS I put these together and noted, 'Here, unhappily, the K.M. and the BBC Mass seem to merge into one.' It is, indeed, confusing, but that the A.K.M. is a Low Mass and the BBC a High Mass is becoming ever more clear to me; so these must go with the BBC MSS. Something else, moreover, is now becoming clear to me — from the writing, disposition on page, paper, style — that the composition of the two poems overlapped. I think David must have been working on the two at the same time; he put the BBC-High Mass material to one side, meaning at some time to link it completely with 'The Old Quarry', and, when he wished to produce a continuous text for *Agenda* in the spring of 1974, he concentrated on the simpler A.K.M. Low Mass — simpler, that is, when he began it, but growing to unmanageable complexity when he came to continue it and found he had opened so many different lines.

(12) Here we have what (10) and (11) above disguised themselves as, source MSS for the A.K.M. 54 sheets — A4 size, in conformity with the late date (*c.* 1972–4). These are variations on successive themes in the printed A.K.M.: the opening

---

pray; the second starts *Oramus,* we beseech you. David uses them both.) Yet all the printed versions, the galley-proof, the *Agenda* special issue, and the Agenda booklet, print *Oremus* correctly for the first prayer, and *Oramus* for the second. Surely the poem was not printed somewhere else at the same time? The date of the letter is just or not long before the publication of *The Sleeping Lord* (early 1974, I think?). It was at the time of the three-day working week — remember? The answer may be quite simple. The galley-proof read OREMUS. D. has corrected — no, changed — this to ORAMUS, and then written 'E stet' over the struck-out 'E', but has left the 'A' in the margin. He may have taken fright and thought, with the short working week, that ORAMUS would be printed. But, hell, no, heaven! that is enough about that detail.

invocation, Helen — with glances, of course, at Hector — the British Helen, the emperor sleeps, 'Brazen-faced Phoebus' and the meet, dawn cockcrow, all leading up to 'What of the Fisherman?' What, indeed — he will be leading us up number-less garden paths, to our frustrated delight. There are several notes. One emphatically draws attention to Melchisedec, who was to become increasingly important to David. Long after 'Balaam's Ass' had first been completed, he forcibly introduced him into the version printed in *The Sleeping Lord*. Melchi-sedec's appearance on p. 108 of *The S.L.*, in an ingenuously and distressingly macaronic setting, may seem to other readers as unfortunate as it does to me. David had ample justification for his view of M., if not for his use of him at that point, and he explains his reasons in the next group,

(13) 7 sheets, f'cap except for one 4to, all headed 'The Mass Notes p. 20' (or some similar wording). What 'p. 20' was we cannot say. It may have been at some time the number of a draft of the sheet mentioned above in (12). We have here several drafts of a short essay, we might almost say, on the relation of M. to the Christian doctrine of sacrifice, based on the Old Testament, the Epistle to the Hebrews, ch. 7, and patristic writers. A fine piece of exposition, even in its in-complete form.

We now come to the A.K.M. continuation. 14 sheets of MS were found together, and it was assumed that these had been put on one side by David as a source for the continuation of the A.K.M. These were cobbled together with paste, hope, scissors, stamp-paper, disappointment, industry, inspiration, stupidity etc., and the result could at least be read and furnish some idea of how the poem would develop. Our assumption (see below, (15)) was mistaken, but even so I am keeping these 14 sheets together, since they are reproduced in the Agenda edition. They form group

(14) Of those I need say no more, for they can be read. We may finally (so far as this poem is concerned) move to

(15) 68 sheets of A.K.M. continuation. These fall into several ill-defined, because overlapping or repetitive, groups. Thus we

have first 22 versions of the opening, 'What of the Fisherman'; 5 that are based on the difference in speech and way of life 'Up in Tetrarchate', and introducing the fair-haired Celt; 7 that develop the 'fair-haired labourer'; 29, very mixed, in which Peter gets into conversation with the Celt (who is unloading timber — there's a suggestion of the timber of the cross) and learns that his name is Akannon, a name we meet in the *Ana*. (p. 184 n. 4). We have a glimpse of Pilate washing his hands, and of the police in the Garden, but we never have a straight run for more than one page. The general drift of all these sheets is to run into 'The Old Quarry', but I doubt whether we can make a satisfactory join.

THE GRAIL MASS

I find it tempting to annotate all these MSS at some length.
I hope that anyone who reads this will forgive me for pointing
out to them much that they (and others, no doubt) know
much better than I do.

p. 106

Inclined in the midst...: The priest has said the opening
psalm, *Judica me, Deus,* and the *Confiteor,* has ascended the
steps to the altar and said the prayer *Aufer a nobis* (with
which the K.M. starts). *Deinde, manibus junctis super altare,
inclinatus dicit.* Bowing, with his hands joined over the altar,
he says the prayer, *Oramus te, Domine, per merita Sanc-
torum tuorum (osculatur altare in medio) quorum reliquiae
hic sunt, et omnium sanctorum tuorum: ut indulgere dig-
neris omnia peccata mea,* We pray thee, O Lord, by the
merits of thy saints (he kisses the altar in the middle) whose
relics lie here, and of all thy saints, to deign to forgive all
my sins.

Note that D., as so often, prefers a latinized English word,
'inclined', based on *inclinatus.*

and invoking... *the cist*: For these lines D. looks forward
to the prayer, at the end of the Ordinary of the Mass,
Suscipe, Sancta Trinitas, hanc oblationem, Receive, O holy
Trinity ('the life-giving persons') this offering... The offer-
ing is to be in memory of the Passion, Resurrection and
Ascension of Christ, and in memory of Our Lady, John the
Baptist, SS Peter and Paul, *et istorum, et omnium sancto-
rum* (of those, *istorum,* those just mentioned) and of all
the saints. A draft of these lines notes those names in the

margin. *Istorum* is wrongly but legitimately applied by the poet to the saints whose relics are 'dusty in the cist', i.e. enclosed in the altar stone.

He turns to ask of the living: i.e. at the *Orate, Fratres*. The rubric reads, *Postea osculatur Altare, et versus ad populum, extendens, et jungens manus, voce paululum elevata, dicit,* Then he kisses the altar ('the place of sepulture'), turns towards the people, stretches out and then joins his hands and in a somewhat louder voice says, Pray, brethren, that my sacrifice and yours etc.

Ceres... Liber... the naiad: Familiar, as symbols or metaphors for corn (bread), wine and water, from *The Anathemata*. They 'have heard his: Come who makes holy', because, before the *Orate Fratres,* the priest has said the prayer *Veni, sanctificator omnipotentes aeterne Deus,* Come, thou who makest holy, almighty and eternal God, which calls for a blessing upon the sacrificial gifts. They are still 'tokens', because until the consecration they are but symbols of the reality.

the horns of the mensa: A number of passages in Exodus refer to the horns at the four corners of the various altars and tables, for the making of which exact instructions are given: 27 : 2; 30 : 2; 37 : 25. 'The name has been carried over to indicate the four corners of the Christian altar, the word "corner" being derived from, and "horn" cognate with, Lat. *cornu,* a projection' (*Catholic Encyclopaedic Dictionary*). The purpose of the horns was to hold the whole-offering in position over the fire. A disgusting thought — no wonder our poet was tempted to look towards Marcion and his rejection of the God of the Old Testament. The horns are conventionally attached to, for example, the 'altar of incense'; and here, with an eye to the replacement of the Old Covenant by the New, D. imagines them as part of the Christian altar.

An earlier passage in Exodus (25 : 10–22) speaks of the making of the Ark of the Covenant. The N.E.B. refers to the contents of the Ark as the 'Tokens of the Covenant'. The

A.V., R.S.V., Douay, Jerusalem Bible, all have 'Testimony' (Vulgate *testimonium*). Although D. could not tolerate the language of the N.E.B., he may well have borrowed 'tokens' from it. This may seem a small point to labour, but the instructions for the carpenters and other craftsmen were valuable to D., not least because of the central position of the *Foederis Arca,* the Ark of the Covenant, the title applied to Our Lady as the immediate warrant of the new dispensation.

'they' are the bread and wine, which await consecration, the consecration being introduced by the prayer in the Canon, *Quam oblationem* (see *Ana.,* p. 49, with the commentary, p. 13).

You are ... doubly signa: In 'You' the poet addresses the bread and wine. They will be 'doubly *signa*' because after consecration they will be both the reality signified and present (the Body of Christ) and a sign or sacrament. This seeming absurdity is dealt with by de la Taille in his *Mystery of Faith and Human Opinion,* 211–15, and at greater length in *Elucidatio XL* of *Mysterium Fidei* ('In eucharistia corpus Christi veram habet rationem *rei* et *signi.*' In brief: 'The Body of Christ, which is the thing signified and contained under the species, is also in its turn a sign, the sign of that Church which fills up all times and all spaces, and forms with Christ but one flesh, *et erunt duo in carne una,* in a unity which is itself the effect of that sign.') Or, to put it more simply, bread and wine may be seen, even in their natural state, as symbols of life. At the Consecration they are the matter of the sacrament or effectual sign, and are therefore doubly *signa.*

Unde et memores: 'Remembering, therefore, the Passion, Resurrection and Ascension of Christ...', the prayer, appropriately, that follows immediately after the Consecration, which we have not yet reached. It is worth noting that this prayer is known as the *anamnesis,* the true meaning of which it makes clear.

O no, not flee away ... brighted you ever: The whole of this part, an embroidery upon, and contradiction of, stanzas 19–26 of Milton's 'Nativity Hymn', is an expansion of the reference to Anubis on the last page of the *Ana*.

p. 107

Yes, brutish you: D.'s alteration on the script, which read, 'Not brutish you', gives a slightly different sense. Instead of saying of these foretypes, 'You are not brutish; you are, on the contrary (but), his forerunners,' he says, 'For all that you are brutish, you are his forerunners' or 'Yes, you *are* brutish, but etc.'

Need peculiar powers...: Peculiar in the sense of having a special attachment to one particular group, people or cult — the *Indigetes* — with the added force of 'consecrated' from the Biblical phrases 'a peculiar people' etc. 'Stalls': obviously in the sense of their appointed places. It would be too crude, I think, to attach the word closely to the choir-stalls in church, or, with an eye on zoomorphic representations of divine beings, to the housing of animals.

glast: To yelp, yelp at, bark, greet. D. took the word from *glatissynge, glatyssaunte, glasting*, used of the Questing Beast in the *Morte Darthur*. Some drafts read 'bark'.

QUI VENIT: All stand during the singing of the Preface and the Sanctus, and then kneel for the beginning of the Canon. In the Sanctus is sung *Benedictus qui venit in nomine Domini*, Blessed is he who comes in the name of the Lord.

Lar... numen... tutelar (the last being David's word for the two former): these are the *di indigetes* who care for particular places and activities. David concentrates on the Roman setting, and so urges us to a rereading of Warde Fowler's *Religious Experience of the Roman People*.

terra, pontus: From the Matins hymn sometimes ascribed to, but in this version earlier than, Fortunatus: *Quem terra, pontus aethera/Colunt, adorant, praedicant*, You whom land, sea, sky, serve, worship, proclaim. It follows aptly after the reference to *Benedictus qui venit in nomine Domini*, for it emphasizes that all the pre-Christian numina may be said to 'come in the name of the Lord'.

the strait bathysphere (spelt 'batho' in script and fair copy; correctly spelt in other drafts): The underworld, the domain of Pluto and Proserpine, of Anubis (cf. above and 'the jackal's head' [p. 110]), the 'hell' into which Christ descended after his Resurrection, the 'fourth land', if we so wish, of *Ana*, p. 209, n. 4.

Now constellate ... ever: The meaning is that all that is bright in, true and valuable in, the many foretypes of pagan antiquity, now shines with (is 'constellate of', forms a constellation with) the risen Christ. Alternatively, we may take 'are constellate of' to mean 'are made to shine together by'. This is effected by the lifting of the 'Lode'; and this we may interpret in several ways. First, we may say that it is the lifting up on the Cross of Christ the Lode or Lodestar, the central point to which all is related. Secondly, it may be seen as the Resurrection and Ascension. Thirdly, we may take both the two earlier meanings as symbolized in the elevation of the consecrated host (though in so doing we have to anticipate the consecration). Finally, there may be a reference (in a rather unhappy pun) to the lifting of the load of sin. The poem, it should be remembered, was read aloud by D. for the BBC to record; and anyone who heard it would, I should think, hear 'lode' as 'load'. 'What light else brighted you ever?' echoes the 'How else?' argument of Part 1 of the *Ana.*, in particular pp. 78–80.

He stands upright ... dead time: Cf. the first two lines of the *Ana.*, p. 50. Here the 'incongruity' is particularized in the 'tubular blacks', the trouser ends showing below the vestments — 'dittoes' in other drafts.

In file of two ... all the years): The deacon and sub-deacon take their places behind the priest, on the steps of the altar, the sub-deacon standing on the lower step. The 'patrician tunicas': they wear the tunic-like garments proper to their office. The deacon wears the dalmatic and the sub-deacon a simpler form of the same. (For such details the quickest,

neatest and most reliable guide is the *Cath. Ency. Dict.*)
The tunics are patrician — or at least the deacon's is —
because the two vertical strips (*clavi*) sewn upon it repre-
sent the *latus clavus* (broad stripe) worn on the *tunica* of
the Roman senator (see Stuart Jones, p. 239). 'The year
that measures all the years', i.e. the year of the foundation
of Rome, 753 B.C., is something of an exaggeration.

He hunches free... folds: The distinction is between the
ample, circular, 'gothic' chasuble and the narrow, more
'practical', 'Roman'. The latter is narrower, straight-sided,
and sometimes cut in, like a violin, towards the waist — a
'fiddle-back'. Some of the drafts read, 'give us a fiddle-back
any day'. 'Planet': planeta, the ordinary Roman word for a
chasuble.

p. 108

Loudly he clears...: The throat-clearing comes from D.'s
memories of Father O'Connor (of Canon Gray, too). In cor-
respondence he mentions it more in connection with the
breaking of the silence of the Canon at the *Nobis quoque
peccatoribus*. Here it comes after the priest has said the
'secret' prayer. The poem is following the course of the
Mass correctly but not fully: the Epistle and Gospel, for
example, and the washing of the hands, have been omitted.
We are about to conclude the Ordinary of the Mass and,
through the Preface, move into the Canon.

when he says Per omnia: *Per omnia saecula saeculorum,* the
words that end the Secret. D. was much moved by such an
ekphonesis, the words said or (as here) sung in a clear voice
after silence. Six phrases are sung alternately by priest and
choir, and then the former, at *Gratias agamus Domino Deo
nostro,* moves into the singing of the Preface ('And now he
sings out and alone').

the gleemen and the Powers: The choir and the angels (*ado-
rant Dominationes,* in the Preface). The 'Nine Bright Shiners'
(from the song 'Green grow the rushes O'): the nine choirs
of angels. The whole heavenly host (*militia caelestis*) joins
in the singing of the *Sanctus*.

247

substitute to the Man in the Mock: Frazer is full of such surrogates; here 'Mock' refers more particularly to the crowning with thorns and the mocking of Christ by the Roman soldiers. But 'substitute' refers to the priest's position as the representative of Christ, sharing his priestly power.

(you, dark-membraned ... somewhat winged): That the reference is to bats (from the homely 'bats in the belfry') is no doubt obvious, but it is made perfectly clear by the use of 'bats' in several drafts. 'Awned', i.e. bearded — a picture of a bat shows the resemblance to the awn or beard of a head of barley. 'Sanctus-pent': bell-tower. *'Cum angelis* exult': 'exult' from the Holy Saturday *Exultet jam angelica chorus* at the blessing of the Paschal candle. That the 'clerestory concelebrants' are angels is clear both from the words of the Preface *socia exultatione concelebrant,* together celebrate, i.e. honour, in common rejoicing, used of angels (cf. 'exult' above) and by a draft which reads 'and with clerestory angels mix your fragile webs' — carved angels, I take it, like the gargoyles a few lines further on. In 'purblind, yet, somewhat winged', man and the bat are brought together in a neat comparison. As the bat is blind, so man sees through a glass darkly; and as the bat is winged, so man is made but a little lower than the angels. In 'Faustian spaces' the adjective is an unwelcome intruder from Spengler — unwelcome, because to accept the word as poetically suitable comes too close to unqualified approval.

He thumbs a page or so ... clear of the instruments: These lines cover the prayers before the Consecration, leading up to the complete silence which surrounds the murmur of the words of institution. (Hence the variation of 'You could hear a penny drop': whose penny? The penny, I would say, of some Phryne or Lais, as in *Ana.,* p. 180, destined for a candle.)

p. 109

His recollected fingers ... : That we are past the Consecration now is shown by this line (after which we need a stop), the meaning being that the priest is keeping the thumb and index finger of each hand closed together: *nec amplius pollices*

248

et indices disjungit, nisi quando Hostia tractanda est, usque ad ablutionem digitorum, nor does he again (i.e. after the consecrating of the Host) open his thumbs and index fingers except when he has to handle the Host, until the washing of the fingers, at the 'last ablutions' just before the end of Mass. Thus, too, the ringing of the bell or bells at the Consecration after the movements peculiar to, that is proper to, the man who has been transfigured by sharing in the priesthood of Christ; and 'the work done at The Tumulus'. 'his supports': the deacon and sub-deacon, now one on each side of the celebrant.

Madelene in fox . . . : Many drafts, and the opening of 'The Old Quarry', greatly expand this description of the congregation.

deep calls: Psalms 42–3 (Vulgate 41–2), which are a single poem: *Abyssus abyssum invocat, in voce cataractarum tuarum,* deep calls to deep at the thunder of thy cataracts. This psalm is the song of an exile, with memories of the Temple and (in the phrase used by D.) the river Jordan — with 'cataracts' (cf. 'down-rusher' of *Ana.* p. 224 and n. 1). The word 'deep' has been transferred by D. from the Jordan to the ocean, and this has suggested the name Calypso, as though the girl were isolated in her pew as Calypso was isolated in her sea-girt island of Ogygia, but could say with the psalmist, 'These things I remember . . . I remember thee from the land of Jordan and Hermon, from Mount Mizar. Deep calls to deep . . .' (vv. 4, 6–7). The psalm was well known to D., and from the opening of the first part (Psalm 42) he retained and made much use of the simile, *Quemad . . modum desiderat cervus ad fontes aquarum,* As the hart panteth after the water brooks (*Ana.* p. 237 and n.2, for example).*

* Soon after writing the above I saw, through the kindness of David's niece, Stella Wright, a little pencil sketch (7″ by 5″) of D. by Dom Theodore Bailey, dated 1927; 'Isle of Caldey. Portrait of the artist by another'. It shows D. standing on the sandy shore, looking out over the sea, and is headed 'ABYSSVS ABYSSVM INVOCAT'. A very different application of those words, but it brought to my mind the parallel between the cataracts of the Jordan and the constant calling of the streams in the rocks and dingles of the Llanthony valley.

The movements peculiar ... to be rung: The 'movements' are the priest's elevation of the host and chalice, marked by the ringing of the bell. 'Transfigured man' may be read in two senses: to mean Christ himself under the sacred species, and the priest as a man transfigured by his priestly character.

quarantines: a period of forty days, the word being used only and anachronistically in connection with indulgences — as though to the dog his confinement in the porch were a long Purgatory.

The worn bronze toe ... :   The statue of St Peter, the toe of which is kissed by the devout. Peter holds the keys as a symbol of the power to bind and to loose: 'troia', both because of Peter's position as bishop of Rome, the successor to Troy, and because of the maze-like pattern of the wards. This statue, the tower, the spaciousness of the roof, suggest that Westminster Cathedral was in the poet's mind, but overlaid by the memory of a smaller and more intimately known church.

equinoctial hat: a new hat ('Easter bonnet') for the spring equinox. With the coming reference to Anubis it is appropriate that this should be Eastertide.

p. 110

And does the sacristan ... :   It was not usual — for once I must use the past tense — for the congregation to go to Communion at a High Mass, that is to say at the High Altar at which the Mass was being celebrated. At the Cathedral, for example, Communion might be given from the Lady Altar by another priest. We may, at a pinch, refer to him as 'the sacristan' (though we may also account for the word in another way as being applied to a figure seen in a half-dream — see below in the reference to the 'Caillech MS'). He may be said to bring out the jackal's head, that is Anubis, the escort and god of the dead; and the jackal's head may thus be seen as the Christian viaticum. All who would eat the bread must die in two senses — they must accept the common lot of man, for the curing of which they need the life-giving bread; and they must die in the sense — two of many

250

examples — of 2 Timothy 2 : 11 and 2 Cor. 6 : 9. I must confess that it is with some diffidence that I suggest this more explicit identification of the Egyptian jackal-headed god with Christian Redeemer; but such an interpretation is suggested by a similar passage in the *Ana.*, p. 205 and n. 5 — 'He whose foretype said, in the Two Lands, I AM BARLEY'.

A MS draft of this passage confirms me in the belief that we must find a literal interpretation: there must be some remembered action or fact, something occurring in the Mass and observed in the same way as the rest of the action has so far been observed; and we cannot be satisfied with some vague parallel between the bread of the Christian sacrifice and the association (through the jackal-headed escort of the dead and the Egyptian king's identification with Osiris and barley) of the life-giving grain with a foretype of the Redeemer. We have two drafts that are appropriate, but as they are very similar only one needs to be quoted:

> Did the sacristan
>   fetch out the jackal's head
> as Finnegan's shawl-wrapt Caillech swore
> she saw he did from behind the dust-hung,
> neglected half-broken side-altar of
> Honoratus of Lerins
>   but that was away back,
> in Medb's own green Connacht — a decade of
> years twix the 'goomboil'
> of Bradford and about the same
> time spell in lodgment far worse
> in the purlieus of Bootle and now
> in a regular tan and black, first
> floor back, at twice the rent,
> a step or so from

The Caillech is a familiar figure in Irish and Scottish legend, about whom much has been written. (Frazer, for example, notes the use of the name for the last corn cut at harvest.) Here, however, and in a longer sequence that we may call 'The Caillech MS' [pp. 97–105], D. uses the word simply as a Christian name, applied to a washer-woman who hears Mass in a Dublin church. (We may digress for a moment to note Father O'C.'s imitation of the Bradford accent in 'goom-

251

boil'. He was a clever and amusing mimic of Yorkshire. Cf. the story of the working man with his child on his knee, 'I were joost teaching the little booger to say booger.') While this quotation makes it clear that a definite event is being recorded or suggested, that some distinct act connected with the Mass was in the poet's mind, the very introduction of the carefully noted detail, the reference to St Honoratus and, through the island of Lerins, whose monastery was founded by Honoratus before he became Archbishop of Arles, to St Patrick (who studied at Lerins) — all these make it even more difficult to pin down the meaning. Time, I hope, or some friend who may read this, will bring illumination.

A reading of the Caillech MS is helpful, for it starts with a dream-like musing as Caillech listens to the sermon in a Dublin church and remembers her home in Connacht and her travels; and this could account for the combined precision and odd inconsequence of the memories.

In the north porch ... howls outright: Here we have a difference in method, familiar enough to readers of the other poems: a scene is suggested to the poet's imagination and it is described as though it were actually taking place. We have had the dog 'realistically' tied up in the porch, and the notion of someone or something outside the church has suggested a scene in the *Morte Darthur* (Book xvii, ch. 15), 'How Sir Launcelot was afore the door of the chamber wherein the Holy Sangreal was'. This was the nearest that Launcelot came to the achieving of the Grail, as we are told in the next chapter: 'Sir, said they, the quest of the Sangreal is achieved now right in you, that never shall ye see of the Sangreal no more than ye have seen.' Whilst Launcelot's exclusion is not to be interpreted literally in the poem, the moral is the same as that emphasized in the *Morte Darthur,* that salvation depends upon integrity of will.

his quillon'd cleddyf-*hilt*: Of the MS variations of this phrase, I must confess that I prefer that which has no adjective; and the correction on the script (followed here, for 'Aryan pommel') seems to me to try to introduce too much too crudely.

right through that chamber door: The memory of 'Frankie and Johnny' is even more pointed in a draft, which reads 'that hardwood door'.

the Cyrenean deacon: The deacon, at the right hand of the priest, assists him as though he were Simon of Cyrene.

to relieve the weight ... surcharged with that great weight: Malory: 'And then Launcelot marvelled not a little, for he thought the priest was so greatly charged of the figure [of Christ, placed in his hands by the Father and the Holy Ghost] that him seemed that he should fall to the earth.'

Argos: Specific to dog ever since the Odyssey — so *Ana.*, 79, 192.

That the Last Supper itself was in the poet's mind as he wrote this BBC Mass is shown by the MS of 'The Old Quarry'. In this we have Launcelot trying to force his way in and the howling of the dog Argos; and then it continues [p. 122]:

'The hymn is sung, the memorial crumbs are gathered. The heavy file circuits the Ophel by-ways, out water-gate, by horse-gate, to known copse. The ascertained place, the place of ill-vassalage, the shameful thicket. The wormwood cup won't pass...'

And so we move into the betrayal by Judas.

THE OLD QUARRY
and the Judas sequence
[Part III]

From a letter of 14 July 1976:

I have been looking at this ['the Judas sequence': i.e. 'The Agent'] again, in the hope that it might be possible to extract pages that could be inserted in the appropriate place in 'The Old Quarry'. That latter, you may remember, branches off from a description of some of the congregation as Mass is being celebrated. The Mass itself is being described, and when the Canon is reached, we are told that 'Here a maker turns a hard corner' [p. 115]. This allows a transition to the Upper Room and the Last Supper, so to the betrayal by Judas, the move into the garden of Gethsemane and the arrest. There is then a sharp break, at which a completely new section and new theme begins. It is marked 'Begin here Section XIV' (a tantalizing figure, for it is impossible to form any coherent sequence of such figures), and from there to the end of the MS we have a long conversation between an old man, experienced in Roman administration, his daughter, who has an interest in the Oriental religions that were then fashionable, and a young soldier, a subaltern in the Twelfth Legion (Fulminata), which served in Syria and Judaea — the Roman equivalent of what some London friends of mine call a 'Woof-woof' — the sort of youngish man, with a rather military moustache (though he's probably in advertising), who stands in an elegant bar and says in a loud, rather high-pitched voice, 'Woof, woof, have Nigel and Fiona arrived yet?'

Since there is a large pile of sheets, all concerned with the betrayal by Judas, I had hoped that some of them might be incorporated in 'The Old Quarry'; I now see that I was mistaken, for 'The Old Quarry' has been written out continuously (or more or less continuously) and the Judas sequence cannot be inserted — that, at least, is what I think at the moment.

A note of 22 July 1976:

As I typed out these sheets I modified my views [of 14 July]. First, it is true that there is an intimate connection between 'Judas' and 'The Old Quarry'. In fact there is more than one coincidence in the wording: see, e.g., 'The heavy file circuits the Ophel by-ways', and the 'Who will betray me' scene and Judas's reference to 'the Party', and the 'Why is John the favourite' passage. There is also a close connection with the *Ana.*, p. 51 ('There's conspiracy here...'). But I now see that 'Judas' is a complete fragment in itself, with four well-marked and perfectly coherent sections. This is a very great acquisition...

Can we just boldly include in one volume two very similar pieces? Though when I say 'very similar' I am going too far. The treatment in 'Judas' is precise, condensed, and direct; in 'The Old Quarry' it is much more allusive, and elusive, and indirect ('Aphrodite of the indirect approach! pray for us,' says David somewhere), and, to my mind — though here I may well be wrong — less finished. I must read 'The O.Q.' again very carefully...

A note of 19 November 1979:

This MS sheet [p. 131, the end of 'The Old Quarry, Part One'] illuminates David's method of writing and his intention; it also helps to explain the difficulty of understanding the earlier part of this piece.

The first three words of the last line I have typed above are 'a nice fork'. On the same line D. continues, 'That's the crux of it/how the hell can you tell, it's a pretty/burden for a white man —'. Later, he put a large star between 'fork' and 'That's' with a note in the margin 'NB [star] Begin [big star] here Section XIV'. This gives us the piece which we are calling

'The Old Quarry, Part Two' (the dinner-table conversation). It is clear that words and ideas came to David more readily than form: looking back on what he had written, he found that, almost unconsciously, he had drifted into a sequence that could be lifted out from the mass of writing and made into a separate section.

THE OLD QUARRY
Part One

From a memorandum of June 1980:

These notes are not offered as part of the book [i.e. *The Roman Quarry*], but were written in an attempt to at least partly clarify my mind, and are included in case they may interest and perhaps even stimulate the exegetical skill of anyone who sees this typescript.

pp. 113–14

This one fetches ... his household their bread: Here we have no trouble. It will be remembered that the beginning can be taken as a continuation of or overlap with the end of 'The Grail Mass'. We are present at a High Mass and are approaching the Consecration. Attention is turned to the congregation, including the choir. We have moved back a little and are at or just after the Offertory, when the various coverings are removed from the chalice. There is a danger here (which the poet, too, had to avoid) of appearing what used to be called 'spike'. (I have a friend who still uses the word, in no disparaging sense, even of himself.) However, there is nothing sentimentally ritualistic in learning, and bearing in mind when reading these Mass sequences, both the rubrics of the Roman Mass and the names and functions of the persons, objects, vestments and linen to which they apply. Associated with the chalice are the veil, the burse, the corporal, the paten, the purificator, the pall. The old *Catholic Encyclopaedia* is useful here (such articles as *Altar*, with the sub-section *Altar-linen, chasuble, deacon* etc.); even quicker and more convenient is Donald Attwater's [D.A.] *Catholic Encyclopaedic Dictionary.*

'This one fetches...' refers to the lighting of a candle at or near the altar from the Sanctus to the Communion. 'This good custom', says D.A., 'is generally omitted except by the Dominicans.' I would wager that it was observed by Father O'Connor, as it was at Pigotts.

The 'ewer', we need hardly say, is one of the cruets, and the reference is either to the pouring of the wine and water into the chalice or to the washing of the priest's hands at the *Lavabo*. The 'coverlet board' cloth is the corporal, now spread out under the chalice.

Two lines on we should doubtless read 'unsheathe' for 'unsheaf'. There is a double meaning in the prohibition: first, it is an expression of fear at the anticipation of the Passion, symbolized by the uncovering of the chalice; secondly there is a reference to Luke 22 : 38 (just before the Agony in the Garden), 'But they said: Lord, behold, here are two swords. And he said to them: It is enough' — i.e. 'That will do; I want no talk of swords'. (Cf. D.'s 'Night-drops tarnish their two swords' [p. 122].) This is a characteristically unobtrusive way of introducing the parallel between the Supper and the Mass, and of preparing us for the transition to the former.

'In file of three' is accurate. The deacon and sub-deacon are standing on the lower steps of the altar, immediately behind the priest.

From here to 'His recollected fingers' [p. 114] we meet no difficulty; but we may note that there are, in the source MSS, other versions of the inscription on the stone: 'General Sir Jack Mary Gabriel Gaunt Ball', 'Colonel Titus Gabriel Bates', 'Brigadier-General John Gabriel Mary Bates', 'Colonel John Cornelius Benit Vaux'. Wherever the stone was, it made a great impression on D. I used to think that it was in the church at Harrow, of Our Lady and St Thomas of Canterbury, until I understood that he was writing of such a stone long before the move to Harrow.* What is an onion stone?

* What put the false idea into my mind was that, in the last year of his life, David spoke to me at length and with great assurance about a stone in the Lady chapel at Harrow telling me that it was in memory of an old friend of mine, Bernard Coldwell. I went round to see and found that David was mistaken; but he stubbornly refused to believe me.

('Onion' appears only in this version of the passage.) Does it possibly refer to the grenade of a Fusilier (and Grenadier) regiment badge, which has some resemblance to an onion?*

'Fiddle-back' may puzzle some readers — the straight-sided chasuble that is cut in on each side of the back, towards the waist — waisted, in fact. [Cf. note on 'The Grail Mass', p. 107.]

'His cuisses on his thighs' (*I Henry IV*, Act IV, sc. 1): cf. *I.P.* p. 173 and letter of 9–15 July 1973, with D.'s remarks about 'beaver up' and 'beaver on', 'young Harry' being his friend in the R.W.F., Harry Cook.

The deacon is 'Cyrenean' because, like Simon of Cyrene, he is helping to carry the burden. The notion of 'relieving the weight' comes from the Malory passage we have met before, where Launcelot wished to break into the chapel. The deacon's move to the left-hand side of the priest, where he can hold the chasuble clear of the sacred instruments, is according to the rubrics. The action is both symbolic and utilitarian. So Fr. Herbert Thurston, S.J. (a name from that past!), in the *Cath. Encycl.*, under *Chasuble*: 'While this shortening' — of the primitive chasuble — 'was still in progress, it became the duty of the deacon and subdeacon, assisting the celebrant, to roll back the chasuble and relieve as far as possible the weight on the arms'. Thurston was writing (1908) before the general reintroduction of the 'Gothic' chasuble, when the 'fiddle-back' was normal.

In 'You can hear... quarantines' we cannot avoid the repetition of the end of 'The Grail Mass'. The imagery of the next lines is familiar.

pp. 114–15

The anointed man ... half-waking Zachary: Here, with the gradual change of scene, we have a change of mood: as there is a change of mood as we enter the silence of the Canon.

---

* [*12 July 1980*] From Walter Shewring I have learnt, to my great relief, and with gratitude, the origin of 'onion stone... General Gandolf': cf. Browning's 'The Bishop Orders His Tomb': '— Old Gandolf, with his paltry onion stone,/Put me where I may look at him'. (*Cipolla*, onion: *cipollino*, a variety of marble.)

So Martin D'Arcy in *The Mass and the Redemption,* pp. 50–1, in a passage which ends: 'And this change all four Gospels attest, for they fix on one incident — that of the betrayal, the departure of Judas — as the beginning of the Passion which they are about to narrate. And with unerring instinct, it is the same incident which the Church has fastened upon in her Liturgy, for, as we know, in the drama of Holy Week the prologue of the tragedy is the treachery of Judas.' It is this which lies behind the *Anathemata*'s 'and one, gone out' (p. 51).

We now meet metaphors that are reminiscent of *In Parenthesis*: in particular ('the drummed assemblies') the terrifying comparison with a court-martial's death sentence and the repetition of Leslie Poulter's *morituri te salutant* on the morning of 10 July 1916 (see *Dai Greatcoat,* 229). Accompanying this is the metaphor taken from another change, from bride to working mother.

The general drift here is clear, but there is some difficulty in the language. 'He's at the frontier...' [p. 115] may be taken as saying, The march, the border-land between the triumph of the Cenacle and agony (first in the Garden and finally on Calvary), the sharp line ('demarcation') drawn by the Old Covenant, has been crossed and so removed; there is now freedom from the Law and the Kingdom is open to the Gentiles.

'Ap Erbin' is Geraint. Lady Charlotte Guest's *Mabinogion* (pp. 260–1 of the Everyman edition) illuminates the 'wall of wove brume'. The ellipses in 'find the way far... as contrapunctal' are D.'s, and indicate not a pause, I believe, but the absence of what was needed to complete that sentence.

If we see the Preface as corresponding to the 'march', then 'Ninth choir's sweet mode' will refer to the *militia caelestis* — the nine choirs of the celestial hierarchy — who join in the singing of the *Sanctus*. With this we may take also Matthew 26 : 30 (*et hymno dicto* etc.), the Psalms of the Hallel, sung at the end of the Passover meal. See, too, 'The hymn is sung...' [p. 122]. The repetition is surely an indication of incompleteness.

With various auxiliaries at hand — a couple of Prophets,

Malory, the archaeologists, Jessie Weston, a map of Jerusalem (most important) — the localizing of the Waste Land in the Hinnôm and Kedron Valleys is eminently reasonable.

At 'the young man stirs' we meet what is more difficult to explain — Absalom. He was associated with this group of ideas at least since 1939, for in January of that year D. writes to H.J.G., 'I am absorbed in my Absalom, Mass, part now'. He reappears in *The Kensington Mass,* where there is a further connection with the Golden Bough, suggested by his fair hair entangled in the oak tree; a parallel is obviously drawn between the 'pierced and hanging son' of David and the Son of God on the Cross. Do we need to enquire more closely into the peculiar fascination that Absalom held for D.? I think not. He was obviously, if superficially, an appropriate symbol for D., who could close his eyes to the less attractive aspects of his character; and the choice of Absalom must have been confirmed by the position of the so-called Tomb or Pillar of Absalom in the Kedron Valley, on the way to the Mount of Olives.

Going back to 'Ninth choir's sweet mode', we are hard put to it to paraphrase the meaning. There is the general sense that with the emergence into the Kedron Valley things appear in a very different light. The hymn sounds out of place in the grim gully. The Kingdom of God had come (Luke 22 : 18, following de la Taille's interpretation of that passage), and from that peak there was now a collapse. This could be expressed in terms of looking at a natural scene or even a building — there are two worlds to be seen, the concrete world seen by 'flesh-eye' and the world of the spirit. The 'unknowable baulk' bars our way, it must be confessed. How do we read that sentence? Possibly: 'The unknowable baulk runs in this way so nearly that "that" was "this" when I looked with my flesh-eye: the mystery is such that what we see with our eyes is almost completely transformed.' At the same time, remembering that we are still to some degree in an actual church at the most solemn moment of the Mass, we may say that the very church itself, including the roof-beam, vaulting, arches, takes on, for the observer, an indescribable and mysterious vagueness. (Those last words, at least, are appropriate.)

Soon will be the fracture...: Here we start a new section. The Branch is a Messianic title (Zachariah 3 : 8, and 6 : 12); we would say 'shoot' rather than 'branch'. The Septuagint has *anatole,* the Vulgate *Oriens,* Douay 'the Orient'. But there is no need to linger over points and references that the reader can easily pick up for himself: the howling of the shepherds (Matthew's 'I will strike the shepherds: and the sheep of the flock shall be dispersed', 26 : 31), Chaucer's 'Hide, Absalom', the Absalom story, the sheep-shearing in Ephraim and the vengeance on Amnon ('for all the guile in Ephraim grove'), the memory of the entry into Jerusalem (Zechariah 9 : 9, with Matthew 21 : 5, etc.). A newcomer is the Prodigal Son, as presented in Wyclif's Bible: but if we keep the general type of imagery in mind and its application to the successive stages of the Gospel narrative, we can move ahead and leave aside for the time being the tracking of detail.

But what does the aged man cry... vengeance on the tall man: Here we take our cue from the Culhwuch and Olwen story in the *Mabinogion,* to explain the long list of things to be fetched or done. There are many things I would like to know, and with luck may learn — who was the Barber to the King of France (the latter appears in Culhwuch and Olwen), why did D. introduce the fourteenth-century mermaid-like Mélusine 'as damp as an eel' — but I do not think we shall be shirking our duty if we say that once D. has started on a list his imagination is given a free rein. All this I take as an elaborate building-up of imagery to emphasize the grandeur and universality of the last stage of the divine enterprise.

Not so fast... howls outright: The imaginative balloon is deflated by 'Not so fast'. The tangled skein has shown how 'diversely he speaks, and by types prefiguring', and at 'The appointed man' we return to the narrative. The repetition of

Launcelot's battering — or I should say the introduction of Launcelot, later to be repeated in 'The Grail Mass' — shows us that we have here an incomplete draft: and this allows us some convenient freedom in interpretation.

The hymn is sung... their two swords: There is admirable compression in these lines, which form a short separate section. Ophel is the site of David's original Sion, the spur that runs south between the Tyropoeon Valley and the Kedron. The 'heavy file' of disciples (heavy because of the terror of the approaching end) moves down from the Cenacle, across the Tyropoeon valley, through 'Ophel by-ways' and out into the Garden. Christ is alone in the Agony (*agonia*, struggle, justifies the military metaphors). 'Ill-vassalage' is reminiscent of *Roland* and the treachery of Ganelon. The twelve legions of Matthew 26 : 53 will not move. We are on the verge of the arrest.

pp. 122–4

Under the tree... on Barbary?: Again a new and straightforward section — with some freedom in the use of allusion, as, for example, in 'Tell me, gentle friend' — in which the betrayal is arranged.

D'you mean be me... would have some part: This continuation of the conversation between Judas and Caiaphas, with some soliloquizing by Judas, introduces the notion of following the Party Line. Both Marxism and National Socialism will come into this (Judas will later develop the notion of the dialectic). The March purge* gives us a date after which these pages must have been written. The concluding lines are

---

* I fear that I may be mistaken about this. I took 'the March purge' to mean Hitler's purge in 1934. That was in June. David may, of course, have forgotten the month. It was in January 1939 that he wrote to Harman that he was busy with his 'Absalom, Mass' part, and in March 1940 that he wrote again that he was continuing his 'conversation at the time of the Passion', which is the second part of this 'Old Quarry'. That Hitler had been in his mind for a long time before that we know very well; and that he was particularly so at this time is certain from the events of 1939–40. A further indication of this is the appearance of the word 'Reich' [p. 115]. (On second, or third, thoughts, I believe D. put down the wrong month, quite possibly deliberately.)

a prelude to Judas's despair. 'Dark fissues spider' must surely be a mistake in the writing.*

pp. 124–6

Why's he elect ... Please repeat. Thank you: The poet's meditations, often expressed through Judas, will become clearer as our eyes become accustomed to the darkness, which corresponds to the darkness in Gethsemane. The arrest, 'The informer walks ...', is clear enough in D.'s transmutation.

pp. 126–7

The venerable man ... *one end to this*: The high priest rends his garments (Matthew 26 : 65); the Sanhedrin. The brazier and Peter's remorse as the cock crows. The 'ubblye' is mysterious.†

p. 127

The sahib eagle ... *the fellaheen*: Pilate and the message from his wife.

O popule meus! ... *who is our mother*: The realization of foretypes.

pp. 127–30

By Hagar's incomprehensible penalty ... *cherry ripe*: The Redemption (following the line of the preceding section) as the reality foreshadowed in pre-Christian rituals.

pp. 130–1

You could not bunch ... *on a nice fork*: The crucifixion. The sponge filled with vinegar ('Tarragon vinegar is very good vinegar' — Mrs Alice Jones, in song or rhyme, to the child D.). The Coat without Seam. The two thieves.

The reader will see that I am running out of steam. However, I may say this, that the main structure of the poem is

* A friend says 'fissues' may be a misspelling of 'fichus', the subject of 'spider'. The shawl, netting, veils, form a web-like tangle.

† 'Ubbley', or (better) 'obley': the host (*oblata*). What is signified by the consecration of the host is now being effected (Walter Shewring).

clear to me; much of the detail is pretty clear, and I am sure that time and attention and other, keener minds will clarify the rest.

This must be presented to the general reader as the *material* from which a poem would have been constructed.

THE AGENT

Some fragmentary notes from a first typing of 'the Judas sequence', July 1976:

p. 133

Bride Ishtar! Hamans...: What exactly brought the book of Esther to D.'s mind? The hanging of Haman, of course: his position as a key-man, his control of money, and his attempt to start a pogrom against the Jews. This could be seen as a betrayal of the Jews, though he was not a Jew himself. And his attempt rebounded upon himself. He was 'integral to the pattern', obviously. D. could therefore represent Judas as seeing in Haman his own forerunner as one who tried to destroy the people of God. But Esther? Her rare beauty, of course, demands notice.

p. 134

More: we'll take a rise... a faction-war in hell: The Ezekiel passage, and the commentators, should be read. The sin, it later becomes apparent, is the sin of trading. The passage is an 'oracle of doom against the king of Tyre'. D. shares the theological belief that you go to Hell only if you wish to do so; as does this unfortunate, who puts it even more plainly in the lines that will conclude this section.

pp. 134–5

Let's fetch our precepts... smells more factual: It is entrancing to watch how the meaning emerges with such clarity from the closely packed but carefully constructed writing.

266

On page [134] Judas says that he will choose the side of evil: that he will be even more evil than Satan, he'll 'sell him as well' (as he has sold Christ) and lead a 'faction-war in hell'. But he breaks off: he is being over-dramatic. If he turns to other interpreters, he may find an even more terrible, more evil end — complete annihilation, which is a denial of being, even a betrayal, the final and ultimate betrayal — better even than betraying Satan.

So, in the next lines, he turns to the Sadducees, upon whose interpretation of the Law he can build his hopes. 'Fur our tippets in the Zadoc school': cf. Milton's 'budge doctors of the Stoick furr' — which was in D.'s mind also on *Ana*. p. 129, 'the budged owls'. The Sadducees are 'cynic doctors' because they are 'men of fact' and have no ridiculous ideas about angels or physical survival — they've 'made a job' of, i.e. 'polished off', eschatology.

The key phrase is 'Do not the under-silences keep interminable jubilee?' — so cleverly put, for it makes the complete negation (the utter darkness and gloom of Sheol) into a positive affirmation.

'Shammai... Hillel', 'stiff as their texts' — the phylacteries of the Pharisees. More seems to be known about H. than about S. H. died about A.D. 20. He was liberal and gentle in his interpretation, as opposed to S. There were many stories about H. I like the one about the man who wanted to know if he could learn the whole of the Torah (Law) standing on one foot. S. dismissed him savagely, but H. told him that all he had to learn was never to treat another person in a way in which he would not care to be treated himself. Poor doctrine for Judas — hence (partly) 'Hillel's noodledom'. Hillel is spoken of as head of the Sanhedrin, with the title of 'Nisa', a word that occurs in another version of this passage.

p. 135

Let sweet oblivion... all antithesis: Not the only indication of D.'s interest in our old friend the dialectic, whether Heraclitean, Hegelian or materialist: cf. 'The Narrows' [p. 63]:

> I wonder how the Dialectic
> works far-side the Styx
> or if blithe Helen toes the Party Line
> and white Iope and the Dog
> if the withering away
> is more remarked
> than hereabouts.

That is dated *c.* 1941 and 1973 — you may remember that at the beginning of the war (Nazi-Soviet pact) and later, when Hitler attacked Russia, there was a good deal of talk about 'the Party Line'.

p. 136

The son of Didymus ... :   I preface section 2 with these lines from the head of one of the several versions of the opening of this section, because they prove unmistakably that the whole of this Judas sequence branches off from *The Anathemata*, p. 51 (alternatively, though less probably, the *Ana.* passage is a distillation of this part of the Judas sequence):

> as one who speaks
> where a few are, gathered
> in high room, battened, and one gone
> out.
> There's conspiracy here and birthday:
> he plants the vine.
> The new code is promulgated in
> the oral style: he would have
> only intimate ears hear.
> The wary Didymus tries the shutter etc.

The *Anathemata* passage reads:

> In a low voice
> as one who speaks
> where a few are, gathered in high-room
> and one, gone out.
>
> There's conspiracy here:
> Here is birthday and anniversary... etc.

On second thoughts, I think that it is *The Anathemata* which is a condensed version of the Judas passage. It must be obvious to anyone who looks through the MSS that what first came from D.'s mind poured fluently, almost excessively, on to the paper; word followed word and idea or image followed idea, so that his problem was what to reject and how to concentrate what he chose to keep — the same problem as that which faces the humble typer of his work who wishes to make a coherent series of passages.

Both views, of course, may be true. The Judas sequence is a branching-off from the *Ana.*, a small part of the branch being then used for the final text of the *Ana.* It is by no means impossible that a betrayal and arrest section might have been included in the *Ana.* just before or, better, in the middle of the final section.

THE BOOK OF BALAAM'S ASS

From a memorandum of 29 February 1980:

The notes that follow were written in an attempt to satisfy the mind of the compiler; and are included here in case any patient and kindly reader may wish to look at them.

p. 187

like when pale flanks: The fruit of many visits to draw at the Zoo in London. I take 'lace' to be a verb — the tiger's pale flanks lace the bars with her stripes. It is 'impertinent', unfitting, to cage the tigress, but necessary if you are to appreciate her beauty at close range. (It may well be better to take 'necessary' as meaning 'inevitable'.) 'by which' etc., which echoes the words of the Canon of the Mass ('Per ipsum, et cum ipso, et in ipso, est tibi Deo Patri... omnis honor et gloria') is a reminder that the poet never sees the making of the beautiful or the taking of delight in the beautiful, except as a form of worship.

the man from Amsterdam: He remained in D.'s mind ever since he saw Charles Hawtrey in *Ambrose Applejohn's Adventure* some time in the late 1920s. Many years later he would roar with laughter at 'the man from Amsterdam'. What of the 'Amiral of Balasquez'? Carroll? Gilbert? Lear? coinage?

when Northumbrian brides: Continuing the analogy — 'she' gives form as does the tigress in the cage, as does the Northumbrian bride to the vulgar church. David must have had in mind a wedding to which he went from Rock in Northumberland. In 'stucco twiddlings' he is referring, as he does at the beginning of *The Anathemata,* to Browning's 'Bishop Blougram's Apology':

> It's different, preaching in basilicas,
> and doing duty in some masterpiece
> Like this of brother Pugin's, bless his heart!
> I doubt if they're half baked, those chalk rosettes,
> Ciphers and stucco-twiddlings everywhere.

The pillars (and cf. 'a pillar of the Church') are Erastian because it is an Anglican church, established by and subject to the state. 'The patriarch of Uz' (Job) originates in a poem by John Gray, from his *Poems 1931,* which we printed at Pigotts. It is entitled, with an appropriate double meaning, *Audi alteram partem,* and ends

> Listen, the Patriarch of Uz
> Is singing in the Temple Church.

The reference is to a gramophone record of a treble voice singing 'I know that my Redeemer liveth'. The poem is worth looking at: but the book is difficult to find. Were it not too long, I would quote it in full.

p. 188

a living sail: So again, the entry of a ship into the bay (which must be Sidmouth) transmutes the whole landscape.

space itself, they say, leans: See *The Anathemata,* 'the bent flanks of space', p. 68, and my *Commentary,* pp. 62–4.

antique tea-pots: The point is emphasized in the title of the watercolour reproduced in the Penguin Modern Painters D.J. book, *Hierarchy — Still Life 1932,* which shows the tea-pot. It was often drawn and is still in existence.

stiff-legged calves: The Balaam notion is introduced with D.'s customary smoothness as a further analogy. The positions of man and beast are reversed by the language: 'you come on hind-legs at them; you come fore-paws waved to shoo them off', and the cattle try to remember what it is that their race-memory tells them of such creatures. Note the Hereford, by far the most popular breed in the Llanthony valley when D. was there, and the 'long-lashed' Channel

271

Island cattle he would associate with Ditchling Common and Pigotts.

p. 189

Pray stone bulls: Man may well pray that the cattle shall not remember (stone bulls being associated with Mesopotamia) what happened to Nabuchodonosor (hence the Babylonian 'irrigation ducts').

Should the stone whisper: A sentence I have found puzzling. I am pretty certain that 'whisper' is used absolutely, i.e. D. is not saying, 'Should the stone whisper, "By Christ, drover, etc." ', but, 'if there should be a whisper from the stone, then, by Christ, drover, etc.'. The MS reads 'you'll treck a china-shop'. The typescript which accompanies the MS reads 'you let trek' and one can see how the MS 'you'll' could be misread as 'you let'. I think we are justified in reading 'you'll wreck'. It will be you, drover, not a bull, who will be infuriated, maddened, who will wreck a china-shop.

Dialectical incoming: The dialectic proceeds from thesis to antithesis, and, ironically, David anticipates, in the reversal of human and bestial roles, a heavier dose of the dialectic than would be palatable to those who speak of it, those who maintain that the very measures which capitalism introduces to secure its own safety are, dialectically, bound to produce the conditions that lead to a classless society.

David was writing (or had started writing) in the Thirties, the time of Fascism and Nazism, the Spanish Civil War, the 'Peace Council', 'fellow-travellers', the time when Herbert Read was writing of 'revolutionary art' as 'constructive, international' and was wondering what the art of the future would be, 'the art of the classless society' (dear God! But who is entitled to throw the first stone?). Against this David reaffirms the validity of Christian belief, and refuses to have Christianity dismissed as bourgeois ideology. There are other references to Marxist-Leninist vocabulary in this poem, for example (on this page) 'She'ld make your exploiting governance wither away all right', and we find the same in 'The Narrows', 'the Party Line' (a phrase that was often heard in some circles when Stalin reversed his policy toward Germany), and the 'withering away' of the state.

Lords of Creation: (We may notice in 'hierarchy of use and delectation' a coincidence with the title of the picture which was suggested by the mention, earlier, of the 'antique tea-pot'; and notice, too, that here the companion or contrast for 'use' is not 'the gratuitous' or 'sign', as so often, but 'delectation': when D. quoted Poussin (from Maritain) to the effect that 'the goal of art is delight', 'delight' represented 'délectation'.) Here we have the animal sarcastically re-proaching man for regarding himself as the only being who knows both use and delight — just as he ascribes only to himself a 'rational soul' and 'corners' for himself memory, understanding and will. In that last phrase we recognize the three-fold Thomistic division, intellect, understanding and will.

She'ld make a Balaam of you: This brings the meaning into the open: it was when the path narrowed that the ass lay down and finally spoke, putting Balaam in his place as she (the cow) would do, says the poet. This paragraph is full of Scripture and liturgy. The animals share in the patrimony (i.e. are 'co-heirs with Christ', Romans 8 : 17); it was He (the Creator) who made her as she is; the 'windy advent' is the *Dies Irae;* the breaking-down of the 'thousand middle-walls of partition' is from Ephesians 2 : 14, 'For he is our peace, who made both one, and hath broken down the middle wall of partition between us', where Paul is saying that Christ, by extending God's covenant to the Gentiles, broke down the wall which separated the court of the Gentiles in the Temple from the court of the Jews. Similarly with the eschatological rending of the veil of the Temple. Lucy, Agatha and Perpetua are from the prayer *Nobis quoque peccatoribus* in the canon of the Mass. With the partition passage, cf. in 'The Grail Mass': a number of persons and objects 'obscure everything for Mr Todd, who kneels in the atrium Gentium twenty pine-pens back from the carmine baize reserve'.

more than two bugbears: The bugbears are from Marx, I am fairly sure; but I cannot remember what he says. Religion and money? commodity? Immediately after this we have the Marxist 'idiocy of agriculture', a re-phrasing of Marx's 'idiocy of rural life'.

turned so like to the bifurcated steel: The horns of some cows (Ayrshires, for example, and there was a part-Ayrshire cow at Pigotts) when seen from the front are elegantly curved, upright, very like the prongs of a hay-fork or pike. Such weapons (in a peasants' revolt, for example) found the flowered (embroidered) groins of the nobility fair game.

sweating out his chrism: i.e. if the cow could remember Nabuchodonosor, the anointed (chrismed) king. As I am writing only for myself there is no reason why I should not say how endearing, and admirable, I find it in David that he should think of poor N. with no tail to ward off the flies that settled on him as he grazed.

On the back of the page which faces this page of the MS is the word 'Bukharin', an indication of what was in D.'s mind. B. opposed Stalin's agricultural policy.

pp. 189–90

Of course there is another possibility: That man's technical capabilities should outrun his common sense. With that increased power goes a contempt for traditional teaching and culture. Here I meet two difficulties. The first is at the foot of [p. 190]: 'Their professorial two-piece sapphic cut' etc. The place seems to be a class-room, lecture-room, art-school, or some such place, with potted cacti, bulbs being forced; but what is 'two-piece sapphic cut', and why the spelling 'saphique' in the MS? Leave it to time and the Muse.

The second difficulty is less serious, and perhaps no difficulty at all. David is saying that an exploding of illusions is being taught, and that this is dangerous: but suggests that you would *expect* their teaching to be sufficient, whereas in fact they retain much of the old superstition, and he quotes the rime as an example. Maybe the difficulty is solved simply by stating it, i.e. the old beliefs cannot be completely killed. Isobel Berners is from *The Romany Rye:* which I have recently re-read — but forgot to note whether that rime is used by Belle Berners in her dingle. Or is it in *Lavengro?*

p. 190

for these being dead, speak: Hebrews 11 : 4 (of Abel), '... he being dead yet speaketh' — next door, we may note, to Enoch, to whom there is an allusion later.

like literature done in 13pt: An odd phrase that would hardly have survived, I imagine. It would not have been used had it not happened that *In Parenthesis* was printed from 13pt Perpetua type. They treat their perilous situation as though it were no more than a story of war.

pp. 190–1

They don't give a bugger: This will provide the introduction to the factual passage that was printed in *The Sleeping Lord,* and which follows here. The *S.L.* extract starts with 'regular at the rails'. The Pauline type of catalogue has a wonderful mixture: Malory ('pukka' — which glances at *I.P.* — 'men of their hands'), old-fashioned Catholic ('regular at the rails', i.e. communion rails, but with an echo of, say, Trollope, of persons like his abominable Captain Doodles in *The Claverings,* who speak of women as though they were horses, 'a straight runner', 'she'll never go the wrong side of the post' etc.). I do not doubt that David was pleased with 'gun-powdered reason' in the last line of this paragraph.

p. 191

Pamela-born-between-the-sirens: This raises a problem of dating. 'Balaam', we know, was written in the '30s and '40s — and this is confirmed by the reference to air-raids on London. But Pamela must be grown up at the time of the conversation that is reported. The writing and paper show that the MS we have cannot be a revision made in the '60s or thereabouts, so that David is looking forward to a conversation that will take place some twenty years after the time at which he is writing. He complains that 'Balaam' would not 'come together', and 'Under Arcturus', written later than the Passchendaele insertion, may have been another attempt to solve that difficulty: I say 'written later', but the overlap between 'Arcturus' and Passchendaele shows that the former was already in David's mind when he wrote the latter. The many drafts of the Mass sequences show that a theme would come to his mind and flow freely from a sentence he had just written, but that he had great difficulty in deciding when and how he could return to the starting point. In the *Sleeping Lord* pieces, he was able to use a knife on what was intended to be a long continuous piece, but here there was at the beginning no joint into which he could insert the cutting edge. The end, and the fresh start, came naturally enough.

p. 193

Tilly Vally Mr Pistol: 'You're romanticizing... seeing this war in terms of Christian hymns (Ambrosian* racket) and Shakespeare — but watch! I remove the hat, like a conjuror, and what do we now see?'

Just one small difference (among a number of such) I may note. The MS reads 'Ploegsteert is Broceliande' (the enchanted forest in Yvain) while the printed version reads 'The salient is B.' — and P. was too far south for D. to describe it as the salient.

Sgt. Michael Mary Gabriel Aumerle [p. 194] is expanded in the *S.L.*, and in precisely the more elaborate, later, style which you, H.J.G., note in the Melchisedec addition. Sord Columcille, incidentally, is the modern Swords ('Sword of C.') near Dublin airport. The bodies of Brian Boru and his son Murrough were taken to Swords Abbey after the battle of Clontarf in 1014.

p. 194

Amis and... Amile: Is it in Anstey's *Vice Versa* that the German master explains at great length his Wortspiel? A

---

* i.e. *Te Deum* ('Ambrosian hymn').

warning to say no more than that I see William Morris made a version of the O.F. *chanson*: so, too, did Frazer — 'retold for the young in modern French', 1903. The initials are the same, so presumably it is the F. of the Golden Bough.

Hilton and ... Rolle: 'Two jokers from one womb', both being fourteenth-century mystical writers.

pp. 194–5

Goater Grover Bunker and Cobb: On the back of the MS sheet facing this, D. has noted 'Hampshire names'. Similarly he notes the name 'Hycga', from whom Hughenden (Collingwood and Myres, *Roman Britain*, 452–3). Pigotts lies at the head of the Hughenden valley.

p. 198

That Tommy was no infantryman: 'Infantryman' has been written several times, and always crossed out. A note on the facing page of MS reads 'get German for footslogger', but David had to accept 'infantryman' in the end.

p. 200

Enoch's shining companion ...: Enoch, who 'walked with God', Genesis 5 : 21–4.

The Lord of Noe: In the *S.L.* version, Melchisedec takes the place of Noe. There are several MS drafts of a long note on the unique position of M. which show that his introduction was an afterthought.

p. 202

Mrs Balaam: A false prophetess, as Balaam would have been a false prophet, had he not been prevented. She is the disillusioned person, the person who 'cannot see the angel', as Balaam could not until his eyes were opened, who does not recognize the 'sweet influence', who sees things in a purely factual and utilitarian way, who (see the concluding section) would be at home in the Zone.

The poet says that there are two ways of looking at everything, and all things are balanced, one against the other. (This will be elaborated later.) Mrs B. is 'disillusioned'. Nevertheless she sees silver lining in the modern world: so much so, indeed, that she makes it all lining and no cloud. On the other hand, when she looks at the real world, by which the poet is moved, she can only 'show a mockery and grim futility'. David corrects her: she cries wolf, but David says, What more noble and magnificent: see him on the steps of God's throne, and consider too the wolf who was (as in D.'s picture) the mother of the western world.

With the paragraph beginning 'It always comes down on its feet', 'She' re-enters; but 'she' is here the 'sweet influence'; she is human and super-human love, and she is *poiesis*, who works gratuitously; who is, you might say, a grace. There is no need to ask Coleridge's Abyssinian maid to please us, not to bribe the hedgerows to delight us with their tangles. We have a change of pronoun because behind her lies he.

p. 203

King's-eye is pierced...: There is no way of determining what price is to be paid for the artefact: it is freely given for delight. So Harold is pierced and his thanes grieve that a queen may delight in the Bayeux tapestry. This is put with force in the next paragraph, beginning 'He is hardy indeed...'. This is a plea for accepting a universe which is ordered to worship, in spite of apparent injustice and cruelty. The owl is wiser — quoting Milton on his blindness.

pp. 204–7

Her owlish wisdom...: An argument for the acceptance, against the 'levellers' of the 'fantastic hierarchy' — a most unwelcome argument in the days when it was used, and one that has not endeared itself since then to the Balaams. It would take too long to go through the catalogue of 'this for that' but all who know D.'s work will see how fruitfully it can be unravelled.

All this section is studded with David's reading, and there are some fine examples of much in little. For example,

'For Emma a wooden wall' — into which is compressed Emma Hamilton, the Royal Navy, Nelson, Salamis, Herodotus; and 'For John Wesley a horse and the opium of the word' (here again we see that Marx was before him).

The three sonnets mentioned are all of the same nature — 'Not marble, nor the guilded monuments', 'When in the chronicle of wasted time', and 'My mistres eyes are nothing like the Sunne'; these are echoed in the paragraph which starts 'Who shall say the measure...', and in that paragraph [p. 206] David asks a question which he does not, so far as I know, raise elsewhere — how far does love of earthly things interfere with love of the divine?

To return to the 'this for that' series: It is clear enough as far as 'A schism and a division' (I must stray for a moment, once more: how touching is 'this one withered tree to eke-out a half-line for this poet in his poverty'). It suddenly came to me (maybe I am peculiarly dense not to have seen it before) that David is referring to the Reformation and the new humanism of the Renascence. (This bears on the origin of 'the Break', whose effects are apparent at different times in different fields.) Hence the 'split inheritance for you and me' and the opportunity for theologians to 'talk the hind leg off a donkey'. Hence the 'torturing of prayer-wallahs', where the Reformers are associated with what we ourselves have to call, after the changes in the liturgy, 'prayer-meetings'. Hence 'no trouble for the Vicar of Croydon', who is a disguised Vicar of Bray; and hence, and how perfectly, 'the fire lit by candle-light', when Latimer and Ridley were burnt. 'We shall this day light such a candle by God's grace in England as I trust shall never be put out.' The same sociological rift gave us tinker Bunyan's *Grace Abounding*. The original Jack Horner was enriched by the suppression of the monasteries, as were contractors who stripped the lead off churches, while the Lords of the Council received grants of land and the paraphernalia (used, I think, in the strict sense of property retained by a married woman, i.e. the Church; the word is important in Trollope's *The Eustace Diamonds*); John Peel's hounds (who reappear in *The Anathemata*) drink from a carved font thrown out of a church, and the sanctuary bell is made into a cowbell. Fine vestments adorn Elizabeth, the Faery Queen. All God's children (Paul Robeson) have the consummate prose of Cranmer's liturgy and the Authorised Version. And, as a result of the new infusion, social, religious and economic, that came with the Tudors, we have Milton and Shakespeare (and how right David is in seeing the sharpness of the break between S. and Chaucer, or, even more, Langland — a point to which he returns at [p. 206]. So, too, from the Tudors, and later the Stuarts, we have the Royal Navy and Britain's sea-power, and (following the flag) African missions. Chinese Gordon will have to wait for a moment — but (again as in *The Anathemata*) Britannia receives the emblems we know, and is mistress of the seven seas (aquatic hills).

p. 207

I've known him cut a square stone: We now have a straight run home. I am not content with my own reading of the opening lines, but they take us almost immediately into the Zone, and the Zone speaks for itself. It is both the world of the utile, to adopt David's word, and, in a more particular way, it is based on the camp near Winchester at which David was stationed before embarking for France in December 1915. What the Zone really means, however, is shown in the paragraph, 'O Mrs Balaam if you want a long thirst to quench after a long burden of prophecy — go to the Zone, you won't be troubled by the sweet influence in the Zone.' The version of the poem 'A, a, a, Domine Deus' (which opens *The Sleeping Lord)* clinches the matter. It is, I believe, a better ending than it is a beginning. Or perhaps I should say that the more diffuse form we have in the MS is a better and more logical ending, while the tighter version in the *S.L.* is a better beginning.

It may be worth adding that David probably — well... possibly — first noted Jeremiah's exclamation in Maritain: p. 88 of John O'Connor's translation of *Art et Scolastique,* p. 99 of the French: a heavily pregnant paragraph.

280

THE SEQUENCE OF D.J.'S UNPRINTED MSS
and their relation to *The Anathemata*

From a memorandum of 5 January 1980:

A stray sheet among the MSS (which I have numbered to follow on after the last sheet of pieces to be included in a new volume) reads as follows:

(1) Commence Book on p. 3 of Manuscript B
'We already etc.' to 'doubts if they be sufficient'
on p. 7 MS. B.
(2) Insertion from pp. 3 & 4 & 5 (?) & 16 & 17 of Manuscript A
'You can hear a penny dropt' 'this one fetches more light'
to bottom of p. 6. MS. A
(3) Continue with p. 7. MS. B
'On night gust etc' to
p. 57 MS. B
pp. 58–143 MS. C intact

From p. 7 MS. A
'Soon will be the fracture of Branch'
to end of MS. A.

Figures in the left margin are mine. All except the first line has been scribbled through in pencil. The scribbling-out of lines 5–6 is explained by the addition of more page numbers to line 4. It should be remembered, too, that when D. scribbles through a page it often may mean no more than 'this has been dealt with'.

(1) 'We already etc' is the opening of the *Ana.* 'doubts if they be sufficient' appears on p. 17 (not page 7) of 'The Judas Se-

quence' [i.e. 'The Agent']. Although D. calls this MS B, it must be MS C (see below, on (3), where another MS is quite certainly (again in spite of D.) to be identified as MS B). It may well be, of course, that D. rearranged and re-lettered the MSS. Unfortunately only one of the three main groups of MSS that we have bears a letter. This is what we call 'The Roman Quarry'. The cover is marked 'MS. B', and at the end (p. 143) it says 'End of section XII, End of MS. B.'

If you look at (3) above, you will see that after p. 143 of MS C we are told to continue 'From p. 7 MS. A, "Soon will be the fracture of Branch" to end of MS. A.' And p. 7 of 'The Old Quarry' starts with 'Soon will be the fracture of the Branch', and at the head of the page is written 'after p. 143 MS. C.'

David must have muddled or changed the letters of the three groups of MSS. As we have them now, it seems to me that

> MS A is 'The Old Quarry'. It contains the 'you can hear a penny dropt' passage mentioned in (1) above, and 'Soon will be the fracture of the Branch' passage, followed by a long, coherent sequence (in two parts); and D. attributes both these passages to MS A.
>
> MS B is 'The Roman Quarry'. This is proved by 'MS. B' on the cover, and by 'End of MS. B.' on page 143. It is this MS that provided most of the material for the *Sleeping Lord* volume.
>
> MS C must then be 'The Judas Sequence'.

I shall have to leave the matter there for the present, and I do not think we shall ever learn exactly how and when D. divided and lettered the three groups.

What interests me is that the sheet I copied out at the head of this shows that the original plan for the *Ana.* was very different.* We were to have the 'we already and first of all discern him' passage, followed by a much fuller treatment of the Last Supper; a return to a Mass sung today, which is glanced at the beginning of the *Ana.*; then (I think) a treat-

---

* [*Later*] No! It only shows that the present *Ana.* opening dates back to the '40s or so, and could have started a different book.

ment of Judas and his betrayal, the arrest in the Garden, the Passion, comments by Caiaphas; then a series of Roman-Jerusalem pieces; then a return to the Passion; and finally a long disquisition on the Roman attitude to local cults and beliefs. The muddle with pages and numbers and letters has no doubt led me astray in detail, but I think that what I have just written is more or less true.

Before I found and thought about the sheet which prompted this note, I had taken the three groups — which had been disentangled from primal Chaos by Harman's patience and skill — and constructed from them, with a view to a new book, a series of pieces which, I now see, roughly follows the plan outlined on David's sheet.

'Commence book on P3 of Manuscript B.
'We already etc.' to 'doubts if they be sufficient'
on p. 7 M.S. B.
In sections from pp. 3 & 4 & 5(?) & 16 & 17 of Manuscript A.
'You can hear a harp draft' [illegible]
[illegible]
Continue with Pt. M.S. B.
'On night quiet etc.' to
p 57 M.S. B.
pp 58 — 143 M.S. C. intact
from p. 7. M.S. A.
'Soon will be the practice of Branch'
to end of M.S. A.